For Sebastian

Acknowledgments

I am indebted to Graham Curry for reading the proof-of-concept draft and for sending me fragments of John Steele's impossible to locate book on Hallam FC. Further thanks are extended to my good friend David Patston who proofread the manuscript and provided the author's photograph and to Adrian Harvey for his excellent, revisionist history of football. I would like to applaud my publisher, Randall Northam, for taking a punt on me and for providing invaluable editorial guidance and I would especially like to acknowledge Andrew Drake for being such a rich font of local footballing knowledge and for kindly allowing me to reproduce some of the information he has so assiduously collected. I am grateful to former colleague, Chris Hobbs, for his swift assistance and wonderful website and to Tony Beardshaw for providing a photo of his great great-uncle, the illustrious JC Clegg. Tony must have Sheffield football's bluest blood going; not only were JC and WE Clegg his great-grandmother's brothers but William Pierce-Dix was his great-grandfather (he married Mary-Ellen, the Clegg's sister) and he is a great grand-nephew of William Frederick Beardshaw! I am also deeply indebted to those people (you know who you are) who encouraged me to write and gave me the self-belief to do so. Finally I give my deepest, most heartfelt thanks to my partner, Katrina, for giving me the meaning of life… our son, Sebastian.

Contents

Foreword by Geoff Thomson OBE	11
Foreword by Richard Caborn MP	13
Preamble	15
Chapter One 　In the beginning was the Word	19
Chapter Two 　Birth of the beautiful	33
Chapter Three 　Hallam chase	52
Chapter Four 　A tale of two cities	61
Chapter Five 　A knockout idea	72
Chapter Six 　Ecce Homo	85
Chapter Seven 　Life's a ball	91
Chapter Eight 　Sweet FA	101
Chapter Nine 　Football! Football!	113
Chapter Ten 　The play's the thing	129
Chapter Eleven 　The pay's the thing	135

Chapter Twelve
    La Belle Époque   158

Chapter Thirteen
    Sheffield, England   169

Chapter Fourteen
    A clutter of spiders   174

Chapter Fifteen
    And there were gods   177

Chapter Sixteen
    Vale   197

Appendices
    Australia rules!   204
    The first try   212
    The Old Club's Club   213
    The Eton Wanderer   215
    Elysian fields   216
    States of grace   217

Bibliography   221

Websites   223

About the author   224

FOREWORD BY GEOFF THOMSON

As a Sheffield man, I'm delighted to see my hometown get the recognition it deserves for its role in the history of football. Sheffield FC is indisputably the oldest football club in the world, recognised as such by the Football Association and FIFA. The formation of the club played a crucial part in the early development of England's national sport – now without doubt the world's favourite game.

Sheffield FC was formed in 1857, predating the FA by six years. The club is still going strong today, playing in the Unibond League Division One South and taking part in the FA Cup and the FA Vase. I remember well the club reaching the FA Vase Final in 1977, drawing 1-1 with Billericay before a 14,000 crowd at Wembley and then losing the replay at Nottingham Forest. The city's professional clubs, Wednesday and United, have also made significant contributions to football over the years. I have been FA Chairman since 1999, having served on the FA Council for 27 years, initially representing Sheffield & Hallamshire. I have also had periods as chairman and secretary of the Sheffield & Hallamshire FA.

I am therefore delighted to congratulate Sheffield FC on their 150th anniversary and to see this book recognising this achievement and the city's unique contribution to football and sport in general.

Geoff Thompson OBE
Chairman of the Football Association
Vice-President FIFA

Foreword by Richard Caborn

I think that every football fan born in Sheffield and those who have chosen to live here are rightly proud that they share their home with Sheffield FC – the world's oldest football club – and with the birthplace of football itself. For I believe that the beautiful game was born, like me, in Sheffield.

The recent rise in profile of Sheffield FC means that there can be few genuine fans of the game who are unaware of the club's unique position in the history of the game. By reading this book, however, I certainly learnt a deal about the early years and development of our national sport and the part that the city of Sheffield played. It is a fascinating read.

Congratulations to the author and to Sheffield FC on their 150th anniversary and long may they prosper.

The Rt. Hon Richard Caborn MP
Member of Parliament for Sheffield Central

PREAMBLE

When we went downstairs, we were presented to Mr Skimpole, who was standing before the fire telling Richard how fond he used to be, in his school-time, of football.

Excerpt from *Bleak House* by Charles Dickens, 1853.

I LOVE FOOTBALL like a brother... though, in a way, it is my brother, born in Sheffield as I was. Yes, Sheffield is the cradle of association football and what follows is a potted history of its birth. Although I regularly wander to other places, other sports, Sheffield and football remain central to the story. I hope such inclusiveness emphasises rather than diminishes what I believe is the city's crucial contribution to world sport.

Living in Melbourne, as I now do, surrounded by sports-mad Aussies, it is easy to forget that we Poms are also mad for it and that my hometown thrives on sport. It is home to the English Institute of Sport, the World Snooker Championship, the English Open Squash Championship, the National Rounders Association and – till 2007 – the British Open Show Jumping Championship. It held the XVIth World Student Games in 1991 and was the first National City of Sport in 1995.

The Hallam FM Arena is home to both the Sheffield Steelers, one of the countries leading ice hockey teams – five times championship winners in thirteen seasons – and the Westfield Sharks basketball side, national champions four times in their thirteen-year history. IceSheffield, a venue with two Olympic-size ice rinks, is home to four ice hockey teams while Ponds Forge Sporting Centre has an Olympic-sized pool and is home to both the Hatters – who have dominated women's basketball since 1991 – and to the British diving team; many British Olympic swimmers have also made Sheffield their home. There is a rugby league side, Sheffield Eagles, giant-killing winners of the 1998 Challenge Cup final when they overpowered Wigan, and two union sides, the Tigers and Sheffield RUFC. Owlerton Stadium is home to both greyhound racing and the local speedway team, Sheffield Tigers, who have won the Premier League. Largely thanks to Irish-born trainer Brendan Ingle MBE, the city's recent world boxing champions have included Johnny Nelson, Clinton Woods, Naseem Hamed, Paul 'Silky' Jones and Herol 'Bomber' Graham.

England cricket captain, Michael Vaughan was raised (and lives) in Sheffield as was David Sherwood – the Davis Cup tennis player – and his Olympic-medal winning parents, Sheila and John. James Toseland the 2004 World Superbike champion hails from the city as do Steve Peat – the 2002 Mountain Bike World Cup champion – and two-times cycling Commonwealth gold medallist Malcolm Elliot.

Yet, still there is Joe Simpson, mountaineer and author of *Touching the Void*, and the rock climber Ben Moon; the country's best climbers gravitate to Sheffield, lured by limestone and Peak. Sheffield-born football legends include Derek Dooley and Gordon Banks, while Geoff Thompson, chairman of the FA and vice-president of FIFA, calls it home. Sebastian Coe, another old boy, won two Olympic gold medals and set eight world records, including the 800 metres in 1981 which remained unbeaten for 16 years. More recently he has gained fame as being the man who secured the London bid for the 2012 Summer Olympics. The UK's largest athletics stadium at Don Valley hosts regular international meetings, while waiting for its next homegrown hero, in addition to the annual BritBowl, the British version of the Superbowl. The city is currently contemplating a bid to host the 2014 or 2018 Commonwealth Games. Oh, and there are two professional football teams.

Sport has permeated the business sector with growth industries in sports engineering and medicine and the development of a world-leading sports industry cluster including innovative research carried out at the Sheffield Centre of Sports Medicine, Centre for Sport and Exercise Science, Sports and Leisure Industry Research Centres and the Sports Engineering Research Group. It has even infiltrated politics: the Labour government's

Preamble

former sports minister, Richard Caborn, is a Sheffielder and Lord Sebastian Coe is a former Conservative MP.

The city is also studded with sporting venues to serve its citizens, including fifteen golf courses and Europe's largest artificial ski resort, while just outside lies the sublime Peak District National Park. Every week tens of thousands flock here to walk, hike, cycle, swim, ride, run, fell run, ramble, scramble, orienteer, boulder, climb, abseil, mountaineer, hang-glide, pothole, cave, canoe, sail, windsurf and fish. It really is a sporting nirvana... if you can stand the cold. The combination of the city's venues and parklands and the Peak District just about caters for every conceivable sport... except perhaps surfing.

So here is how it first started one hundred and fifty years ago. The following is not meant to be a sobering sociopolitical history of football or of sport in general – I leave that to the professionals – though for those interested, there is sports-polemic aplenty out there. Rather, it is intended to be a celebratory romp through the early years of football; a fans-eye view if you will. I apologise in advance for the somewhat tangential text but make no apology for its actual content. Originally, the appendices and footnotes, the roots and leaves of this book, took on a life of their own and just grew and grew. I have lovingly pruned them back and subsumed much of their trimmings into the body of the work.

Brendan Murphy
Melbourne, July 2007

Chapter One

IN THE BEGINNING WAS THE WORD

He rolleth under foot as doth a ball

The Knight's Tale from the *Canterbury Tales*
by Geoffrey Chaucer c: 1390

FOOTBALL IN SOME shape or form has existed in England for at least eight hundred years; its hazy origins may even extend back to the Roman occupation. For most of that time it differed markedly from today's moderns: Association, Rugby, Australian Rules, Gridiron and Gaelic. Shared elements include two sides, two halves and a ball, but it was a mob affair, usually played between large numbers of men, who would fight for a makeshift ball, often running from one end of a town to the other. The first reference in British literature to ball playing comes from the *Historia Britonum*. Believed to have been originally written around 820AD, it was an attempt by the original author (generally, though controversially, attributed to Nennius, a Welsh monk) to collate whatever disparate sources were available into a chronological narrative of Britain.

The questionable original sources and the numerous additions and revisions it underwent over centuries raise questions as to the validity of its contents. Nevertheless, it has remained important due its numerous Arthurian legends. One such story concerns King Vortigern, the fifth century warlord responsible for allowing the Anglo-Saxons in as mercenaries, only to see them turn coat and overrun the country, condemning him to the title of most hated man in Britain. It tells of how he was counselled to find a boy immaculately born whose sacrifice would enable a citadel to be built. He duly summoned and sent out his men to scour the lands. They searched fruitlessly until they came upon Glywysing (now Glamorgan) 'where a party of boys was playing at ball', one of whom was the boy in question. If the text is to be believed this occurred sometime around 425–466 AD, the years when Vortigern could have reigned.

Notwithstanding the book's problems it does establish that ball games were played prior to the Norman (and possibly Anglo-Saxon) invasion. Additionally, although it does not establish the type of ball game played, it was a game involving a group of boys, so a form of football cannot be excluded. Incidentally, the tale ended happily. The boy, Ambrosius, revealed his magic powers to the king, showing him two fighting 'vermes' (or dragons) the red one representing the Britons, the white one, the Saxons.

Against the odds, the weaker red dragon overcame the white dragon, just as, explained Ambrosius, the Britons would vanquish the Saxon scourge. Rather than being sacrificed Ambrosius was given a large chunk of what is now Wales and the country later adopted a red dragon passant on a white and green background as its symbol; it belatedly became the national flag in 1959.

Vermes can also be translated as badger, though perhaps a badger rampant did not strike the required tone for this fiery race. Ambrosius was later identified by the twelfth century Arthurian writer, Geoffrey of Monmouth, as Merlin, which means, wonderfully, that the first ever recorded game of ball in Britain was played by a wizard! Football really is the stuff of legends. Myth also has it that Merlin was responsible for the construction of Stonehenge. Temple? Observatory? Sundial? Barrow? Nonsense; it is Britain's first national football stadium – and they were ancient goalposts.

The earliest known depiction of football in England was by William FitzStephen in 1173. He was one of Saint Thomas A' Becket's chaplains and claimed to be one of the three clerics who did not desert the Archbishop when he was murdered in Canterbury Cathedral in 1170. His subsequent biography of Becket (1118–1170) included a long and rather incongruous preface on London life that included mention of youths 'playing with the ball in wide open spaces'. He also went on to comment

In the beginning was the Word

on a Shrove Tuesday match played by many of the city's youths on a large, flat patch of land, just outside the city; the game appears well-established, sufficiently so for FitzStephen to forego a description:

> *After lunch all the youth of the city go out into the fields to take part in the famous game of ball. The students of each school have their own ball; the workers from each city craft are also carrying their balls. Older citizens, fathers, and wealthy citizens come on horseback to watch their juniors competing, and to relive their own youth vicariously: you can see their inner passions aroused as they watch the action and get caught up in the fun being had by the carefree adolescents.*

An annual Royal Shrovetide football match is believed to have been played at Ashbourne in Derbyshire (just south of Sheffield) since the 12th century and probably gives the greatest insight into football's ancient past. It is played on Shrove Tuesday and Ash Wednesday, reflecting the ancient, festival spirit of these Holy Days. Two teams, the Up'Ards and Down'Ards (born, respectively, north and south of the river that bisects the town) try to move a ball from a plinth in the town's centre to one of two opposing goalposts, set in the river, three miles apart. The game is started or 'turned up' by a dignitary – the 'turner upper' – who gets to keep the ball if neither team scores. The teams are made up of dozens of people who move the large, hand-painted ball through the town, en masse in 'hugs', which are similar to scrums.

The ball can be carried, thrown or kicked but is 'goaled' by tapping it three times against the post which signals the end of the game for that day. The earliest existing account of the Ashbourne game is supplied by Charles Cotton, author of the famous fishing manual, *The Compleat Angler*, in 1683; local records, documenting its medieval origins were lost in a fire in the 1890s. It did not earn the prefix 'Royal' till 1928 when the Prince of Wales (the future King Edward VIII) 'turned up' the game; the current Prince of Wales was turner upper in 2003. Shrovetide football historian, Francis Peabody Magoun, in his

From Sheffield with Love

History of Football: From the Beginnings to 1871 (1938) disputes the medieval genesis of Shrovetide football claiming it as a much younger sport. He cited Chester, Corfe Castle (immortalized as Kirrin Castle in Enid Blyton's Famous Five books) and Glasgow as the first recorded venues, as late as the sixteenth century. His argument does not stand if FitzStephen or the good burghers of Ashbourne are to be believed.

Similar rough and tumble games were played nationwide and not just at Shrovetide, but such were their popularity and perceived loutishness that serial attempts were made to ban football completely; not for nothing was it dubbed 'mob' football. From a young age football appears to have been ruled out of contention as the 'Sport of Kings' with monarchs sticking the boot in, seemingly from the whistle. Edward II banned it from being played in London in 1314:

> *forasmuch as there is great noise in the city caused by hustling over large balls… from which many evils might arise which God forbid: we command and forbid on behalf of the king, on pain of imprisonment such game to be used in the city in future.*

Serious stuff, but then again serious injuries were common and, with players running around pell-mell, lethal accidents were a distinct possibility. Only a few years later a football fatality is recorded. During a 1321 football game as Canon William de Spalding kicked the ball his friend rushed him, inadvertently fell heavily against De Spalding's scabbard and mortally wounded himself, dying six days later. Poor De Spalding was suspended from his duties and needed papal dispensation from John XXII in Avignon to avoid censure.

Taking things one step further, in 1349 Edward III outlawed football and other sports nationwide because he was worried they were distracting his Black Death-depleted population from their archery practice; no small worry with Gallic eyes surveying the Cinque Ports. Likewise, Richard II in 1389 and Henry IV in 1401 attempted blanket bans on sport, while James' I and II of Scotland outlawed football there in 1424 and 1457 respectively. It is unclear how football fared under the next five English

In the beginning was the Word

monarchs (Henry V and VI, Edward IV, Richard III, Henry VI) though, of them, perhaps Henry V sufficiently realised the sublimated power of the game loved by 'the happy few' to sanction it amongst his 'band of brothers', while it is rumoured that Richard III hid a ball up his tunic. There is a description of football from the end of the fifteenth century, most likely during the reign of Henry VII that suggests football had regained some acceptability. It describes a surprisingly modern game played out in a field where 'the boundaries have been marked':

> ...the game at which they had met for common recreation is called by some the foot-ball game. It is one in which young men, in country sport, propel a huge ball not by throwing it into the air but by striking it and rolling it along the ground, and that not with their hands but with their feet... kicking in opposite directions.

The rough element had in no way been denuded though, the game 'rarely ending but with some loss, accident, or disadvantage of the players themselves'.

The next king, Henry VIII, actually played football as a youth and is the first person on record to order a pair of football boots. Secured from the Great Wardrobe, the hand-stitched leather boots were made in 1526 by the royal cordwainer, Cornelius Johnson, for a princely four shillings and were used by Henry during a Shrovetide match. But for every king there is a cabbage. In his 1531 book *The Boke named the Governour*, dedicated to Henry, the diplomat Sir Thomas Elyot was less than generous towards football, describing it – in a vitriolic anti-sports rant – as:

> nothinge but beastly furie and exstreme violence; wherof procedeth hurte, and consequently rancour and malice do remaine with them that be wounded; wherfore it is to be put in perpetuall silence.

He may have had the King's ear because in 1540 Henry imposed a ban. By now, however, the previously sports-mad monarch was wracked with pain from leg ulcers (probably diabetic in origin and not syphilitic as is usually assumed) and had become a bit of a grouch. His daughter, Elizabeth I, also imposed a ban in London in 1572, such local prohibition by Good Queen Bess not preventing West Ham United from later naming their ground in honour of her mother, Anne Boleyn. By Elizabeth's reign football was so commonplace that women had begun to play; Sir Phillip Sydney, the poet and consummate courtier mentioning in his 1580 *A Dialogue Betweene two Shepherds*:

> *A tyme there is for all, my mother often sayes, When she, with skirts tuckt very hy, with girles at football playes.*

It was also inveigling itself into the national consciousness as the winter sport; Alexander Barclay, the poet, writing of it in 1598:

> *The sturdie plowman, lustie, strong, and bold, Overcometh the winter with driving the foote-ball, Forgetting labor and many a grievous fall.*

There is evidence that Elizabeth's successor, James I, initially tolerated football; certainly in 1615, during a Royal visit to Wiltshire, the locals entertained him with a football match. Unfortunately a tidal wave of fundamental Protestantism was sweeping through the country, seemingly hell-bent on washing the fun from the nation's fabric.

In 1617, a local dispute between Puritans and Catholic landowners in Lancashire as to what sports could and could not be played on the Sabbath reached the King's court. James sympathized with the liberally-disposed Catholics and rather than imposing a complete prohibition, laid out which sports could (archery, dancing, vaulting) and could not (bowling, football, bear baiting) be played in Lancashire on a Sunday, in his 'Declaration to His Subjects Concerning Lawful Sports'.

The following year the partial ban was extended nationally in his 'Book of Sports'. Of course by banning football on Sundays and Holy days there was very little time left for poor people to play since these were the only days they had off. This was still insufficient to please the po-faced dyed-in-the-wools who never forgave James for his half-measure. Their ultra-orthodox cousins, the Separatists, went one step further and sailed off to colonise Massachusetts to establish the warm and fuzzy fundamentalism we all love today: no surprise that soccer never took off there. James himself was no personal fan of the game; in 1598, when he came to write his overbearing how-to-be-a-king helpful hints 'A Kinge's Christian Dutie Towards God', for his eldest son Prince Henry, football was sent to the dugout:

From this court I debarre all rough and violent exercises, as the foot-ball, meeter for lameing than making able the users thereof.

In turn, Charles I's attitude to the sport was no less cavalier and he reissued the Book of Sports, severely curtailing the practice of football. Of course Oliver Cromwell, that puritanical killjoy, banned football; Parliament even going so far as to publicly burn the Book of Sports. Surprisingly Cromwell had played in his youth, throwing 'himself into a dissolute and disorderly course... famous for football, cricket, cudgelling and wrestling' and somewhat incongruously going by the name of 'royster', which means one who engages in boisterous merrymaking. Eh? What? But football bounced back, receiving royal approval by Cromwell's successor (and the man who had his decapitated head slam-dunked onto a pole for fifty years), Charles II in 1681, when he attended a match between his servants and those of the Duke of Albermarle. Early in his reign over the moon footballers came out of hiding, Samuel Pepys describing 'the street full of footballs, it being a great frost' in 1665.

Unfortunately, the country's Puritan element remained, sulking and pouting, chiding and scolding and, in 1683, the pamphleteer Philip Stubbes wrote his *Anatomie of Abuses*, describing football as a 'develishe pastime' The book, which pretty much had a go at anything even remotely pleasurable that one could do in 1683 – including public dancing, wakes, astrology, church ales and that most heinous of pursuits, morris dancing – polarised opinion and he was viewed as either crackpot or moral redeemer. His description of the early game, however, is unsurpassed:

From Sheffield with Love

Lord remove these exercises from the Saboath. Any exercise which withdraweth from godliness, either upon the Saboath or any other day, is wicked and to be forbidden. Now who is so grosly blind that seeth not that these aforesaid exercises not only withdraw us from godlinesse and virtue, but also haile and allure us to wickednesse and sin? For as concerning football playing I protest unto you that it may rather be called a friendlie kinde of fyghte than a play or recreation – a bloody and murthering practice than a felowly sport or pastime. For dooth not everyone lye in waight for his adversarie, seeking to overthrow him and picke him on his nose, though it may be on hard stones, on ditch or dale, on valley or hill, or whatever place soever it be he careth not, so he have him downe; and that he can serve the most of this fashion he is counted the only fellow, and who but he? So that by this means sometimes their necks are broken, sometimes their backs, sometimes their legs, sometimes their armes, sometimes their noses gush out with blood, sometimes their eyes start out, and sometimes hurte in one place, sometimes in another. But whosoever scapeth away the best goeth not scot free, but is either forewounded, craised, or bruised, so as he dyeth of it or else scapeth very hardlie; and no mervaile, for they have the sleights to meet one betwixt two, to dash him against the hart with their elbows, to butt him under the short ribs with their griped fists, and with their knees to catch him on the hip and pick him on his neck, with such murthering devices. And hereof groweth envy, rancour, and malice, and sometimes brawling, murther, homicide, and great effusion of blood, as experience daily teacheth. Is this murthering play now an exercise for the Saboath day?

Clearly this is more akin to mob football and rugby, but there is evidence both from the description of football during Henry VII's reign and from Sydney's quote that the game had diversified and a less physical, less hands-on variation was commonly being practised. It is probable that the game was arborising into three major forms: one mainly using the feet, another mainly the hands and the third a free-for-all using both. In 1602 Richard Carew described two variants of Cornish hurling, one similar to

In the beginning was the Word

mob football, the other a stickless variety, predominantly using the hand, less physical than mob football and with an emphasis on passing the ball:

> *...that he must deale no Fore-ball, viz. he may not throw it to any of his mates, standing neerer the goale, then himselfe. Lastly, in dealing the ball, if any of the other part can catch it flying between, or e're the other haue it fast, he thereby winneth the same to his side, which straightway of defendant becommeth assailant, as the other, of assailant falls to be defendant.*

A historically important depiction as it renders the game the first known to prohibit a forward pass. Carew goes on to describe something approximating to a modern goal:

> *two bushes in the ground, some eight or ten foote asunder; and directly against them, ten or twelue score off, other twayne in like distance, which they terme their Goales*

The eighteenth century is football's Dark Age with very few literary references though in Strpye's 1720 edition of John Stow's *Survey of London* there is mention that:

> *The lower classes divert themselves at football, wrestling, cudgels, nine-pins, shovelboard, cricket, stowball, ringing of bells, quoits, pitching the bar, bull and bear baitings, throwing at cocks and lying at ale-houses.*

Football was still around but was not thriving as it once had been. It was on the decline. There is no evidence of monarchical prohibition during this era, suggesting that Stubbes and his cronies had tapped into the nation's psyche, linking eternal damnation to Sunday soccer. The result appears to be a marked reduction in football, something no amount of kingly creeds had managed, testament to the power of God and the fear of man. If this is so, we will never know the resulting damage done to the evolution of the game by religious folly or contrariwise the strange game we would now be playing had it not gone into decline. Finally, in 1801, during the reign of King George III, the voice of Joseph Strutt comes ringing through the silence. A philanthropist and writer from Derby, Strutt wrote *The Sports and Pastimes of the People of England*, which chronicles the demise of football:

> Football is so called because the ball is driven about with the feet instead of the hands. It was formerly much in vogue among the common people of England, though of late years it seems to have fallen into disrepute, and is but little practised. I cannot pretend to determine at what period the game of football originated; it does not, however, to the best of my recollection, appear among the popular exercises before the reign of Edward III, and then, in 1349, it was prohibited by a public edict; not, perhaps, from any particular objection to the sport in itself, but because it co-operated, with other favourite amusements, to impede the progress of archery.
>
> When a match at football is made, two parties, each containing an equal number of competitors, take the field, and stand between two goals, placed at the distance of eighty or an hundred yards the one from the other. The goal is usually made with two sticks driven into the ground, about two or three feet apart. The ball, which is commonly made of a blown bladder, and cased with leather, is delivered in the midst of the ground, and the object of each party is to drive it through the goal of their antagonists, which being achieved the game is won. The abilities of the performers are best displayed in attacking and defending the goals; and hence the pastime was more frequently called a goal at football than a game at football. When the exercise becomes exceeding violent, the players kick each other's shins without the least ceremony, and some of them are overthrown at the hazard of their limbs.

Probably in part due to its fall from favour, football was eventually deemed a nuisance rather than a national threat and the Highways Act of 1835 banned it (and tennis and cricket) from being played on public roads. The trend, however, could not be bucked by God or kings or statutes alike; football refused to lie down and its core popularity continued. It was ultimately taken up by, and evolved in, England's public schools. By the 19th century the game being played was a chimera of association[1] and rugby football and allowed running with the ball, scrums and hacking – a sharp kick to the shins of an opponent. Despite each institution developing its own idiosyncratic rules with considerable inter-school variation, the games being played could all be placed somewhere on a continuum that had rugby and football at either pole. Some schools, like Harrow and Eton, placed greater emphasis on the dribbling aspect of the game, while at others, including Rugby and Blackheath, the carrying game prevailed. The variations also began to become codified; Cambridge University are known to have first published in-house rules around 1839–42 though the earliest existing set of football rules was issued by Rugby School in 1845.

A set of common rules were developed by H de Winton and JC Thring at Trinity College, Cambridge University in 1848 to allow for inter-collegiate games. The rules were decided by a committee of fourteen men including representatives from Eton, Harrow, Rugby, Shrewsbury, Winchester and Trinity College. There are no known copies of this first attempt though a set of rules from 1856 survives. With myopic self-protectionism each public school stuck to its own version, and no one set prevailed; visitors were expected to play by house rules. Refusing to give up, JC Thring, who had since become master at Uppingham School, further developed his rules as 'The Simplest Game' in 1862 and, in 1863, Cambridge University revised their code which then became the template for the Football Association's first attempt at their own 'Rules of the Game' later that year.

The long-held view that football was philanthropically saved by the public school system at a time when it was dying out amongst the working classes is erroneous. Prevailing historical opinion has long held that only a mob version of football was played by the lower orders and for some reason (perhaps industrialisation reducing both leisure time and playing areas and/or increasingly effective social prohibition by the new national police force) essentially disappeared around the early 19th century. With noblesse oblige it was taken up by the higher orders and elegantly transformed from a vicious, snarling, scum-scrum of a game into a genteel, skilful and virtuous pursuit; polished and preened and handed back to the feckless masses in the second half of the nineteenth century.

This argument has been thoroughly and stylishly dissembled by Adrian Harvey[2] who points out that while the sport did evolve in public schools, it did so, as mentioned, with great insularity and was neither propagated nor disseminated with any vigour. He goes on to unearth evidence of the existence of numerous working class teams playing nationwide in the first half of the nineteenth century, especially in Yorkshire and Lancashire. Most played with sides of even numbers (usually between 6- and 20-a-side) and with rules agreed between the two sides that had no direct bearing on public school codes.

Middle-class teams also existed nationally, but originated in schools and military regiments rather than from occupation or location, as was the case with working class sides. They were also freer to play on a day of their choosing unlike the working classes whose matches were often limited to public holidays or Mondays. 'Mondayitis' is nothing new; the Victorian working classes would regularly wag Mondays waggishly claiming that they were celebrating Saint Monday. It was also known as Fuddling Day since, rather than play sport, many preferred to keep drinking.

It appears then that football has been played in Britain for centuries and that it became so popular that opposing sides were often huge. It is likely to be this gargantuan aspect of the game that led to it being perceived both threat and crowd-pleaser, leading in turn to recidivistic bans and to it becoming a festival sport, watched by the masses and tolerated by the authorities. The sheer size and glamour of these games is likely to have attracted all the contemporary press but it is eminently possible that matches with far fewer participants had always been played yet gone unrecorded.

The invention of the ball is sport's equivalent of the wheel and surely whenever a ball could be fashioned, men would play with it in teams of two, irrespective of available numbers. In his book, Magoun records numerous instances of football between

In the beginning was the Word

small evenly matched sides being played at locations throughout Britain during the seventeenth century; clearly then, not mob football. Harvey develops the argument and cogently reveals that such games continued during the eighteenth century, especially in East Anglia, Lancashire and London, establishing a temporal link to the more organized team games of the first half of the nineteenth century.

In East Anglia, a particular variation of mob football known as camping was also played, which had been popular since the middle ages. To those familiar with the region this did not involve towing caravans around the Fens using Robin Reliants, rather it was a particularly violent game played with two teams of large numbers, each occupying a camp (half). The object was to drag opposing members into the home camp until their side was depleted; this could only be done if the ball was in the opponent's half, so it was important to hurl the ball back into the enemy camp as quickly as possible. If a large ball was used the game was called 'kicking camp' and the game appears to have been normally played in bare feet since if shoes were worn it was called 'savage camp'. This term clearly implies that the game was not for the faint-hearted and there is documented evidence to support this: one seventeenth century match between Norfolk and Suffolk featured more than three hundred players, nine of whom died!

According to Mrs Gaskell's *The Life of Charlotte Bronte* (1857), in 1750 football was played using stones in the Roses border town of Haworth, Yorkshire. This was seventy years before the Bronte sisters moved into the parsonage in 1820 and the Reverend Bronte's predecessor, who 'made good with the whip', earnestly bid to stop such devilry. In London, meanwhile, football was usually played by apprentices, forming an obvious link to FitzStephen's observation of craft workers six hundred years earlier. In conclusion, although there are no earlier records, smaller games may have always been contemporaneous with, or even predated, mob football: speculative but feasible.

Undoubtedly, football continued to be played by the common man the length and breadth of Britain and is likely to have slowly evolved in this setting too and probably with more homogeneity than the public school system allowed for, though admittedly with substantial local variation. Certainly, from the seventeenth century onwards, football was played with large or small numbers and it is possible that idiosyncratic rules developed depending on the size of the game with smaller games allowing for greater consistency and application of rules. The sport that was taken up by the public schools may have had less to do with the free-for-all that was mob football than with a compact, cultured, working class invention.

Footnotes

[1] I apologise for anachronistically using the term 'association' as shorthand for a game where kicking was preferred to handling; the term was not used formally until the formation of the Football Association in 1863.

[2] *Football: The First Hundred Years – the Untold Story* (2005) by Adrian Harvey

Chapter Two

BIRTH OF THE BEAUTIFUL

*And Eton may play with a pill if they please
And Harrow may stick to their Cheshire Cheese,
And Rugby their outgrown egg, but here
Is the perfect game of the perfect sphere.*

Brighton College Football Song, circa mid-19th century

WHEN SHEFFIELD RECEIVED its royal charter in 1296 it is likely that football in some form was already being played locally. There may even have been kick-arounds when William De Lovetot built his castle there (c: 1100) and established Sheffield as the principal centre in the manor of Hallamshire. Before De Lovetot, the area's main claim to fame had taken place at Dore (now a suburb of Sheffield) in 829 AD. Derived from 'door', the hamlet was the passageway between the two Anglo-Saxon kingdoms of Mercia and Northumberland. King Egbert of Wessex, who had already subjugated all the other Anglo-Saxon lords, travelled north to Dore to receive a pledge of allegiance from the Northumbrians and, in so doing, finally united England and became its first king. In Sheffield united.

The region's connection with Anglo-Saxon lords continued beyond the Norman conquest of 1066: Waltheof, the last of the lords in England, owned the manor of Hallam. His father, Siward the Dane, who had been made an earl by King Canute, was responsible for providing English support to Malcolm and MacDuff in their overthrow of the Scottish king, Macbeth. Despite being married to a niece of William the Conqueror, Waltheof could not help plotting against the Normans, little wonder as the King sanctioned such measures as the harrying (harrowing) of the north, in 1069, where every man over the age of sixteen was reputedly killed. Following his involvement in a third rebellion in 1075, Waltheof was executed, either having confessed and/or having been betrayed by his Norman wife, Judith. He was the only notable Englishman to meet this fate during William's reign though more than a little harrying followed. Waltheof's manor went to his wife and is mentioned in the Domesday Book of 1086 as being managed for her by Roger De Busli to whom it subsequently passed before moving, via his son, to De Lovetot. Sheffield is mentioned in the Domesday Book as both Escafeld and Scafeld (pronounced Shafeld); romantic as the former sounds it was probably a typo by the scribe. The River Sheaf, which passes through Sheffield, now divides the counties of Derbyshire and Yorkshire, just as it once divided Mercia and Northumberland. Its name is derived from a word meaning 'to divide' and so Sheffield is believed to mean 'the dividing field'.

Waltheof's death was a huge loss to the English cause and confirmed Norman hegemony. Interestingly, Waltheof held the title of Earl of Huntingdon, just as Robin Hood is said to have done and some historians, notably Graham Kirkby, are convinced that Robin Hood is a direct descendant of Waltheof's. Despite much myth surrounding the man it is clear that Robin Hood did exist and that it is likely he was from Loxley, now a suburb of Sheffield. He was probably born during the 1190s and lived as an outlaw for 22 years around 1225–1247, possibly engaged in guerrilla warfare against the state.

It is also hypothesised that the Peveril family, who had their castle at Castleton and were the sheriffs of Nottingham, were direct descendants of William the Conqueror. Moreover, the town of Castleton, south of Sheffield, lies just a few miles from the village of Hathersage, where the grave of Little John can be found. Certainly, the Norman lords continued their atrocities and maintained their punitive laws and taxes and it is feasible that the armed Saxon struggle against the Normans continued for centuries, despite significant inter-breeding between the two sides. By Robin's time, however, the fight may have been morphing from an ethnic struggle into a class war.

Birth of the Beautiful

It all seems a bit too neat – William and Waltheof having direct descendants slugging it out one hundred and fifty years later but it is, doubtless, allegorical and despite Robin of Loxley being a real person who probably was an outlaw, it is easy to see how the legend of Robin Hood grew and became so embellished. It represented no less than the nation's collective resistance to foreign invaders, injustice and discrimination. The myth wove itself into the nation's psyche with the ease of a Bayeux weaver.

What it was that they were kicking around and outside De Lovetot's castle is unclear but anything roundish and smallish was probably fair game. We have seen that the men of Yorkshire were using stones in 1750, just as 220 years on my friends and I would, around the hopscotched yard of our infant school, before and between classes. We have probably been kicking stones forever. At some point attempts would have been made to procure a more toe-friendly object, perhaps more uniformly round and with an element of bounce and this is where the notion of using pigs' bladders must have arisen. The decision to encase the delicate bladders within a more robust outer layer seems a logical progression (as pigs would attest to) though before this bladders were often filled with peas or beans and these continued to be used later by those unable to afford the leather variety.

The chapter's opening refrain refers to the balls used (and still in use) by different public schools. Both the Eton field game and wall game use a ball half the size of a standard football while the Brighton game used a standard size. The Harrow game uses a ball flattened on its sides and larger than a football, the origin of its shape probably stemming from early attempts at making a round ball. The earliest surviving football in the world was found in the roof beams of Stirling Castle, Scotland in 1999. It is believed to be about 430 years old (c1570) and was found above the room occupied by Mary De Guise, wife of James V of Scotland. Interestingly, James V's father, James IV of Scotland, had his servant, James Doig, order footballs in 1497. Since the Stirling Castle ball was estimated to have been made during the reign of James V's grandson, James VI of Scotland and I of

England, it appears that the later heads of the House of Stuart took a rather more lenient view of the sport than their football-banning predecessors, though the tolerance may have ended with James' ascension to the English throne. As we shall see, Scotland assumed a lead role in football's development.

The ball is constructed from two circular pieces of leather stitched to a rectangular strip of leather, approximating to a sphere but actually forming a shape like a wheel of cheese; the Harrow ball is made using the same method. The old leather caseys in use till recently employed the same basic outer design but with more leather strips, conferring a rounder shape.

Incidentally, in 1542, six days after Mary had a daughter James V died and the infant became Mary Queen of Scots, future bane of Elizabeth I and mother to her successor, James I of England (and VI of Scotland). Cousin Mary just couldn't seem to keep away from plots to overthrow Elizabeth and take the throne herself and, in 1570, she was sent to Sheffield Castle, where she resided at Her Majesty's pleasure for fourteen years. Within two years she was plotting with the Duke of Norfolk, and while she survived, he lost his head. As we shall see, it was his descendant who granted the land on which Bramall Lane was built in 1855. On her release Mary was at it again, this time with Anthony Babbington who fled to Harrow, presumably *sans balle*, before being apprehended and ending up *sans tête*. Mary was executed for her persistent perfidy in 1587.

While it is probable that football had been played locally for centuries, the first known recorded football match in Sheffield was not until 1793, when a six-a-side game between Sheffield and Norton took place at Bents Green. Bents Green is, and was, a Sheffield suburb whereas Norton, although now a suburb of Sheffield, in 1793 was a hamlet, south of the River Sheaf and therefore in Derbyshire. The match then constituted a county tie attracting much rivalry; testament to this is the fact that it lasted for three days and deteriorated into mob football:

> *There were selected six young men of Norton, dressed in green; and six young men of Sheffield, dressed in red. The play continued*

for three consecutive days. At the arch which was erected at each end of the place selected, there was a hole in the goal, and those on the Sheffield side would prevent the ball from passing through the hole. Then those on the Norton side (not being so numerous as those of Sheffield) sent messengers to the Peak and other places in the county of Derby; in consequence thereof, a great number of men appeared on the ground from Derbyshire.

Then those of Sheffield sent fife and drum through the streets of the town, to collect recruits and sufficient force against Derbyshire men. The fashion then was for all responsible gentlemen, tradesmen and artisans of Sheffield to wear long tails. Hence, at the end of the third day, a general row or struggle took place between the contending parties, insomuch that the men of Derbyshire cut and pulled nearly all the tails from the heads of the gentlemen of Sheffield.

I understand there were many slightly wounded, but none were killed; thus ended the celebrated football match which aroused the bad passions of humanity for many years afterwards, insomuch so that the inhabitants of Norton felt a dread in coming to Sheffield, even about their necessary business.

It is 1857 however, that is the milestone year. It was the year of the Indian Mutiny, when locals rebelled against brutal British colonialism. Napoleon had been defeated forty-two years ago, New Zealand founded just seventeen years before and both the Communist Manifesto and Texas were less than a decade old. As a result of the Industrial Revolution, the population of Sheffield had rapidly grown in size from around 35,000 in 1800 to almost 200,000 in 1857 (and by 1900 that figure had doubled). In the 1740's Benjamin Huntsman had invented the crucible steel process, allowing the production of much harder, higher quality steel in large quantities. The same decade had also seen Thomas Bolsover create Sheffield Plate by fusing a thin layer of silver over copper, giving the appearance of solid silver at a fraction of the price and affordable to many. Steel and silver had galvanised the city and transformed its fortunes, creating mass employment for the working classes and vast wealth for a new elite upper-

Middle-class. Two years before Sheffield FC's inception, in 1855, Henry Bessemer had invented a cheap process of mass producing steel and the city stepped up a gear. Daily, thousands swarmed from tumbling terraces to fearsome factories which heaved and roared night and day, fuming and bellowing, incandescent and terrible. Molten metal flowed from fiery furnaces; crimson crucibles cried volcanic tears. Room-sized vats poured liquid steel into giant chambers which pumped lava-life through the vessels of Sheffield.

All of her was aglow with the warm hammerings of grinders and turners, smithies and smelters, buffers and cutlers. She shone in the sheen of shiny Sheffield steel. Cutlery, jewellery, ornaments and silver-plate, filigree and delicate; forged in her hands. And later, weapons too: bombs and bullets, tanks and guns, ships and planes, wrought in Sheffield, sending all to the four corners. The world was showered in Sheffield steel, beauty and beast, enamoured and en-armoured. Little wonder that Sheffield adopted Vulcan and Thor as its emblematic gods.

In May of that pivotal year, two men – Nathaniel Creswick and William Prest – decided to form a football club. Nathaniel Creswick (1831–1917) was a solicitor and all-round sportsman whose family of silver plate manufacturers dated back to 14th century Sheffield. William Prest (1832–85) was a wine merchant who, as a cricketer, had captained Yorkshire and played for the All-England XI. Two other Prests from York – John Beevor Prest (1826–71) and Charles Henry Prest (1841–75) – also played first-class cricket (John played for Sheffield) and it is probable they were related, possibly his brothers. Legend has it that Creswick and Prest hit on their idea while promenading in the local countryside, deliberating about how to keep fit during the cricket close season.

After five months gestation Sheffield Football Club was born, the oldest football club in any code in the world. It was officially founded on October 24th 1857, at a meeting at Parkfield House in the suburb of Highfield, home of Harry Waters Chambers, whose family were to enjoy a long connection with the club. Several sources claim 1855 as the year of inception, but there is

Birth of the Beautiful

no corroborative evidence for this and the first minutes known to exist are from 1857. Percy M Young in his book, *Football in Sheffield* (1964), concludes that football had been played since 1855 by many of the men who would become the first board members and players but they had not yet formed the Club. Fittingly, the first headquarters for the infant club was a nursery – well, more of a greenhouse really – at the bottom of friend (and first president of the club) Frederick Ward's house in nearby East Bank Road. Ward was the son of Thomas Asline Ward (1781–1871), the nonagenarian elder statesman of Sheffield, former Master Cutler, editor of the *Sheffield Independent*, President of the Literary and Philosophical Society and member of an elite circle of local famous figures including the sculptor Sir Francis Chantrey, the historian Joseph Hunter and poets James Montgomery and Ebenezer Elliott – the 'Corn Law Rhymer' and 'Poet of the Poor'.

Creswick and Prest were members of the local Clarkhouse Road Fencing and Gymnasium Club and believed in a sport with a common set of rules that could be played by anyone. The Clarkhouse Road club had been playing football since 1852 and, as noted, Sheffield FC appears to have played informally since 1855. Both numbered a great many ex-Sheffield Collegiate School pupils, the city's preeminent private school, opened in 1836; seventeen of the Club's fifty-seven members had schooled there. Creswick himself had attended whilst Prest lived close by on Collegiate Crescent.

Creswick's brother, AJ, was another old boy, who also played for Sheffield FC, turning out for them against Notts County in 1865 – the first match played by an existing professional team. The relation of the two brothers to Henry Creswick (1824–92) is unclear but captivating. Born in Sheffield in 1824, he and his brother emigrated to Australia in 1840. They settled in country Victoria in 1842 and the gold rush town of Creswick was named after them, in 1854. Henry became a successful wine merchant (like Prest) and settled in the Eastern suburbs of Melbourne in a grand house called 'The Hawthorns', built in 1845 on what is now Creswick Street. The suburb he lived in was originally known as Wattle Hill but later became known as Hawthorn, local historians remain baffled as to why. Some suggest it was named by Charles Latrobe after the native hawthorn-like white blossoms reputed to have grown on the hill, though it was already named because of the profusion of wattle, so it seems curious to change it for this reason. Others believe Latrobe named it after Lieutenant Hawthorne of Her Majesty's ship *The Phantom* and, in truth, some early maps show the spelling as Hawthorne.

The suburb was not officially ratified (as a municipality) till 1860, when supporters of the Phantom theory claim a town clerk omitted the 'e' in error. It is eminently possible that neither of these is accurate and that it was named after Creswick's house which had already stood for fifteen years, just as the neighbouring suburb of Burwood had been named after a local titular residence in 1852. This raises the fascinating possibility that the local Australian Rules football club, Hawthorn FC, was named after a house owned by a relative of the founder of Sheffield FC.

Henry Creswick's Sheffield–Melbourne connection may not end there. As described later, Sheffield FC formalised its playing rules in October 1858. A mere seven months on Melbourne FC were formed and a few days after that, on May 17th, 1859, the founders met to develop the first set of rules for the game that would become Australian Rules football. The rules bear some surprising similarities to those of Sheffield FC, including the laws for kicking off, kick outs, throw-ins, and the use of a clean catch (or mark) to gain a free kick.

While both also sanctioned pushing and outlawed hacking, the most intriguing similarity is not in what is included in the codes but what is not mentioned in either: an offside rule. These were the only two football codes in the Victorian world (including Cambridge University and all the public school codes, but excluding Gaelic football which was not codified till 1887) that did not include an offside rule. All these similarities raise the fascinating possibility of Melbourne knowledge of the Sheffield game, and that Sheffield's rules strongly influenced Melbourne's and, by proxy, today's Australian Rules. Perhaps it is Sheffield-born Henry Creswick who provides the missing link. Of the four men who founded Melbourne FC, three – Thomas Wills, William Hammersley and James Thompson – were eminent cricketers who played for Victoria in the late 1850s. Henry Creswick also played first-class cricket for Victoria during the '57–58 season: around the very time the Sheffield code was developed. Maybe he was a relative of Nathaniel Creswick's and maintained correspondence with his Sheffield relatives, passing on details of the new code to his Victorian cricketing teammates, who, it seems, included Wills, Hammersley and Thompson It is highly likely that he would have met at least one of them during this time, especially Thompson who was a fellow Yorkshireman.

Henry was also a well-respected member of Melbourne society and if he blunderingly failed to meet them at the crease there is every reason to suspect that he would have met at least one of them elsewhere. If any of them had even hinted that they were keen to develop a sport to keep them fit during the winter months, then surely Henry, as a relative of Nathaniel's, would have been only too eager to boast of his family connection to Sheffield FC and to divulge details of their newly developed rules. There is even a chance that Wills and Creswick knew each other during the 1840s and (possibly) early 1850s, when they both lived in the Ballarat district of Victoria. Admittedly Wills, who was born in 1835 and was eleven years younger than Creswick, would have been young but their families may have been acquainted; there were also Hammersleys and Thompsons living in the area at the time.

Meanwhile, back in their loaned potting shed, Creswick and Prest sat mulling over the terms of reference for their new club, unaware of the historic import. They soon came up with the Sheffield Football Club's code of conduct which, despite its dreary verbosity, still makes for interesting reading one hundred and fifty years on:

Rules and Regulations for the Government of the Sheffield Foot Ball Club, established 1857

1. *That this Club be called the Sheffield Foot Ball Club.*
2. *That the Club be managed by a Committee of five members (three to form a quorum) of which the*

officers of the Club shall be ex-officio members, to be elected at the annual general meetings.

3. *That the annual general meeting of the Club shall be held on the second Monday in October in each year for the purpose of electing officers for the ensuing year and for other purposes.*

4. *That the Committee shall be empowered to call a special general meeting of the Club on giving seven days notice by circular to each member, specifying the objects for which such meeting is called, and the discussion at such special meeting shall be confined to that object alone. The Committee shall also call a special meeting of the Club on the written request of six members.*

5. *That each member on his admission to the Club shall pay 2s. 6d. subscription for the current year and that the annual subscription shall be due on the first day of November in each year.*

6. *That it shall be necessary for members wishing to retire from the Club to give notice in writing to the Hon. Secretary on or before the first day in October.*

7. *That the Committee shall have power to make a further call in addition to the annual subscription if they shall deem it necessary for the purpose of the Club, such further call not in any case to exceed 2s. 6d. per year.*

8. *That the Committee shall (during the season) meet once in every fortnight for the dispatch of business.*

9. *That the season shall commence on the first day in November and end on Easter Eve in each year.*

10. *That the play day of the Club be Saturday from two o'clock until dark.*

11. *That every candidate for admission to the Club shall be proposed by one member and seconded by another, his name and usual place of residency having been given to the Secretary, the Proposer and Seconder each subscribing his own name. The candidate will be balloted for by the Committee according to the priority of their nominations.*

Birth of the Beautiful

12. No ballot shall be valid unless three Committeemen vote, and two black balls shall exclude.

13. That all disputes during play shall be referred to the members of the Committee present at the ground, their decision to be final.

14. That the officers for the season be: – President: Frederick Ward; Vice-Presidents: JA Sorby and I Ellison; Committee: Messrs. W Prest, I Pierson, W Baker, JK Turner and JE Vickers; Honorary Secretary and Treasurer: N Creswick.

15. That each member shall have the privilege of introducing one or more friends in company with himself during each season if within six miles of Sheffield; such friends shall be introduced once only.

16. That the Committee shall take immediate cognizance of any infringement of these Rules, and it shall be their special duty in case any circumstances shall occur likely to endanger the stability or to interrupt the harmony and good order of the Club to call a general meeting in the mode above described. In the event of two thirds of the members present at such meetings deciding by ballot on the expulsion of any member such member shall cease to belong to the Club.

17. That the Rules, together with the Laws relating to the playing of the game, shall be forthwith printed and afterwards, as often as the Committee shall think fit, and one copy shall be delivered to any member on application to the Secretary. Any member may obtain additional copies at the rate of sixpence each copy on a like application.

Clearly the Club was being run along the lines of an old boys club, black balls and all. In truth they were an elite lot, being made up of steel and silver manufacturers, dentists, doctors, lawyers and architects, and they were known to their early opponents as 'the Gentlemen'. This may, in part, explain the Club's subsequent haughtiness in refusing to play more working class Sheffield clubs. While the working classes were not explicitly barred, Rule 10 declared Saturday as play day, a full work day for the poor.

From Sheffield with Love

For all that though, they were no dilettantes: the game in those days was very physical, often violent and not for the lighthearted. Nor were they sexist: though Rule 11 refers to the admission of male candidates, a female was admitted as a member as early as 1859 – the first in football history – and by 1864 one in nine of their 252 members were women.

The Rules reveal several gems. Firstly, that they were originally called Sheffield Foot Ball Club; the foot was yet to connect to the ball and would not for several years. Secondly, repeated references to the 'Club', while belying lofty aspirations, also gave rise to their nickname 'the Club' still used today, altogether appropriate given their uniqueness in being the only club in existence at the time. Thirdly, Rule 13 makes the first reference in football to adjudicators; the world's first referees were to be whichever Committee members were following the game, presumably by majority decision. Finally Rule 15 makes it very clear that the Club was to be a local club for local people – and you only got one stab at joining.

At the same time Creswick and Prest were ensconced in their botanic headquarters developing these Rules they were also up to something far more important: creating their own version of football. The fruits of their labour ultimately bore harvest with a set of eleven laws – modernising the Cambridge rules of 1848 and further removing football from the carrying game common in English public schools. They are first known to have been published, together with the Rules and Regulations outlined above, in October 1858.

Original Sheffield Playing Rules of 21st October 1858.

N.B Immediate changes were made as indicated in brackets and explained in the subsequent text.

1. *The kick off from the middle must be a place kick.*

2. *Kick Out must not be from more than twenty-five yards out of goal.*

3. *Fair catch is a catch direct from the foot of the opposite side and entitles a free kick.*

Birth of the Beautiful

4. *Charging is fair in case of a place kick (with the exception of a kick off as soon as a player offers to kick) but he may always draw back unless he has actually touched the ball with his foot.*

5. *No pushing with the hands or hacking, or tripping up is fair under any circumstances whatsoever. (Amended)*

6. *Knocking or pushing on the ball is altogether disallowed. The side breaking the rule forfeits a free kick to the opposite side. (Removed)*

7. *No player may be held or pulled over. (Became Law 6)*

8. *It is not lawful to take the ball off the ground (except in touch) for any purpose whatever. (Became Law 7)*

9. *If the ball be bouncing it may be stopped by the hand, not pushed or hit, but if the ball is rolling it may not be stopped except by the foot. (Removed)*

10. *No goal may be kicked from touch, nor by a free kick from a fair catch. (Amended and became Law 9)*

11. *A ball in touch is dead, consequently the side that touches it down must bring it to the edge of the touch and throw it straight out from touch. (Became Law 10)*

12. *Each player must provide himself with a red and dark blue flannel cap, one colour to be worn by each side. (Became Law 11)*

These were the original Playing Rules; however, several immediate amendments took place. This infers that in addition to the club having had experience with these Rules (as Creswick later confirmed) they had also played around with some alternative rules during the '57–58 season, which the majority of board members clearly preferred. Certainly Creswick declared that he and Prest had developed a set of rules soon after the club had been formed, though if he did, they no longer survive. The following changes were made:

Laws 6 and 9 were expunged and replaced with the rule 'The ball may be pushed on or hit with the hand but holding the ball, except in the case of a fair catch is altogether disallowed' (this became the new Law 8).

Law 3 was altered to 'Fair Catch is a catch from any player provided the ball has not touched the ground or has not been thrown from touch and is entitled to a free-kick.'

Law 5 changed to 'Pushing with the hands is allowed but no hacking or tripping up is fair under any circumstances whatever.'

Law 10 was changed to 'A goal must be kicked but not from touch nor by a free kick from a catch' and became Law 9.

As can be seen, even with the amended rules for the '58–59 season, hands still played a considerable role in the game. It was not till 1860 that the new Law 8 was changed to 'Holding the ball (except in the case of a free kick) or knocking or pushing it on is altogether disallowed'. In fact, one alternate rule that did not make the final cut was that players should carry half a crown in each hand to prevent pushing with an open hand.

It is generally considered that the Sheffield Rules were an amalgam of different public school codes, since Creswick and Prest wrote to them asking for copies of their rules. Creswick dismissed this during a speech he gave at Sheffield FC's jubilee dinner in 1907. The major schools playing a soccer-type game included Eton (field game), Harrow, Westminster, Shrewsbury, Winchester and Charterhouse.

Their rules, however, were so varied and had developed such idiosyncrasies that it would have been extremely hard to conflate them without some prior knowledge and Creswick attested to this in his jubilee speech. Certainly from '55–57, before they had officially formed, Sheffield FC played with few rules and any number of players. At this time there were many other teams playing informally in southern Yorkshire, especially around Penistone (which had a rich history of football: one of England's first documented – non-Shrovetide – football matches took place there in 1648) and Holmfirth and it appears just as likely that the rules were of local origin.

As Adrian Harvey points out, some of Sheffield FC's rules had been anticipated by Edinburgh University, Glasgow College and Surrey FC and it is probable that the rules were an amalgamation of local, public school and other college practices with laws 3, 4 and 7 (which became 6) most likely to have possible public school roots. The notion that only public school codes were used is probably perpetuated by the myth, still current in contemporary publications, that Prest and/or Creswick attended Harrow. In contrast, when the Gothic-sounding Yorkshireman, Ebenezer Cobb Morley, drew up the Rules of the Game for the Football Association (FA) in 1863 his remit was to amalgamate the rules of various public schools and he appeared to manage the task with few problems, though in fairness he was greatly assisted by the 1863 Cambridge Rules, itself a synthesis of public school codes.

Those schools that preferred the dribbling game as opposed to the carrying game were over-represented by the FA including Harrow, Eton, Westminster and Winchester though Rugby's rules were also considered. The later exclusion of their hacking clause provoked the subsequent schism.

Initially without competition, the Club held games internally, playing the first half of the alphabet against the rest, professional occupations versus the others, law versus medicine or married men versus unmarried. Players had no kit but were distinguished by a red or dark blue flannel cap, which they were required to possess under article eleven of the Sheffield Rules: this is the origin of players receiving caps when representing their country at football.

They played on Saturdays, at Strawberry Hall Lane Park, around the corner from the new Bramall Lane cricket ground, which had been opened two years earlier. Prior to the 1858 rules, they played with any number of players (usually around 20-a-side) and no time limit – though usually from 2pm till dusk on Saturdays; goals were as wide as both sides agreed to and the pitch was only marked out at the corners: in other words just like the kick-around I have with my mates in the park every Sunday.

The Club's sporting activities were not confined to football and in April 1858 they drew their first real crowd when they held an athletics meeting. This is no surprise, with Prest and Creswick both members of the Clarkhouse Road Fencing and

Gymnasium Club and keen sportsmen. Creswick, in particular, enjoyed diverse pursuits, including cricket, running and pedestrianism; his prowess had practical applications too – he once saved a boy from drowning.

Pedestrianism originally referred to both walking and running races and became hugely popular in Britain in the 19th century. A Captain Barclay Allardyce (1779–1854) was the undoubted early champion of pedestrianism and once won a handsome £16,000 by walking 1,000 miles in 1,000 successive hours – averaging a mile every hour for forty-two successive days – before a crowd of 10,000 at Newmarket in 1809.

By the 1850s pedestrianism had become a synonym for athletics, with Sheffield one of the leading centres: in 1843 the town was reported to be 'standing high in reputation for pedestrianism' and it continued to flourish throughout the 1860s. Sheffield runner Jem Sherdon was regarded as the fastest mile runner of this era while Ghanaian, Arthur Wharton (q.v.), one-time Sheffield United goalkeeper and England's first black professional football player, moved to Sheffield in 1887 to become a professional pedestrian and establish himself as the fastest man in Britain over 100 yards.

In 1875, the newly-founded *Athletic News* reported that 'the town of Sheffield is proverbial all over England for being the most sport loving place in the country' and by the 1880s athletes were flocking to Sheffield, attracted by numerous meetings at multiple venues including Newhall, Queen's Grounds, Sheaf House Gardens, Hyde Park and Bramall Lane.

They were also no doubt lured by prize events including the famous Sheffield Handicap run over 130 yards (120 metres) with a gold purse prize. Despite falling from grace in England, similar prize sprints are still competed for. The oldest, the Powderhall Handicap, started in 1870, is run every New Year's day at Mussleburgh raceourse and others include the Bay Sheffield Gift in Adelaide and the world-famous Stawell Gift in Western Victoria.

Then, as now, Sheffield had an embarrassment of sporting venues including Blackburn Meadows, Hunters Bar, Machon

Bank, Meersbrook Park, Myrtle Road, the Old Forge Ground, Olive Grove, Quibell's Field, Sandygate, Sharrow Vale bicycle ground, Glossop Road skating rink and the Sheffield & Hallamshire Lawn Tennis Club.

At that first sports day, four thousand people crammed into the field, adjacent to Frederick Ward's house on East Bank Road (where Sheffield FC practiced and occasionally played) to see William Prest win eleven of the events including the hammer, hundred yard dash, wrestling, backward sprint and sack race. So popular was the day that an additional playing rule (Law 12) was added on October 28th 1858 that 'the season be closed by a variety of sports but no gentleman can contend who has not been a member for at least two months. A committee shall be appointed to arrange a scheme for the same'

Although the first football club (possibly the first club of any kind in Britain) to host athletic days, the first recorded athletics meeting was at the Royal Military Academy, Woolwich in 1849 and the second at Exeter College in 1850. Athletic clubs did not come online till the 1860s with Liverpool Athletic Club being founded in 1862.

The following year, anticipating the plot for a Carry On film about pedestrianism by almost a century, the Mincing Lane Athletic Club was formed in London, though unlike East Anglia they did not carry on camping there. In 1866 the Mincing Lane Athletic Club became the London Athletic Club, patronised, amongst others, by Charles Craven Dacre.

The club moved to Lillie Bridge (home of the 1873 FA Cup Final) in 1869 before finally settling at nearby Stamford Bridge in Fulham, in 1877. Later, in 1905, the new home underwent a refurbishment with designs by football's premier architect, Glaswegian Archibald Leitch. The intention was to incorporate a football club into the venue; Fulham FC were given first refusal but turned it down so the new owners, the Mears brothers, formed their own club – Chelsea FC.

They were immediately granted entry into the Football League's Second Division for the '05–06 season, finishing a creditable third and gaining promotion the following season, when they finished second. A hundred years on and they are still doing rather well. In the '05–06 season Chelsea, the designer club ignited by a rich philanthropist, played Manchester United in a top-of-the table clash in front of a crowd of 67,000. The nation's journalists were crowing that Chelsea's owner: 'evidently does not believe in doing things by halves, and has spared no expense in the furtherance of his hobby – for hobby it undoubtedly is – as it is obvious that it is a matter of impossibility for many years at any rate that he can receive anything like an adequate return for the money he has spent.'

Sound familiar? Well of course it does... except that the season was '05–06, the clash in Division Two, the owner referred to was one Mr Mears and the article appeared in *Athletic News*.

Incidentally, Archibald Leitch was a prolific worker designing stadiums almost at will including: Celtic Park, Ibrox, Anfield, Goodison Park, Old Trafford, Maine Road, Villa Park, Molineux, Highbury, White Hart Lane, Craven Cottage, Selhurst Park and the Den. The first English stand he built was Bramall Lane's two-tier John Street Stand, complete with mock-Tudor press box, which opened in 1901 and seated 10,000. Thirteen years later the Wednesday replaced the old Olive Grove stand they had carted across town, with a Leitch design, at the same time changing the ground's name from Owlerton to Hillsborough. Archibald Leitch is not to be confused with Bristol-born Archibald Leach who changed his name in 1931 to Cary Grant.

The Sheffield Club finally found some one else to play soccer with, in December 1858, when it beat the local 58th regiment in the world's first competitive game played by a football club; testimony to the roughness of the early game, two soldiers suffered fractured ribs.

The next competitive outing, however, was to be the following year's end-of-season athletics meet held in April 1859, where Creswick almost won the most outstanding shirt contest and Prest once again impressed and was awarded a silver cup inscribed with the motto *Toujours Prest*. Football's first decade bowed out with an exhibition match at Newhall, second billing to a mammoth 42-a-side hurling game.

Birth of the Beautiful

Footnotes

[1] *The Perambulations of Barney the Irishman* by Bernard Bird, 1850. Bird lived and worked in Sheffield for more than forty years.

[2] Association football was born in the neighbouring suburb to the one in which I was born (Nether Edge), less than a mile from the house I grew up in and a stone's throw from the local library where I had borrowed books on my first favourite football team, Celtic, when I was five.

[3] My family and I live in Hawthorn, close to Creswick Street.

Chapter Three

HALLAM CHASE

'Ay, ay, ay!' resumed the old man, catching the last words. 'I remember 'em well in my school time, year after year, and all the merry-making that used to come along with them. I was a strong chap then, Mr Redlaw; and, if you'll believe me, hadn't my match at football within ten mile. Where's my son William? Hadn't my match at football, William, within ten mile!'

Excerpt from *The Haunted Man and the Ghost's Bargain* by Charles Dickens, 1848

WITHIN A FEW years the Club had a rival, Hallam FC. The new club had existed as a cricket club since 1804, the landlord of the Plough Inn agreeing to allocate some of his land for a cricket pitch. By the time it was decided to incorporate a football club, allowing sporting activity during the winter months, it had become one of the key northern cricket clubs with more than 300 members. In 1860, the second oldest club in the world to play the dribbling game was formed by two Sheffield FC members – Thomas Vickers, a steel magnate, and John C Shaw, an attorney's clerk. It was not to be the world's second, third, fourth, fifth or even sixth oldest club in any football code however, those honours appearing to go to: Liverpool Football Club (c: December, 1857); Edinburgh Academicals FC (c: 1857/58); Blackheath FC (c: 1858); Melbourne FC (c: May, 1859); Geelong FC (c: July, 1859). The first three played a rugby version of the game while the last two played under Melbourne Rules, the precursor to today's Australian Rules.

The Aussies even stole a march by claiming the world's first ever inter-club football match when the two sides met on the Argyle ground in Aberdeen Street, Geelong West – then known as 'Little Scotland' – in 1860.

Hallam Chase

Hallam FC was born at Sandygate, Sheffield; the location for the home it still plays at today, Sandygate Road, the world's oldest football ground (in any code!). It was there on Boxing Day 1860 that Sheffield FC beat Hallam FC 2-0 in the world's first inter-club association football match. It was also the first red v blue rivalry with Sheffield FC turning out in scarlet and white, Hallam in blue and white. *The Sheffield Daily Telegraph's* match report on the 16-a-side game was a world-first in football journalism:

> *This match was played on Wednesday upon the Hallam cricket ground in the presence of a large number of spectators. Owing to the severe weather several players were absent from each side, but the spirit exhibited by those who were present prevented the game from flagging or becoming uninteresting to the observers, who were extremely liberal with their plaudits on the successful 'charge' or quiet 'dodge', and equally unsparing in their sarcasm and Country 'chaff' on the unfortunate victims of the slippery ground or the 'pure' scientific.*
>
> *The day was beautiful and the 'uniform' of the men contrasting with each other and the pure snow had a most picturesque appearance. The Sheffielders turned out in their usual scarlet and white, whilst most of the Country players wore the blue garment of the Hallam Club. It would be invidious to single out the play of any particular gentleman when all did well, but we must give the palm to the Sheffield players as being the most scientific and also more alive to the advantage of upsetting their opponents. No serious accidents however occurred – the game was conducted with good temper and in a friendly spirit – and when darkness closed upon the scene, the Sheffield Club, not withstanding their inferior numbers, counted two goals to nothing, and went home fully satisfied with their victory.*

The journalist reveals that players were missing and it is likely that a 20-a-side match had been anticipated. He also refers to Sheffield's 'inferior numbers' indicating that the long-held belief that it was a 16-a-side game is erroneous.

Certainly, Sheffield was known to offer a handicap by playing with fewer men. In December 1861, sixty-eight years after that 1793 Sheffield–Norton ruckus, the Club offered three players against six of Norton and were made to eat humble pie when they lost 3-0. The following month they avenged themselves 4-0 with four against six, Creswick reminiscing half a century later about how 'very personal' the three-hour game got by the end; bitter memories no doubt resurfacing.

Around the same time they beat them again, 1-0, fielding twelve to Norton's eighteen. That first match report also refers to Hallam as Country, the name presumably deriving from their location on the outskirts of the city; this also gave rise to their nickname of the Countrymen. Almost one hundred and fifty years on both teams are in the Premier Division of the Northern Counties Eastern League so, delightfully, the world's oldest football derby continues to be played.

The nascent game was in no hurry and things rumbled along slowly. There was a return match in March which the Club lost 3-0, no doubt hindered by allowing Hallam to field more men (18 vs. 15): a gesture to offset their superior strength which, as mentioned, the Club offered to any local fledglings. The accompanying newspaper report of the three hour game was the first time the men of Hallam were referred to as the Countrymen.

In December 1861, the two teams played their third game and the world's first inter-club charity match, for the benefit of a new Sheffield hospital. The 14-a-side fixture played at the local Hyde Park ground attracted a noteworthy crowd of 600. Time and again we see that teams were a family affair, with brothers turning out for the same club; Hallam's victorious 2-0 lineup illustrates this admirably:

Hallam FC: JC Shaw (captain), B Elliott, G Elliott, A Hobson,
  H Moore, A Pearson, JW Pye-Smith, J Snape, F Vickers,
  T Vickers, F Warburton, A Waterfall, GH Waterfall, W Waterfall.
Sheffield FC: N Creswick (Captain), W Baker, HW Chambers,
  AA Dixon, R Favell, Gould, Hall, Moore, W Prest, D Sellars,
  W Turton, A Wightman, J Wild

Sheffield's third club, Norton, were now on the scene and had played Sheffield FC several times before the Club once more faced off with the Countrymen, in March 1862. The fixture was a 14-a-side charity game to support the Hallamshire Volunteers, one of many regiments established nationwide in response to Napoleon III's sabre-rattling and fears of an imminent French invasion. Creswick was instrumental in the regiment's creation in May 1859 and later became a colonel, while Prest also joined and rose to the rank of major.

With measured detachment and a pinch of schadenfreude, Marx had written his treatise *The Invasion Panic in England* in London, in November 1859, but jingoism was at such fever pitch that even 'willowy' Pre-Raphaelites John Everett Millais and William Holman Hunt executed anti-French paintings. Both became members of the Artist's Rifle Corps (another volunteer regiment), as did Frederic Leighton and William Morris. Neville Barnes Wallis, designer of the bouncing bomb – which was road-tested by the 'Dambusters' on Ladybower Reservoir, just south of Sheffield – also served in the regiment during World War One. By wonderful coincidence, Derbyshire-born Barnes Wallis was employed by Sheffield steel magnates Vickers in 1919 to design airships.

Vickers had been founded in 1828 by Edward Vickers, his sons, Thomas and Albert joining the firm in 1854. Both sons had attended Collegiate School and were senior members of the Hallamshire Volunteers, but more importantly, Thomas was one of the five original Sheffield FC committee members and co-founder of Hallam FC. Thomas later became Master Cutler – in 1872 – and with a nod to his artist compadres-in-arms, immortalised his family in a series of three paintings by the American artist John Singer Sargent, the greatest portraitist of his era.

With Barnes-Wallis' help, Vickers successfully manufactured a commercial dirigible, the R100. It was a whopping 700 feet long and 133 feet in diameter and could carry 100 passengers (the German-built Hindenburg had the same dimensions but only carried 50). Romantically known as the Trans-Oceanic Airship, it sadly realised just one return trans-Atlantic flight, in 1930.

From Sheffield with Love

It was grounded following the tragic crash, in France in October 1930, of the government-built R101 on its maiden flight to India; 48 perished. Incidentally, Sheffield was bombed by a Zeppelin during World War One on the night of September 25th 1916; it missed its munitions targets but 28 lost their lives in the Burngreave area. Far worse aerial assaults were to follow during the Blitz in World War Two; over two nights (December 12th and 15th, 1940) German bombers pummelled the city. Over 660 civilians died, 1586 were injured, 40,000 made homeless and 78,000 houses damaged. Even Bramall Lane took a direct hit from a bomber.

The Volunteers fixture was a no score bore draw with few talking points, something that could not be said about their next charity game. On December 29th 1862, Sheffield and Hallam met in the world's third charity game with the two oldest clubs literally fighting it out in Bramall Lane's first ever football game and, in so doing, christening the ground as the world's oldest major football stadium. Donations were going to the Lancashire Distress Fund set up after the cotton trade had been heavily affected by American export embargoes resulting from the Civil War. The game lasted three hours, ended 0-0, deteriorated into a fight involving all 26 players on the pitch and was dubbed 'The Battle of Bramall Lane' by a reporter from the *Sheffield Independent* newspaper.

The first half appeared to have passed charitably enough and when both teams went in at half-time it is doubtful the crowd had any inkling of what would unfold. The interval dragged on and while the crowd awaited the second half, the players were tucking into some festive victuals and maybe more than one or two had more than one or two. The brawl allegedly began in response to either William Waterfall of Hallam striking Nathaniel Creswick of Sheffield FC or vice-versa. Creswick was 'dangerously in possession' when he was body checked by Waterfall and Shaw. Creswick's fist uppercut Waterfall – 'accidentally' reported Sheffield FC; 'deliberately' rebuffed Hallam in an open letter to the Sheffield press – who needed no invitation to get stuck in. The *Sheffield Independent* reported:

Hallam played with great determination. They appeared to have many partisans present, and when they succeeded in 'downing' a man their ardent friends were more noisily jubilant.

At one time it appeared that the match would be turned into a general fight. Major Creswick had got the ball away and was struggling against great odds – Mr Shaw and Mr Waterfall (of Hallam). Major Creswick was held by Waterfall and in the struggle Waterfall was accidentally hit by the Major. All parties agreed that the hit was accidental. Waterfall, however, ran at the Major in the most irritable manner, and struck him several times. He also 'threw off his waistcoat' and began to 'show fight' in earnest. Major Creswick, who preserved his temper admirably, did not return a single blow.

There were a few who seemed to rejoice that the Major had been hit and were just as ready to 'Hallam' it. We understand that many of the Sheffield players deprecated – and we think not without reason – the long interval in the middle of the game that was devoted to refreshments

The Hallam player's version of events as subsequently published in the *Independent* has more of the ring of truth about it:

The unfair report in your paper of the 29th ult. and again on the 3rd inst. of the football match played on the Bramall Lane ground between the Sheffield and Hallam Football Clubs calls for a hearing from the other side. We have nothing to say about the result – there was no score – but to defend the character and behaviour of our respected player, Mr William Waterfall, by detailing the facts as they occurred between him and Major Creswick.

In the early part of the game, Waterfall charged the Major, on which the Major threatened to strike him if he did so again. Later in the game, when all the players were waiting a decision of the umpires, the Major, very unfairly, took the ball from the hands of one of our players and commenced kicking it towards their goal. He was met by Waterfall who charged him and the Major struck Waterfall on the face, which Waterfall immediately returned.

From Sheffield with Love

As claim and counterclaim sallied forth across the pages of the local papers, Nathaniel Creswick's silence was audible. Perhaps he remained discreetly quiet, a gentleman having no wish to wash his dirty laundry in public or perhaps he was guiltily keeping his head down, keen to avoid the mudslinging. Whoever started it, it soon kicked off big style. Spreading to implicate all the players and dozens of spectators 'a general riot ensued' until 'older and cooler heads prevailed' to clear the pitch some minutes later. The match resumed, but a bitter Waterfall was consigned to goal for the remaining spell.

The fallout was grave. Shaw was forced to fall on his sword and resign from the Hallam board, albeit temporarily, while the Bramall Lane committee was vindicated in its snooty opinion that football was not a suitable sport for its hallowed turf. Indeed, proceedings were so acrimonious the two teams did not play each other for more than 42 years! The truth is that the sport was still uncomfortably close to the carrying game with plenty of explosive physicality fizzing around the pitch. William Clegg (q.v.) wrote of an early game against Hallam:

Down one side of the field there ran a stone wall only a foot or so off the touchline. I was running down the wing with the ball and after me came hurtling a great big fellow, twice my weight. I knew he was up to some mischief, and suddenly he launched himself at me with all his weight. I swerved quickly to one side and he went smack against the wall with such force that he knocked several stones out of position!

Interestingly, the Sheffield–Hallam match report was only the second time that a goalkeeper had been mentioned and the first time for two hundred and thirty years. In his 1633 book *Vocabula*, David Wedderburn, a teacher at Aberdeen Grammar School, detailed a football game where different sides pass the ball forward and try to get a goal by kicking it past a goalkeeper.

This is consistent with the theory that more structured games, not just mob football, were practised at the time. It is the only known reference to goalkeepers before the 19th century. The book also details the game of golf in Scotland for the first time. Popularly believed to be a Scottish invention, the first written account was actually by a Dutchman in 1545. References to golf in Scottish Acts of Parliament in 1457 (half a millennium before Sheffield FC were formed) are believed to refer to a type of hockey or shinty played in Britain at the time, with the word golf derived from 'kolve' an old Flemish word for hockey stick. Golf is now believed to be a continental European creation.

With enmity seething between Hallam and Sheffield FC, it was lucky that other local teams sprang up; Collegiate, Engineer, Norton, York and Pitsmoor all kicking off in 1861. By 1863, at least sixteen amateur clubs were playing against each other (using Sheffield rules) and the city was, far and away, the leading force in football. Sheffield FC's paramount position was rapidly challenged and they soon began to falter against the new teams; between May 1863 and January 1865 they did not score a single goal in eight outings. Hallam managed to consolidate their position but it was Pitsmoor who rapidly became the preeminent side, losing a mere three of their 26 recorded matches from 1862–65. The number of players on each side varied but gradually reduced year-on-year; for example out of Sheffield FC's matches the sides were as follows:

'60–61: one 16-a-side and one 18 vs. 15-a-side
'61–62: between 14 and 18-a-side
'62–63: 11 to 14-a-side with Sheffield FC's first recorded
   11-a-side at the end of the season
'63–64: 11-a-side except for two 16-a-side fixtures against
   Mackenzie
'64–65: predominantly 11-a-side, some 12 to 14-a-sides, one
   18-a-side (v Nottingham)
'65–66: all 11-a-sides recorded

Sheffield FC had actually declared at the start of the '63 campaign that it would only play 11-a-side games, though they bent the rules to suit themselves, for example when they wanted to play Nottingham.

Team formation and tactics developed slowly over a number of seasons. There were few fixed positions initially and play proceeded with most of the players moving forward with the player who had the ball, so that if he lost possession someone else could pick it up; the distant relative of an unravelled scrum. In the absence of an offside rule, a 'kick through' roamed behind the defence ready to pick up an easy ball and as a result a 'cover goal' player was employed to remain behind the pack. His job would have been to protect the goal in the absence of a goalkeeper or to assist one if present. In the very early days goals had no crossbar and kicking the ball between and above the posts at any height resulted in a score, which rendered goalkeepers somewhat redundant such that they were not always used. We have seen, however, that Waterfall was consigned to goal in the 1862 match so goalkeepers were definitely used at times. The following quote from William Clegg, which continues his theme on how tough the game used to be, implies they were used more often than not, and also explains why:

> *If you couldn't take the knocks, you didn't play, and the man who was given the hottest time in terms of physical ill-treatment was the goalkeeper. Those were the days when there were two outer goals, in which rouges were scored, as well as an inner goal, and, if it wasn't enough to have to defend this large area, a goalkeeper was constantly shadowed by an opposing forward. It was this forward's sole task to wait until the ball was kicked towards the goal and then knock the poor goalkeeper about as much as possible.*

Throughout these early years athletic meetings held by the clubs were still the big crowd-pullers and football games were almost the private recreational preserve of club members and their families and friends, drawing small attendances and revenues. The emphasis on sports days ranged from the downright silly to the highly competitive though the latter became the norm as the decade waned, with national contestants competing for ever grander prizes. Money for clubs flowed in from the entry fees charged, though some lesser income also accrued through subscriptions; nevertheless they generally operated as not-for-profit organisations contributing much towards local charities.

Chapter Four

A TALE OF TWO CITIES

In football everything is complicated by the presence of the other team

Jean Paul Sartre

NATIONALLY, THE GAME developed more leisurely, though teams sprang up in many towns. Not all agreed with Sheffield FC's rules and some developed their own codes, including the neighbouring cities of Nottingham and Leeds. Progress was most rapid in London and, on October 26th 1863, a meeting was held at the Freemason's Tavern, in Lincoln's Inn Fields, to form the Football Association (FA). For the record the founder members at that first meeting were: Barnes, Blackheath, Blackheath Prep School, Crusaders, Crystal Palace, Forest, Kensington School, No Names Kilburn, Perceval House, Surbiton and War Office Club. Charterhouse School, though present, did not join. Over the next six weeks a series of meetings was convened to develop a national unified code of play, with representatives from several London clubs and schools and a few independent observers; Harry Chambers of Sheffield FC was allegedly present at the final meeting.

Sheffield FC's secretary, William Chesterman, wrote requesting that the Club be admitted to the FA and encouraged changes to the FA's draft rules, suggesting that they include a clause on the use of a crossbar. The idea did not become a feature of FA Laws till 1866 when tape was introduced; until then a goal could be scored by kicking the ball between the posts or at any height over the space between the goalposts.

Ebenezer Cobb Morley, of the FA, finally saw sense after attending a match in Reigate where someone scored with a ninety foot up and under; a fixed wooden crossbar finally became mandatory in 1882, although Sheffield had long since been using them. Chesterman also discouraged the clauses on running with the ball, charging, holding, tripping, hacking and wrestling the ball from a player. For good measure he also informed the FA that, although there was no Sheffield offside rule, they had always played it. JC Thring, who was instrumental in the Cambridge Rules of 1848 and who had written his own code of rules The Simplest Game earlier in 1863, also offered guidance.

Although there was a more or less equal split within the FA between those who preferred the carrying game to the dribbling game, the powerbrokers favoured the latter. They may have been influenced, or at least encouraged, by the updated Cambridge Rules of 1863, which had excluded hacking and running with the ball. It is unclear how much weight Chesterman's letter carried; in fact, when the FA read it on December 1st it appears to have been the first time that they were aware of the details of Sheffield Rules. Nevertheless, the final version presented at the FA meeting on December 8th, 1863, contained significant changes and hacking and running with the ball were outlawed, a move that incensed Blackheath FC who refused to ratify the rules and immediately resigned from the committee. Others followed and the schism ultimately led to the formation of the Rugby Football Union in 1871 and the modern game of rugby. Ironically, hacking, one of the main bones of contention, was dropped by Blackheath themselves within a few years.

Development was rapid in rugby: the first Roses match took place in 1870 with four Sheffield footballers playing for Yorkshire while a year later, in March 1871, the world's first rugby international, Scotland v England, took place in Edinburgh – Scotland won. This became an annual fixture and led to the Calcutta Cup in 1879. The Indian-designed Cup, complete with three king cobra handles and elephant lid, was presented to the Rugby Football Union by the disbanded Calcutta Football Club of India (founded 1873) in 1878. Locally, in March 1872, The Garrick Club played an exhibition game of rugby against Manchester Free Wanderers at Machon Bank, Sheffield (3 goals,

A tale of two cities

3 tries, 17 rouges to nil) and by 1873 Great Britain had beaten The World by one goal and one try to nil in Lausanne, Switzerland.

By 1893, rugby had become as huge as football but remained amateur and controlled by the elite-heavy London-based Union. Yorkshire teams, having seen what association football had achieved, suggested the restoration of six shillings 'broken-time' payment to compensate their poorer players for lost earnings but the Union baulked. In response, in 1895 the northern teams broke away from the amateur Union to form the professional Northern Rugby Football Union complete with modified rules; it became the Rugby Football League in 1922.

The FA Laws actually included many Sheffield elements and the Club became one of the eighteen FA members – the only one from the provinces. The FA still countenanced handling of the ball, a feature of the game that had been eschewed in Sheffield by 1860, such that Sheffield clubs continued to play a purer form of the kicking game.

The Football Association Laws of 1863 Published in *Bell's Life* Saturday, December 5th 1863:

1. *The maximum length of the ground shall be 200 yards, the maximum breadth shall be 100 yards, the length and breadth shall be marked off with flags; and the goal shall be defined by two upright posts, eight yards apart, without any tape or bar across them.*

2. *A toss for goals shall take place, and the game shall be commenced by a place kick from the centre of the ground by the side losing the toss for goals; the other side shall not approach within 10 yards of the ball until it is kicked off.*

3. *After a goal is won, the losing side shall be entitled to kick off, and the two sides shall change goals after each goal is won.*

4. *A goal shall be won when the ball passes between the goal-posts or over the space between the goal-posts (at whatever height), not being thrown, knocked on, or carried.*

5. *When the ball is in touch, the first player who touches it shall throw it from the point on the boundary*

line where it left the ground in a direction at right angles with the boundary line, and the ball shall not be in play until it has touched the ground.

6. *When a player has kicked the ball, any one of the same side who is nearer to the opponent's goal line is out of play, and may not touch the ball himself, nor in any way whatever prevent any other player from doing so, until he is in play; but no player is out of play when the ball is kicked off from behind the goal line.*

7. *In case the ball goes behind the goal line, if a player on the side to whom the goal belongs first touches the ball, one of his side shall he entitled to a free kick from the goal line at the point opposite the place where the ball shall be touched. If a player of the opposite side first touches the ball, one of his side shall be entitled to a free kick at the goal only from a point 15 yards outside the goal line, opposite the place where the ball is touched, the opposing side standing within their goal line until he has had his kick.*

8. *If a player makes a fair catch, he shall be entitled to a free kick, providing he claims it by making a mark with his heel at once; and in order to take such kick he may go back as far as he pleases, and no player on the opposite side shall advance beyond his mark until he has kicked.*

9. *No player shall run with the ball.*

10. *Neither tripping nor hacking shall be allowed, and no player shall use his hands to hold or push his adversary.*

11. *A player shall not be allowed to throw the ball or pass it to another with his hands.*

12. *No player shall be allowed to take the ball from the ground with his hands under any pretence whatever while it is in play.*

13. *No player shall be allowed to wear projecting nails, iron plates, or gutta-percha on the soles or heels of his boots.*

Although it joined the FA, Sheffield FC also went its own way, keen to protect its autonomy and its rules and, in 1865, began playing newly-formed clubs outside the city, no doubt

Nathaniel Creswick, one of the two founders of Sheffield FC.

*John Charles Clegg who featured in the first
England v Scotland international (photograph courtesy of his
great great-nephew Tony Beardshaw).*

CW Alcock.

Top: Football in Crowe Street 1721.
Bottom: Football at Winchester School.

Top: Football at Rugby School (note the round ball)
Harper's Weekly 1870.
Bottom: Bully football at Eton and the Wall Game by Syndey P Hall (wood engraving).

Sketches from the first international, between Scotland and England in Glasgow on 30 November 1872.

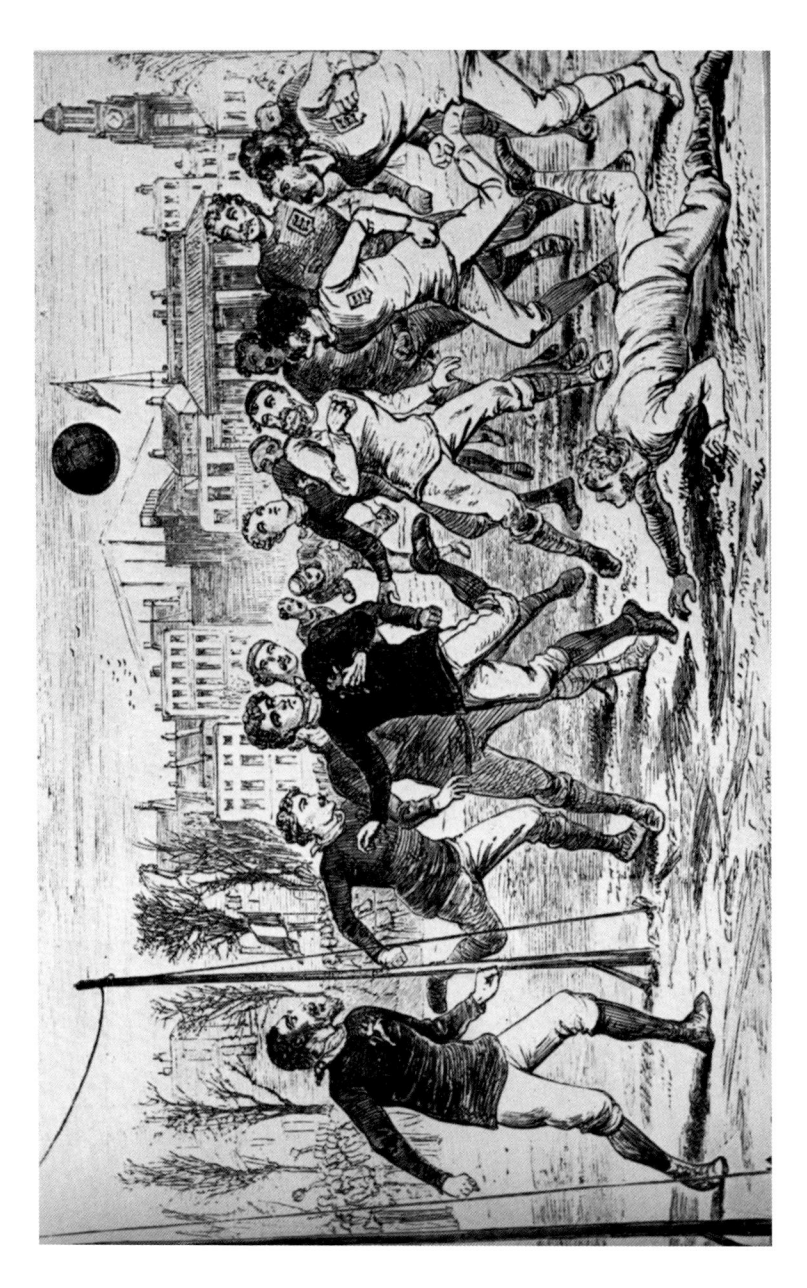

Kennington Oval. England v Scotland in 1878.

Lord Kinnaird.

A tale of two cities

eager to propagate its version. At this time, for several reasons, considerably more clubs were playing by Sheffield Rules. Not only had they been around longer but the FA had also caused considerable rancour with its split from rugby; furthermore the FA's offside rule was proscriptive.

The rule determined that, as in rugby, any player ahead of the player with the ball was offside and clubs complained that this led to a boring afternoon. Sheffield used a much more exciting one man offside or, at times, dispensed with it altogether. The original Sheffield Rules (as well as its subsequent amendments) contained no offside rule, which, as discussed, may have influenced the Australian code. Chesterman, however, had written to the FA in 1863 pointing out that although there was no written rule the one 'which is always played by us' was to be entered into the rules. According to Harry Waters Chambers, rather than it having always been played, the following one man offside rule had only been in use since the beginning of the '63 campaign:

> *any player between the opponent's goal and the goalkeeper unless he has followed the ball there is offside and out of play. The goalkeeper is that player in the defending side who is for the time being nearest his own goal.*

As mentioned, at this time Sheffield teams employed a 'kick through' who sat behind the defence and near to the goal, ready to collect an easy ball; a position that would not have been available had there been an offside rule – the same position is still in practice today, except we call it goal hanging. News reports of early Sheffield FC games rarely mention offside and when they do the inference is that it was used a one-off for that particular game.

Of thirty-five games played between 1860 and 1865, use of an offside rule is only reported on two occasions: that first out-of-town fixture pitting Sheffield FC against Nottingham in January 1865 and Sheffield FC against Mackenzie in October 1865. Of course newspaper articles are not entirely reliable but it does seem as if the offside rule did not sit

From Sheffield with Love

well with Sheffield and, though they dabbled with a liberal version, preferred to keep it out of the rule book. When it was finally incorporated in 1863 it may well have been initially (and subsequently) ignored. Chesterman certainly seemed to be exaggerating the use of an unwritten rule, which was in reality, loosely and infrequently applied.

Sheffield later dabbled with the FA offside law (in '65–66) with a view to adopting the FA code but found it dried up goals and it was given short shrift, the rules reverting to a loosely-applied one man offside the next season. As a result of the Sheffield experiment the FA (during the February 1866 meeting at which they accepted Sheffield's use of a crossbar into their game), fearing its rules would not be nationally adopted, relented and downgraded to, a still conservative, three man offside law.

Unlike Sheffield, an object lesson in pragmatic flexibility when it came to adapting rules to fit the situation, the FA were grudging and glacial; they did not further soften the rule for nearly forty years when they introduced the two-man offside clause in 1925. In summary, then, it appears that in Sheffield there was no offside law from 1857–63, a poorly-applied one man offside law from 1863–65, London's draconian rule 6 from '65–66, a loosely applied one man offside law from 1866–77 and finally a three man offside law when Sheffield accepted FA Laws from 1877 onwards.

In 1866, Chesterman again wrote to the FA, this time suggesting a match between London and the Club. The invitation was accepted and the worlds' first representational match took place at Battersea Park in March 1866. The teams consisted of the following players, many of whose names recur throughout this book:

London: A Pember (captain), CW Alcock, A Baker, CW Barnes, J Barnes, ED Elphinstone, AF Kinnaird, JM Martin, DM O'Leary, C Tebbutt, R Willis.

Sheffield: W Chesterman (captain), W. Baker, HW Chambers, J Denton, AA Dixon, F Knowles, JC Shaw, J Knowles, JK Swift, JD Webster, A Wightman.

A tale of two cities

In front of a small, shivering, rained-on crowd, Sheffield lost by two goals and four touchdowns to nil. The FA Laws had still retained touchdowns, which came into play in the event of a draw and although they had just got rid of the rule at the February meeting (trading them for the Sheffield corner kick), still used it for this game.

The Sheffield contingent were not happy, believing that they had been misled over which of the old and new rules (including no touchdowns, a three man offside and the use of a crossbar) were to be employed. The match also has historical significance in being the first ninety-minute game, previous ones generally lasting three hours.

The wet and wintry weather conditions prompted the lily-livered Londoners to attempt to abandon the game but, despite losing, the hardened Northerners, feeling somewhat duped over rules, insisted on playing on, refusing to give up both on point of honour and to get one over on their nesh[1] southern opponents. From then on Sheffield FC preferred to play ninety-minute matches; it did not become an FA Law until 1877. Another match was proposed for March 1867 but, perhaps unsurprisingly, rules could not be agreed upon.

By the time of an FA meeting in early 1867, the FA had shrunk to just ten member clubs, with Chesterman of Sheffield (the only non-London based member club) one of only six delegates who bothered to attend. He urged them to see sense and include more Sheffield laws, requesting that they include rouges, a one man offside and a free kick for handball, but the FA declined.

The rouge system, derived from Eton Rules field football, was first used by the Sheffield Club in 1860 and included in the first revision of their rules in 1862, because of the excessive number of goalless draws with the existing four-yard goalmouths (it is unclear if the Club had thought of just widening the goal). It consisted of two goalposts four yards apart (connected by a crossbar nine feet from the ground) with two further posts four yards either side.

Getting the ball between the goalposts led to a goal but a rouge was scored if the ball landed between goalpost and rouge post and was then touched on the ground by an attacking player following through. Games were won on goals scored but, in the event of a draw, rouges came into play. It was discarded in 1868 though a similar post system exists to this day in Australian Rules football.

The Eton Field game no longer has extra posts but still has a rouge system of touchdown point scoring. Not as well known as the school's other ball game – the Eton Wall game – the field game is something of a chimera. It is played with a round-shaped ball and picking up the ball is forbidden but points are scored by touchdowns and conversions. It is unclear which game came first, despite the first known Wall rules being recorded in 1841 and those for the Field version in 1847. Football at Eton (possibly an ancestor of both versions) was first mentioned in Thomas Gray's *Ode on a Distant Prospect of Eton College* in 1742: 'What idle progeny succeed, to chase the rolling circle's speed, or urge the flying ball?'

The FA's unwillingness to consider Chesterman's suggestions was symptomatic of the indecision of a weakened central administrative body and signalled the clear supremacy of the Sheffield Rules in regard to their popularity and playability. Chesterman had not even mentioned several other features the Sheffield game had at this time that the FA had not, including, referees, the opposite side – to the one that put the ball out of play – throwing it back in (as opposed to whoever got to the ball first) and changing ends at half-time if no one had scored (as oppose to changing ends every time someone scored).

Seizing the initiative, in 1867 the Club formed The Sheffield Football Association (SFA) to further develop the Sheffield Rules, to administer those clubs adhering to the rules and to encourage more clubs to use them. At this time, the SFA had more players and clubs than the FA and nationally Sheffield Rules were favoured.

The FA, probably alarmed at the SFA's ascendancy, began in earnest to lobby support from clubs and although the SFA tacitly supported the FA, the two codes essentially vied for national dominance. An example of the battle to win the hearts and minds

A tale of two cities

of the country's clubs took place in Nottingham in '67–68 when the Nottingham club (later called Notts County) adopted FA Laws while Nottingham Forest adopted the Sheffield code. The following year the FA increased its committee to nine members and in 1869 reached to the provinces, admitting Chesterman and representatives from Nottingham, Newark and Lincoln to the board.

Sheffield and London did not play each other again till nearly five years after the formation of the SFA, in December 1871. The previous year the FA had cautiously admitted sixteen SFA clubs, allowing them to play FA clubs under Sheffield Rules, an arrangement that was to continue till 1877. More formal relations were established when the SFA became affiliated to the FA in 1871; at last the FA was exercising Machiavellian astuteness. The match almost never happened. The London-based Wanderers had challenged any team in the world to play them but when the SFA picked up the gauntlet, suggesting two matches using FA and Sheffield rules respectively, they did not reply.

The Sheffield Association then challenged the FA to home and away games but the FA churlishly demurred on the grounds that it could not countenance another code; clearly some rivalry had been established. Luckily the FA secretary, Charles W Alcock, agreed to select a team of London-based players and make the trip to Sheffield on an informal basis, ensuring the viability, though not the legitimacy, of the fixture.

Held at Bramall Lane using Sheffield rules, the world's first (albeit unofficial) inter-association match ended 3-1 to Sheffield. London was apparently the better team on the day but just could not get their heads around the lack of an offside rule, constantly forgetting to cover the bog-lining kick throughs. A Sheffield team playing long ball, who ever would have thought?

In that 1871 game, JC Shaw, co-founder and captain of Hallam FC and president of the SFA from 1869–85, played in goal for London, who were a man down. Shaw (no relation to the great Joe Shaw who made 714 appearances for Sheffield United) had also played in the 1866 London game and continued to play football till the ripe old age of 56. Incidentally, in 1862 he organised the

69

From Sheffield with Love

first Hallam Chase fell-run still held today, coming second and winning the following year.

The famous Chase was originally 10 miles but was changed within a few years to 3.25 miles. It is the second longest running cross-country race in the world (and the oldest open to any age; held 126 times); only the 10 mile Crick Run in Rugby is longer (c: 1838; 17-18 year-olds only; held 159 times)[2]. Twenty-one years after that first Chase, the Hallam FC annual end of season sports day was as popular as ever, attracting a crowd of 20,000 to the world's oldest football ground at Sandygate to see, among other things, Billy Mosforth – England international, darling of Wednesday Club and local sports pin-up – win the 440 yards run.

A return match between Sheffield and London took place in the capital in January 1872 using FA Laws. Following this, games were played thrice yearly, twice in Sheffield and once in London, with half the game under Sheffield Rules and the other under FA ones. Potential Sheffield players were nominated by their clubs and then selected by the SFA, sometimes, taking the spirit of fair play to new heights, by picking names out of a bag.

It was Sheffield who had urged the FA to introduce a tape between the posts at a height of eight feet but no sooner had the FA agreed to do this (in 1866) that the SFA then raised their tape back to nine feet.

They did not lower it again for some time, which meant that for the March 1872 London-Sheffield fixture the crossbar had to be lowered at half-time from Sheffield's nine feet height to London's eight. These were important fixtures in the footballing calendar (CW Alcock (q.v.) regularly captained for London) and according to the 1879 *Dickens's Dictionary of London*, edited by Charles Dickens Junior, the matches were only equalled in importance by the England-Scotland games and the FA Cup final.

Playing two halves under different rules was fair but absurd and the situation was untenable. The final match held in London was at The Oval in 1890; ironically it was abandoned due to fog,

A tale of two cities

with Sheffield winning 2-1. Sheffield won convincingly (4-1) the following year in front of a home crowd of 10,000 but something had to give – and something did. The antecedents to the crucial move that decided who would reign supreme were contained in a cup.

Footnotes

[1] colloq. 'intolerance of cold, northern English

[2] Neither the Crick nor the Chase took place in 2001 due to the foot and mouth epidemic. Of all the Sheffield clubs, Hallam FC had a particular penchant for athletics; the famous Hallamshire Harriers Athletics Club is a direct descendant.

Chapter Five

A KNOCKOUT IDEA

*'And how does the world use you, Mr George?'
Grandfather Smallweed inquires, slowly rubbing his
legs. 'Pretty much as usual. Like a football.'*

Excerpt from *Bleak House* by Charles Dickens, 1853.

DURING ASSOCIATION FOOTBALL'S first decade clubs had formed and played for fun, but all that was about to change. In Sheffield, in 1867, the world's first knockout football competition was proposed and the world was to see its first football trophy.

It gives me great pleasure to reveal that the man behind the idea was an Irishman. Like my father, Thomas Youdan (1816–83) went to Sheffield from Ireland as an eighteen-year-old to work as a labourer. By the time he was 35, in 1851, Youdan had worked his way up to become the landlord of a pub, the Spinks Nest Inn. Given the then current situation in Ireland, with the potato blight and its mass deaths and Diaspora, Youdan had done well for himself and could have enjoyed a comfortable life, but he had bigger ideas: it was to be a rollercoaster ride. His pub was in West Bar, a tenement slum area that was also the music hall quarter of Sheffield; here numerous theatres provided cheap entertainment, injecting transient gaiety into the dreary lives of the poor.

Youdan fancied himself a Boniface and bought the Casino pub and dance hall and the neighbouring Surrey Theatre; he joined the two together and opened the new venture as Youdan's Royal Casino in 1858. Incorporating free music into the schedule attracted a big following and he was soon able to further extend the premises, which reverted to the name, the Surrey Theatre. In 1863 slum clearances saw the tenement buildings demolished, giving Youdan scope to realise his vision – the establishment of a

A knockout idea

theatre to rival the best in London. He spent an enormous £30,000 to expand his theatre, making it the biggest public building in the city. The frontage led to an anteroom housing the biggest mirrors in England, which led, in turn to the picture gallery, an opulent smoking room and a saloon containing concert and dining rooms – all illuminated with huge chandeliers.

The theatre itself seated 1,500 and was festooned with flaming gas jets in the shape of Mr Punch for the lighting of pipes and cigars. Above the theatre was a mirrored ballroom studded with oil paintings and finished off with a magnificent central cut-glass chandelier. The roof was a decked terrace and dining hall for summer dances, and the building was capped with a tower. Beneath the theatre was an underground museum with model cities, Indian and Chinese weapons, marble statues and busts, paintings, mechanical figures, stuffed birds, waxworks and a menagerie. Youdan had realised his dream – it had a reputation as second only to Convent Garden.

In a bid to become the greatest provincial impresario and expand his empire, in 1860 Youdan had leased Sheffield's Adelphi Circus Theatre. Built in 1837 as a faithful copy of Phillip Astley's Amphitheatre (the biggest circus in the world when built in 1771), it had a 42 foot diameter ring which converted into an arena for equestrian acts. In January 1848 Pablo Fanque appeared there with his horse show; the first black circus proprietor and entertainer in Britain. He was immortalised by John Lennon in the Beatle's song *Being for the Benefit of Mr Kite* from the Sergeant Pepper album –

> 'The Hendersons will all be there, late of Pablo Fanque's fair.'

Two months after his appearance, his wife died in a freak accident. While watching her son perform a tightrope act, the wooden gallery seating 600 collapsed; she was the only fatality. Distraught as he was, Fanque picked himself up, dusted himself down and started all over again, marrying a circus rider in Sheffield three months later.

The Adelphi theatre sat on the banks of the River Sheaf with its rear end projecting on stilts to the water's edge. By the time of Youdan's lease it appears to have been shut down as he immediately used it for costume, props and set storage. On March 11th 1864, Sheffield's newly-built Dale Dyke Dam burst on its first filling and six hundred and fifty million gallons of water burst out in what became known as The Great Sheffield Flood.

Robin Hood's Loxley was first to be hit followed by Sheffield Wednesday's future home, the suburb of Hillsborough, before continuing to the city where a bend in the River Don diverted the water to where the Don Valley Stadium and Hallam FM Arena now stand. Two hundred and fifty people died in what was one of England's worst man-made disasters and, for those interested, there exist fascinating first-hand accounts of heroism, tragedy and even comedy.

There was also considerable damage to property; amongst these was the Adelphi whose riverside location was in the direct line of water. Much of Youdan's stage property was destroyed but this did not stop him contributing £100 to the relief effort – the largest contribution by an individual businessman.

Worse was to follow for Youdan a year later. He had matched the Surrey Theatre's lavish surroundings by staging ever more ambitious operatic and theatrical projects and in March 1865 put on *The Streets of London* by Boucicault, the Irish dramatist. The play climaxed with the Great Fire of London of 1666 and Youdan staged it by spectacularly setting fire to a huge onstage house façade, which dramatically crashed to the ground; the conflagration put out by local firemen to the relief of the thrilled audience.

Unfortunately following the Friday March 25th show the fire may not have been fully extinguished as the building was found aflame at 2:30 am. It burned like fury until nothing was left but charred walls. (Interestingly the building that replaced it was itself engulfed in flames when it was destroyed by German bombers in the Blitz. The new law courts now occupy the site – fingers crossed.)

Youdan was inconsolable and faced financial ruin, but in great theatrical tradition he once again went on with the show. Like

A knockout idea

many others he had filed for compensation from the Sheffield Water Company and in July 1865 he was granted £66 or about half of what he had claimed. The particulars of the claim make for interesting reading and give an insight into the theatre of the period. Amongst other things he claimed for the loss of:

6 canvas-covered basket horses, a basket frog, a basket goose, a trick clock, a trick star, a trick box, a bass viol, 8 dolphins, a trick turkey basket, a revolving barrel, 2 property guns, two property drums, a property fox, a fish head, a horse for Don Juan, a set of rustic railings, a large working butterfly, a boat trick and the basket body of a man; the latter possibly mistaken for a drowned corpse.

He immediately gave up his lease and purchased the Adelphi, renovated and enlarged it (and fire and waterproofed it!) and renamed it the Alexandra Theatre and Opera House, though it was nicknamed Tommy's, the Old Alex or the Blood Tub. With a 40 by 60 foot stage and seating for an impressive 4000 it was the largest provincial theatre; it reopened in October 1865 and Youdan was back in business.

By 1867 when he offered his cup, Thomas Youdan was once again on solid financial footing and had managed to secure the patronage of the elderly Lord Brougham (1778–1868), the lifelong abolitionist who as Whig Lord Chancellor had pushed through the Slavery Abolition Act of 1833. As a young man Henry Brougham was a radical, friends with Byron and Lamb and sufficiently brilliant to be admitted to the Royal Society at only twenty-five. He later designed the eponymous four-wheeled horse-drawn carriage and is credited with turning Cannes from a backwater village into an international resort. He gained his notoriety defending Princess Caroline and the annulment of her marriage to George IV.

In 1811 George had become Prince Regent after his father, George III, was deemed unfit to rule on the grounds of insanity. A spendthrift hedonist, Parliament demanded that George marry Princess Caroline of Brunswick in exchange for the cancellation of his enormous debts. George agreed but on first meeting the malodorous, short, dumpy Princess declared 'I am not well; get me a brandy' and left the room. The marriage went ahead but he could only face her when drunk, this presumably explaining the birth of their daughter.

They stayed together only for a year, Caroline ultimately removing herself to Italy, agreeing to renounce her title of Queen Consort in return for an annuity and the promise that she would not be divorced. Several times George tried to find grounds for annulment but failed. To his horror, when he became King in 1820, Caroline decided she would return to become Queen. His lawyers went into overdrive, desperate to finds grounds for an annulment. In fairness, George did have a point, albeit a hypocritical one.

Unattractive as she was Caroline had a recidivistic history of scandalous behaviour including frequent indiscretions, flirtatiousness and conversations peppered with innuendo. She was accused of 'romping familiarly' with numerous naval officers – a servant having fainted at the sight, and having both an illegitimate birth and at least one adulterous relationship. George delayed his coronation while the Bill was put forward but Brougham succeeded in having it withdrawn, much to the delight of the public, who had always had a soft spot for her – the Queen of Hearts. Stalemate.

Regardless, and hoping for a future annulment, George went ahead with his coronation on July 19th 1821 to which the future Queen was not invited. Furious, she turned up at Westminster Abbey insisting on admission but was refused as she did not have a ticket! She created such a scene that the gathered well-wishers appear to have turned against her, hissing and hooting until she left. The constitutional crisis was resolved by divine intervention.

Eleven days after the coronation she developed severe abdominal pains while at the Drury Lane Theatre and died on August 7th.

Thomas Youdan had certainly gained a very influential friend and it is possible that without Brougham's patronage in 1865 he may not have got back on his fiscal feet and been able to offer his knockout football competition. Brougham, in turn, may

A knockout idea

not have offered his patronage, had he not made his name with the monarchical crisis. Perhaps then, the world's first football competition would not have happened were it not for George IV's profligate dandyism.

The Youdan Cup was fought between twelve Sheffield clubs though notably Sheffield FC, who from early 1867 refused to play local sides, busy spreading its gospel nationally, declined to enter. After two knockout rounds, three teams – Hallam, Norfolk and Mackenzie – made it to the semi-finals. Norfolk (for unclear reasons though possibly because they had performed best in their first two matches) were given a bye and Hallam beat Mackenzie to set up the final. The other teams competing were: Broomhall, Fir Vale, Garrick, Heeley, Mechanics, Milton, Norton (who were beaten by Hallam, resurrecting memories of that first Sheffield game 74 years previously), Pitsmoor (whose fortunes had slumped) and Wellington.

The world's first football cup final took place on Tuesday March 6th 1867 at Bramall Lane between Hallam FC and Norfolk. Although no goals were scored, 3,000 paying spectators – a world record football attendance – saw Hallam emerge winners, as they slammed two rouges in the last five minutes, stunning Norfolk who had sailed through the preliminary stages. Four days later, Norfolk had to play Mackenzie for second spot rather than being automatically awarded it, presumably owing to the bye. Tommy Youdan was too unwell to attend the match and missed Norfolk's 1-0 win, the team subsequently receiving a silver chalice encircled with athletic figures.

An alternative explanation for the bye is put forward by Adrian Harvey who suggests that after the two knockout rounds the three teams went head-to-head in a three match final but with Hallam playing both their games first and winning, the third game became an also-ran for third place. This does not directly explain the huge attendance at the Hallam–Norfolk game, though the public, having seen Hallam winning their first match and knowing Norfolk's pedigree, may have divined that this would turn into the final proper.

Either way, the Countrymen became the first football club in the world to win a cup and Shaw the first football captain to lift a trophy. Unfortunately, he did not get to pick up the Sheffield-made silver cup on the day, as it wasn't ready. It arrived late and left early, going missing for a number of years. The Cup finally turned up in a Scottish antique shop in 1997 and was bought back by a grateful Hallam FC for £2,000. The world not only saw its first competitive football games, it also saw how hugely popular this combination of football and competition was; here was fiscal potential writ large. Nothing was the same again.

It was the success of the cup that provided the impetus for the formation of the SFA. All twelve cup entrants were rewarded by becoming founder member clubs with Sheffield FC (of course) making up the baker's dozen. The new SFA, however, did not establish the cup as an annual event. After doing nearly everything right, including effortlessly making the near impossible look eminently doable this was an unfathomable error. It was to become its basic fault, its Achilles Heel.

Youdan, understandably, did not realise that he had set into motion what would culminate in truly the greatest show on earth – the World Cup – and perhaps feeling that he had offered sufficient patronage (and received the due publicity) went back to what he did best. Another cup did take place the following year, in 1868, but the SFA had no involvement. Once more a theatre impresario obliged his sponsorship, further forging early links between stage and pitch.

Oliver Cromwell, the Cavalier-moustachioed manager of the Theatre Royal, Sheffield – main rival to Youdan's Alexandra Theatre – entered stage left. (While this must have been doubly galling for the Irishman, a posthumous blow was to follow. After Youdan's death in 1883, Cromwell took over management of the Alexandra.) Cromwell played for the local Garrick Club and confined his titular cup to Sheffield teams less than two years old expecting Garrick to win from the four contenders eligible – Exchange, Garrick, the Wednesday and Wellington[1].

Despite their local stage connections the Garrick were neither associated with the London stage actor (he was deceased) or the eponymous theatre (it was yet to be built; it would open the

A knockout idea

month before Sheffield United came into being), rather they were patrons of the Garrick pub. They did make the final at Bramall Lane though only by beating local whipping boys Wellington by a solitary rouge to nil and that with the help of seven Hallam players 'borrowed' for the tie.

Cup glory ended when they lost 1-0 in extra time to the youngest entrants, the Wednesday (renamed Sheffield Wednesday in 1929, the club in those days were either referred to as the Wednesday or Wednesday Club both of which are used in this text) who claimed their first silverware – still on view at Hillsborough for all to see.

It was the first cup final shock; the Garrick convinced they would easily win after trouncing the Wednesday 8-1 only two months before. The February 15th final was also the first ever to be decided by an extra-time golden goal; the rule had been in place in the Youdan Cup final but was not needed. The goal itself was a fluke: a Garrick player hoofed the ball into the air and it ricocheted off someone and between the goalposts. In an early example of football journalism, the game was described in the following Monday's *Sheffield and Rotherham Independent*:

> *The final match for the above prize was played at Bramall Lane on Saturday. The day, though cold, was very fine for the contest, and upwards of four hundred assembled to witness it. The cup is given by Mr O Cromwell, who has now been established favourite at the Theatre Royal for years, and will be presented to the winning club at the Theatre on the occasion of his benefit.*
>
> *'The prize was given to be contended for by the four junior clubs in the town, and in drawing for the first event the Wednesday were pitted against the Exchange on the first Saturday in February which will long be a memorable day, as the one in which rude Boreas took great liberties with chimney pots, slates, tiles, and signboards, as the writer had good cause to remember, being in imminent peril from a falling signboard of large dimensions in Waingate. With or against the wind, it mattered not, the Wednesday club scored at both ends. On the following Saturday*

the contest, Garrick v Wellington, came off and after a severe struggle the Garrick scored a rouge to nothing.

This was consequently the struggle for the prize, and it was thought by some that the Garrick, comprising as it did seven of the best of Hallam, would 'smother' the Wednesday club. A few who felt so certain speculated a trifle of specie at the rate of three to two. The game began in earnest about three o'clock. Dame Fortune gave the Garrick the wind. Very soon they had the ball down at the low end, and someone sent it direct to the Wednesday's goal. The goalkeeper showed bad judgment by kicking at the ball instead of simply stopping it. He missed his kick, and unfortunately for Garrick it hit the goal post and rebounded. They played until half-time without scoring, and then reversing the ends, the Wednesday Club had the advantage of the wind. Both sides now went at it with great pluck and determination, and the ball was alternately at each goal. When time was called neither side had scored.

They then agreed to play on; the first to score decided the match. In tossing for choice of goals the Wednesday Club were more fortunate, and this time had the wind. The fray recommenced with redoubled vigour. The sides were well balanced, and all went at it ding-dong. J Marsh, the Wednesday captain, kept putting in his toe with the precision, celerity and force for which he is well known. Messrs Denton and Whelan played well. Jenkinson and Broomhead worked like a pair of horses, but what pleased us most was to see A Wood, a slim, diminutive youth, vigorously attack and upset the 'Giant Shang' amidst the applause of the spectators. On the other side, Henry Ash particularly distinguished himself by his celerity and good play. J Donovan also worked extremely hard, and frequently got the ball from his opponents, but never made any good use of it afterwards, his kicks evidently lacking steam. Not so Shang; when he got to her she had to travel, and a very long way too. Messrs J Dale and C Lee also did good service for the Garrick Club.

After playing ten minutes, the Wednesday Club got the ball to the low end, and one of the other side, in making a kick,

A knockout idea

got too much under. The ball went up almost perpendicular, and in dropping cannoned off someone through the goal. The Wednesday men and their friends, who had assembled in great force, gave vent to their voices, and we have not heard such youngest team a shout since the memorable county match v Surrey, so unexpectedly won.

Some excellent play was shown on both sides, but certainly the Garrick showed the most activity, and as a whole we think were slightly the better players. A few of the Wednesday men were well adapted for charging, but a trifle slow. This butting we would have done away with, as it gives the heavy man an undue advantage over the slender, unless the latter has corresponding quickness to compensate. Altogether the match was tolerably free from that unpleasant wrangling which too frequently occurs in football contests.

A very physical game was still being played, then, with plenty of bullish butting and charging going on. It was, after all, only seven years since the 'Battle of Bramall Lane' between Sheffield FC and Hallam. Chesterman wrote of those early Sheffield–Hallam encounters as 'bull-strength' clashes, more akin to rugby, where the object was to charge an adversary and have a 'shot at him' whether he was near the ball or not:

I have often seen the ball lying on the pitch totally ignored, while half a dozen players have been preoccupied with butting each other... men on both sides were more interested in having a go at an opponent than getting the ball.

The evolution of team formations gradually denuded the more physical aspects of the game. More of an emphasis became placed on tactics and playing the ball and less on physicality and playing the man. The introduction of competitions such as the Youdan and Cromwell Cups went some way in assisting this as they refocused attention away from the game's many one-on-one prize fights towards a more cohesive, team-oriented struggle in search of a greater glittering prize.

Existing SFA records patchily chart the evolution of team

formations within Sheffield football. In the earlier days, as mentioned, Sheffield teams played with or without the luxury of a goalkeeper until a crossbar was introduced, when they then became a necessity. In the absence of an offside law, they soon introduced a kick through to hang around the goalmouth, keeping the keeper company and, in turn, a cover goal hovered over the opposing kick through, the rest of the team marauding up and down the pitch. In an 1870 game against Leeds Athletic Club, Garrick are recorded as using two cover goals and two kick throughs, and here we have the rudiments of a defence, a midfield (albeit seven in number and very cohesive) and an attack.

For the December '71 fixture against London FA, the SFA team appear to have used only one cover goal and their kick throughs are described as forwards, presumably because they were playing a code with an offside rule. They also played two 'sides', presumably wingers. The positions of the other five go unrecorded but a year later there is mention of a player acting as half-back, a position now known as centre-backs or central defenders. When established, half-backs (usually three of them), played in a more forward position at the rear of midfield, only later (well into the 20th century) did the central one drop back into a more defensive position; the name now given to them – centre half – is testament to their previous forward position.

Adding in another half-back led to the 2-2-6 formation becoming established, with two cover goals, two half-backs and six midfield/attackers, who still roamed as a pack. In Sheffield this would have been a 2-2-5-1 formation with a kick through, until an offside rule was introduced. In 1877 Heeley travelled to Glasgow to play Third Lanark RV and are recorded as using a 2-2-5-1 formation with Scottish international Peter Andrews in the lone-wolf role.

Scottish Rules included an offside rule so, rather than using Andrews as a kick through, they appear to be trying to use him in an attenuated role trying to beat an extant offside trap. This is an important move. Sheffield's use of a kick through had allowed them to develop a game where a lone striker roamed though, rather than the pack passing short to him, he was more likely to

A knockout idea

mop up any long, loose or lucky balls. By using a kick through within the confines an offside rule there was less chance of serendipity and a greater need for the ball to be passed to him. It was the advent of the modern striker.

Up till now players had dribbled the ball up the field, protected by a pack of roaming teammates. If they lost the ball in a tackle, another from the pack would try to pick up the ball and run with it, with dribbling being the principal tactic and the players so tightly knit there was little need to pass the ball. The increase in positional play and the introduction of cover goals, half-backs and kick throughs, meant that players were becoming geographically remote from each other on the pitch and the need for passing pressing.

It was the Royal Engineers and the Scottish teams who developed the passing or 'combination' game and this proved far more effective. It was soon introduced south of the border and taken up by the northern teams before drifting to the Midlands and beyond, though it took a while for it to take hold in the south, which explains, in part, the early preeminence of the Scottish and northern teams. Heeley's visit to Scotland and their early experience with a Scottish player (the first in England) may explain their early use of an exciting 2-2-5-1 formation.

With the development of positions elsewhere and the threat to the central pack from a passing game, the next logical step was to separate the pack out and at some point this must have become compelling.

It would have made sense for some to hang back and others to hang forward and then for some to steer to the left, others to the right and others to stay centrally. In 1880, minutes of the Sheffield Football Association document that a cautious 2-3-5 formation was used, instead of the usual 2-2-6, by the Sheffield FA side against Berkshire and Buckinghamshire.

Within two years, however, the Wednesday club is recorded as having used a 'traditional' 2-3-5 formation; it had clearly caught on. The formation the Wednesday used was further delineated. There were two cover goals, but they are referred to as full backs and in front of them sit three half-backs. The remaining five are made up an inside left, an outside left, an inside right, an outside right and a centre forward.

Whatever the tactics used in those first two finals (and given that football clubs had only been around for a decade, they were likely to be primitive) the city had been privy to something unique. The nexus between football and competition had produced something special that synergised and harmonised with the zeitgeist. It did not take long for others to take notice.

Footnotes

[1]Cromwell's infamous namesake, the Lord Protector, played football at Cambridge University only to later suppress it as an antisocial influence. His birthday, April 25th, coincidentally marks two important occasions for Sheffield United: their last FA Cup win, against Cardiff City in 1925 and their last appearance in an FA Cup final when they lost 1-0 to Arsenal in 1936.

Chapter Six

ECCE HOMO

Yet, when confinement's lingering hour was done,
Our sports, our studies, and our souls were one:
Together we impell'd the flying ball;
Together waited in our tutor's hall;
Together join'd in cricket's manly toil,
Or shared the produce of the river's spoil;

Hours of Idleness, 12: Childish Recollections
by Lord Byron, 1807

IN 1871, FOLLOWING the popularity of the cups in Sheffield, Charles William Alcock (1842–1907), secretary of the FA, suggested a challenge cup be established: the FA Cup was born. Inviting all-comers and using FA Laws it was won the following year by Wanderers who unexpectedly beat Royal Engineers. The first man to lift the FA trophy, the Wanderers' captain, was none other than Charles William Alcock.

Half forgotten now, Alcock is one of the true giants of football and was one of the dominant sporting personalities of the nineteenth century. His biographer rightly describes him as 'a colossus of Victorian sport, bestriding the worlds of cricket and football', and he did so with the easy genius of the Renaissance man that he was[1]. Though a player of both sports, his genius lay off the field. He was a pioneer and visionary with remarkable organisational and administrative abilities and this story would be incomplete without some idea of his enormous contribution to modern sport.

The second of nine children, Charles was born in Sunderland on December 2nd 1842. His father worked in the family shipbuilding business before moving to London and branching into marine insurance. Charles and his elder brother, John, were

From Sheffield with Love

educated at Harrow School where football and cricket were compulsory. The rules for Harrow football were (and still are) idiosyncratic, though the game resembled association football to a far greater degree than it did rugby. Doubtless this is where Charles Alcock developed his love of cricket and football, though he did not make the first eleven for either.

On leaving Harrow in 1859, Charles joined John in their father's insurance company. By the mid-1860s, however, he had established himself as a sports journalist, beginning as athletics subeditor of the *Sportsman* (est. 1865) and subsequently covering football and cricket for the tri-weekly newspaper.

He also began covering football for the weekly *Field* magazine, the second oldest weekly sporting publication, established in 1853. The oldest publication was *Bell's Life*, which was established in 1822 and merged with *Sporting Life* in 1886. Interestingly the April 10th, 1842 edition of the newspaper claimed that Sheffield Wednesday Cricket Club was formed in 1816 though all current sources cite its year of origin as 1820.

Alcock wrote prolifically on cricket and for twenty-nine years was editor of *Lillywhite's Cricketer's Companion* (and Annual) – which rivalled *Wisden* – till it folded in 1901. The Lillywhite family were a sporting dynasty at the head of which stood William Lillywhite (1792–1854) who had bowled for Sussex, turned the clubs fortunes around and was known as 'nonpareil' (unrivalled).

One of his three sons John was a cricketer. He played in England's first overseas tour – to Canada and the United States in 1859 – which was organised by his brother, Fred, who accompanied the party as a reporter.

Their cousin James Lillywhite captained England in the first ever test match – against Australia in Melbourne in 1877. It was Fred who wrote the *Companion* and other cricketing publications and he also headed up the firm of Lillywhite Brothers, their sports shop in London, still going strong today. It was a Lillywhite's 'Number 5' football (made of heavy canvas saturated in rubber) that was chosen for the first Sheffield-London game in March 1866: Fred died six months after this match aged just 37.

Alcock also founded the world's first cricketing magazine – the weekly *Cricket* – in 1882. Editor from its inception, he remained at the crease of this famous, globally circulated publication till he was dismissed by time in 1907. His old school, Harrow had first played Eton at cricket in 1805. Byron who had fielded for Harrow that day later penned *Cricket at Harrow*; the final line of its famous last quatrain – 'Together join'd in cricket's manly toil' – appeared on each cover of *Cricket* magazine.

Among other publications, in 1895 he edited *Famous Cricketers and Cricket Grounds*, a beautifully illustrated book with 294 plates originally published in 18 weekly parts in the *News of the World*. In 1902 he co-edited and wrote six chapters of *Surrey Cricket*. Perhaps his greatest literary achievement, it is still referred to at The Oval as the 'Old Testament'. There was also the *Cricket Calendar*, the delightful *Cricket Stories: Wise and Otherwise* and dozens more prefaces, chapters, essays and articles.

Football was not ignored. In 1868 he created the world's first football yearbook – *The Football Annual* – editing it from 1868–1903. It served as a barometer of the changing forces in the nascent game and the eddying winds of fortune of the different clubs, essentially charting the evolution of the world game in its early years – testament to this is its original inclusion and subsequent exclusion of rugby.

His first book – *Football, Our Winter Game* – provided a historical context for the game and in 1882 he launched and co-edited *Football*, the sister publication to *Cricket*, though for some reason it did not enjoy similar success (despite its first issue featuring an article on Sheffield football). Similarly, in 1895, he produced *Famous Footballers and Athletes* to mirror his *Famous Cricketers and Cricket Grounds*. He also contributed many articles on football including how-to hints in *Boy's Own*. Had he done nothing else he would have gone down in posterity as the first great sports journalist, but there was more… much more.

He played club cricket with Gentlemen of the South and gained his own first-class cap at Lord's in 1862 for Marylebone Cricket Club (MCC) against Middlesex. He went to Paris with the Butterflies cricket team in 1865 and is believed to have played for the Incogniti and Harrow Wanderers, two 'wandering' sides; at the time there was a penchant for non-county touring sides with no ground of their own. 'I Zingari'[2] (Italian for The Gypsies) was the original wandering club, founded by the Ponsonby brothers in 1845, and, like the Incogniti and the Butterflies, still extant. Perhaps Alcock's most unusual cricketing moment was captaining France once in a match against Germany in Hamburg – *vive le toutcoq sportif*!

Holding the post of secretary to Surrey County Cricket Club for an astonishing thirty-five years (from 1872 till his death), his Oval office overlooked the pitch. The club had been formed in 1845 from the embers of the Montpelier Club and had its own purpose-built ground, The Oval in Kennington. John Burrup had been the inaugural secretary from 1848–55 and was replaced by his brother William[3] and him, in turn, by Alcock.

It took Alcock a while to turn things around on the pitch but by 1887 Surrey were again county champions. They then went on a winning spree till 1895, marred only by a third place finish in 1883; this included winning the first official championship in 1890. And have a guess who organised the new County Championship still played for today? Why, Alcock of course.

While transforming Surrey into a modern, efficiently run cricket club, he was also responsible for organising the national tours of most overseas visitors including Australia, South Africa and the Indian Parsis. Under his stewardship, The Oval was transformed into a major sporting venue and staged the England v Australia encounter there in September 1880 – the first Test match on English soil.

The three-day match attracted 20,814 paying spectators on the Monday, 19,863 on the Tuesday and 3,751 on the Wednesday. England fielded the three Graces (though not the nine Muses) and ran out winners by five wickets with WG Grace scoring England's first Test century (152). Australian, Charles Bannerman, had scored the first ever test century – 165 – in the very first Test in Melbourne in 1877, before retiring injured after a ball bowled by Sheffield-born George Ulyett injured his finger. His score remains the highest individual proportion (67.35%) of a completed innings in Test match history.

Ecce Homo

Footnotes

[1] *The Father of Modern Sport: The Life and Times of Charles W Alcock*, Keith Booth, 2002.

[2] A nomadic club with no ground, it was strictly amateur and remains the only amateur club to have its matches regularly reported by Wisden. Despite its status it regularly beat professional teams and was held in such high esteem that two of its three club colours (the red and the gold – not the black) are believed to have been copied by the MCC in 1860. An Australian counterpart was formed in 1888, the oldest social cricket club in that country. One of the Ponsonby brothers, Fred, was also Surrey CCC's first vice-president.

[3] William Burrup's tenure was characterised by early glory on the pitch and bureaucratic mismanagement off it and when Alcock took over the club was experiencing a slump in its fortunes. They had been proclaimed the first Champion County in 1864 under the captaincy of the legendary Fred Burbidge. That side had also included HH Stephenson who had captained the first English side to tour Australia in 1862 (it was actually a Surrey XI and they only played local sides not a national Australian team) and a wicket keeper by the name of Julius Caesar.

From a cricketing family, Caesar, in 1850, had played in an astonishing match in which his extended family all named Caesar and dubbed 'The Twelve Caesars' (after Suetonius) took on the Eleven Gentlemen of Godalming. They lost their only game by 16 runs: ambition should be made of sterner stuff. Caesar was in the first English side to tour abroad when he accompanied Lillywhite's party to Canada and America in 1859. Fred Lillywhite published a book of the tour – one of the first sporting books in history.

George Parr was captain on the tour and had been the leading player of his day – an awesome batsman – having taken the mantle from Fuller Pilch and handing it in turn to WG Grace. Julius Caesar had a tragic life, his first child died in infancy, his wife died young and his only other child, a son, committed suicide. Broken, he ended up as cricket coach at Charterhouse school where he tutored Sir Aubrey Smith, the famous cricketer-actor, whose oeuvre was significant enough to merit a rosette from the great film critic Leslie Halliwell. Caesar died in poverty 19 days short of his 48th birthday.

Eerily given his name, midway between his dates of birth and death lies the Ides of March, the day Coincidentally on which England played Australia in the world's first Test match in Melbourne. Sheffield-born George Ulyett played in that Melbourne game, taking 3 for 39 in the second innings. Another cricketer who died young (aged 46 in 1898, after contracting pneumonia at Bramall Lane), Ulyett is renowned as possibly the best Yorkshire batsman of all time, giving more than two decades service to

From Sheffield with Love

Yorkshire – from 1873 – and representing England for a whopping thirteen years, from 1877–90.

He was also a goalkeeper of some renown and, in 1874, was selected by the SFA to play in net for a 'colts' match for young players who had yet to play for the first representative team. Ulyett kept goal for Sheffield Wednesday from 1882–84 and represented Sheffield in the SFA match against Berkshire and Buckinghamshire in 1883, keeping a clean sheet in the 6-0 victory. He retired to concentrate on his cricket career.

Chapter Seven

LIFE'S A BALL

*All that I know most surely about morality
and obligations, I owe to football*

Albert Camus

ALCOCK HAD GREATER success playing football than he did cricket and one could argue that as an Old Harrovian football was his first love; certainly his *alma mater* figured heavily in those early years of football. In fact, his idea for the FA Cup was based on the Harrow House football competition – known as the Cock House Cup, with the winning house earning the title Cock House – which is why it was originally named the FA Challenge Cup. The winner of that first season ('71–72), like the Cock House, did not have to play in the following year's competition until the final when they were 'challenged' by the winner of the knockout stages. This rule was dropped for the 1873–74 season so was applied only once.

The club he founded, the Wanderers (previously Forest FC), contained other Old Harrovians, as did Harrow Chequers, NN (No Names) Kilburn and Old Harrovians FC. Of the fifteen clubs that entered the FA Cup in its first year, three had Harrow School connections: Wanderers, NN Kilburn and Harrow Chequers. It should come as no surprise that Alcock's team won. Morton Peto Betts, scorer of the winning goal and the first man to score in an FA Cup final also played for the Chequers, which is why he played the final under the pseudonym AH Chequer.

Alcock would have been the first man to score but had his goal disallowed after a handball by his teammate Wollaston; the first disallowed goal in FA Cup final history. The assist for Bett's goal came from Robert Vidal who was still at Westminster school and, as such, is the only schoolboy ever to play in the FA Cup final. Known as 'the king of dribblers' he is also the only man to appear in the first three FA Cup finals; in the 1873 final he had switched to Oxford, who lost, though they were victorious the following campaign when, once again, he provided an assist. He also goes down in history as being the only person to score a hat-trick without anyone else touching the ball. In those days the scoring side got to kick off and twice after scoring Vidal did so, dribbling past all-comers to tuck the ball home.

Alcock must have been bursting with pride. Not only had he created the cup but the team he founded and captained went on to win it and he very nearly claimed the first goal. And as if all that was not enough, the final was held at his beloved Oval to boot; his Elysian field – and surely the Gods were jealous that day, had a hand in his disallowed goal. That would have been too much for them, that mortal man could rise to such dizzy heights, possess such pizzazz, challenge their superiority. The Gods do not amuse themselves on level playing fields.

In fact, Alcock turned The Oval into the Wembley of its day, football's first spiritual home. Ten football and seven rugby union internationals were held there in those early years including the first rugby international in England. Alcock even tried arranging the first Australian Rules football game in England at The Oval in 1884 only to be thwarted and leave England waiting another eighty-eight years to see the game. Except for 1873, all FA Cup finals were played there till 1893. The date of the 1872–73 final clashed with the Varsity boat race, at that time Victorian England's biggest sporting event.

Since Oxford University were challenging Wanderers, a decision was made to switch the match to Lillie Bridge, a venue near the Thames, with an early kick-off at 11 am, to allow spectators to get to the race in time. Oxford lost both ties. Wanderers retained the cup, being excused the preliminary rounds, having only to beat Oxford University in the final. Alcock was not in the team, which fielded just one Old Harrovian (though ironically Oxford University fielded two), but he was retained as club secretary.

His connection with the cup also continued when he refereed

the finals of 1875 and 1879, both, of course at The Oval. Wanderers would go on to win the cup five times. CHR Wollaston was in all five and was also their most capped player, representing England four times.

Alcock remained club secretary until 1889, seeing his club win the cup three times in succession (1876–78) and be given the trophy outright. Despite the original FA rules stating that a team could keep the cup if it was won three times in succession, Wanderers modestly returned the Sheffield-made, 18-inch high 'little tin idol' to the FA on the proviso that no other team could ever again win it outright.

It was used in cup finals till 1895, when it was stolen from a shop in Birmingham where the holders, Aston Villa, were displaying it. It was never seen again. A replica was made and used till 1910 when it was presented to Lord Kinnaird, fitting really, as he had been a key Wanderer's player. A new, larger trophy was made which was used till 1992 when it was replaced, due to fragility, by a replica.

It is impossible not to mention a little more about The Right Honorable Arthur Fitzgerald Kinnaird, the 11th Lord Kinnaird KT (16/12/47 – 30/01/23), a footballer who, with his bushy red beard, was the most recognisable player of his day. He was also regarded as the finest and was probably more famous than Alcock. He developed his love of football at Eton and went on to play at Cambridge University. He played for London in the 1866 Sheffield game and was elected to the FA in 1868 serving them for a ridiculously long fifty-five years including thirty-three as president!

He played club football for both the Old Etonians (which he created in 1865) and Wanderers, switching several times between the two. Appearing in a mind-boggling nine FA Cup finals, he won three times with Wanderers and twice with Old Etonians. In two finals he scored as an outfield player and in one he scored the first significant own goal in English football when, playing as goalkeeper, he carried a long cross into his own net.

He was captain for the Old Etonians in his final cup victory and encouraged his team to parade the trophy to the crowd, unknown at the time but now cup tradition. He then went on to do a handstand so delighted was he to get his fifth cup winner's medal.

Kinnaird even represented Scotland at football despite being English – he played in the first three unofficial games in 1870–72 and in the second official game in 1873. He qualified for the official game because Scotland were three men down for the away fixture and being a Perthshire landowner he was deemed eligible!

Alcock also gave an astounding forty years administrative service to the FA. Within two years of its formation he was on the committee, replacing his brother, John, and by 1870 was secretary, a post he would not relinquish for a quarter of a century. No sinecure, the post required the sort of dedication only an Alcock could provide; he even found time to factor in the positions of vice-president and honorary treasurer.

He was there at the outset too, harrying clubs to accept a unified set of rules in the 1860s, although it was his brother and not he who was involved in those 1863 meetings at the Freemasons' Tavern. He subsequently acted as go-between for the SFA in a bid to bring in a unified set of rules that pleased everyone, pressuring the FA to accept certain SFA rules. Later, his vision and pragmatism as FA secretary helped to usher in the professional era at a time when payment for playing was regarded as disreputable.

He initially played football for Forest FC, a team he founded with other Old Harrovians, including his brother John, in 1860. They were based in Leytonstone, London (the birthplace of David Beckham) and played one stop down the newly opened Central Line (c: 1856) at Snaresbrook. As well as being one of the founding fathers of the FA, Forest FC are the first known (and, in the 1860s, the most important) 'association' football club to have formed outside Sheffield, are indeed the third oldest after the Club and Hallam FC.

John Forster Alcock (Forster being their mother's maiden name) skippered Forest FC and later played for Wanderers. As mentioned, he was present at the Freemason's Tavern meetings

Life's a ball

where he advocated for the Cambridge rules. Forest FC should not to be confused with Old Foresters FC (est. 1876) who were old boys of Forest School, Walthamstow and, confusingly, also played at Snaresbrook. To make matters more complicated, Wanderers subsequently played fixtures against Forest School itself. Contrary to popular belief neither brother attended the school though two of their younger brothers did. In 1863, with a nod to the nomadic cricket sides, Forest FC left their Leytonstone ground, became Wanderers and played their home games in Battersea Park, before moving to The Oval in 1869.

Kinnaird and Alcock were not the only notable Wanderers alumni. AG Guillemard (18/12/48 – 07/08/09) known as the Father of Rugby Union Football, was another Wanderers founder member and player destined to make a massive impact on the world of sport.

The 1870s were a rich seam in sporting history, giving rise to the first rugby, cricket and football internationals, the FA Cup and the Wimbledon tennis championship. Many of the founding fathers were involved in multiple sports and Guillemard was right up there amongst them.

As a boy of eight and nine he would go to watch Blackheath School Old Boys (who became Blackheath FC in 1858) play their carrying version of the football game, though in those days they employed a goalkeeper. He attended Rugby school, further reinforcing his love of the game though this did not stop him from co-founding the Butterflies Cricket Club with another Rugbeian at the age of eleven.

They played their first game in 1863 against Forest School, Walthamstow and, although initially limited to Old Rugbeians, the following year extended their membership to other public school pupils and old boys. In 1865 when they went to France to play the Paris Club (the first visit by an English team), Old Harrovian CW Alcock was a member of the touring party. By 1872 the club numbered 212 members and in 1882/83 the England Test team which first won the Ashes fielded six Butterflies; thirteen in all have captained England including Sir Pelham Warner and Gubby Allen.

From Sheffield with Love

In fact, just as the MCC admired the colours of I Zingari, so Alcock's Wanderers took on the Butterflies' colors of orange, violet and black. The Butterflies continue to play to this day.

Guillemard did play the dribbling game with Wanderers but he was an Old Rugbeian not an Old Harrovian and he did not stick around for their FA Cup glories, preferring instead to concentrate his energies on his first love. He was involved in the creation of the Rugby Football Union (RFU) on the 26th of January 1871 and, in 1876, began a four-year tenure as its president.

He also served as vice-president, honorary treasurer and honorary secretary and was an international referee on six occasions. He played in the first ever rugby international in March 1871 when Scotland beat England in Edinburgh; he was also in the return match at The Oval the following year to help England get their revenge. In both these games (which were 20-a-side and played with a round ball – teams were reduced to 15 in 1877) Guillemard occupied a fullback position as he did when playing his club rugby with West Kent.

Apropos of the shape of the ball, a round ball was the norm in rugby till the late 1870s. Guillemard, however, would have been used to playing with an oval ball, which was originally used exclusively at Rugby School. The school itself had initially used a round ball but switched to the oval shape around 1835. A reference to this shaped ball was made in *Tom Brown's Schooldays*. Published in 1857, but set in Rugby School in the mid-1830s, it was written by Thomas Hughes, himself an Old Rugbeian. William Gilbert, a cobbler who supplied boots to the school from his shop next door, made the new ball.

His balls were originally made of pigs' bladders encased in hand-stitched leather, the bladders reputed to naturally form into an oval shape though, by the 1860s, rubber replaced bladders thus ensuring consistency of shape. The rubber bladder was invented in 1862 by Richard Lindon, another Old Rugbeian, possibly in response to the death of his wife from lung disease, purportedly due to a lifetime of inflating pig's bladders by mouth, though raising seventeen children probably contributed to her demise.

Lindon also claimed to have invented the rugby ball but did not patent it.

In America a few years earlier, in 1855, Charles Goodyear had used his patented vulcanized rubber to make the first all-rubber football, but it did not catch on in England. Even in America it was not used till 1863 when the Oneida Club of Boston took on a local composite team. Gilbert exhibited both round and oval balls at the Great Exhibition in 1851 and within a quarter of a century use of his oval ball was widespread. In 1892 the RFU enforced the oval shape in addition to standardizing size: the ball used then was larger than now and was reduced to today's size in 1931. Gilbert's company continues to be the world's leading supplier of rugby balls.

His shop became the James Gilbert Museum in 1987 and is now the Rugby Museum.

Charles Alcock's position was forward, though London team formations had progressed little since those adopted in the early days of Sheffield football and many played a 1-1-8 with one man sat in front of cover goal and eight forwards; there was no kick through as there was an offside law. The main tactic was to dribble the ball upfield solo with the minimum of passing. Fellow players would run close by and try to collect the ball if there was a tackle from the opposition, if successful they would then embark goalward-bound.

At five feet eleven inches and thirteen stone Alcock was a handy, physical presence scoring regularly and in 1872, the *Sheffield Independent* newspaper described him as 'a great authority on the game and one of the finest players in the world'. He not only scored for Wanderers – he also played for Upton Park Football Club from 1869–72 and for Crystal Palace. No relation to West Ham United, Upton Park (one of the 15 sides in the first FA Cup) played as the Great British team in the Paris Olympics of 1900 and won, though gold medals were not awarded at that time. In truth, there were only two other teams competing – Club Française and Université de Bruxelles – still it is neat symmetry that the new Olympic Park for the 2012 London Olympics will be built next to Upton Park.

From Sheffield with Love

Footballing world-firsts scatter themselves around Alcock like confetti. As well as founding the first London-based association football club and the world's most famous knockout club competition (and captaining the first winning side) he played in the first official game under FA Laws at Battersea Park in January 1864, when The FA President's XIV beat the FA Secretary's XIV 2-0. He scored both goals! Alcock's brother, John, fielded for the Secretary's XIV, while Harry Waters Chambers, owner of Parkfield House – the birthplace of Sheffield FC – also played for the President's XIV.

Chambers was a lawyer who was both Sheffield FC player and board member; during his twenty-two years as honorary secretary he missed playing in only four matches, and then only because of professional legal commitments. He chaired the extraordinary general meeting in late 1887 that bid to reverse the club's fortunes. Twenty-eight years after first playing for Sheffield FC he turned out for them once more in a veterans v current players; both he and Shaw turned crowd-pleaser when they forgot (or faux forgot) that the handling rule had long since changed and gave away free kicks by gaining a fair catch.

Although the Battersea game was the inaugural game for the new FA Laws, an unofficial match had been held three weeks before. In December 1863 at Mortlake, Barnes played non-FA neighbours Richmond in a 0-0 draw organised by Ebenezer Cobb Morley. Founder of Barnes FC in 1861, it had been his letter to *Bell's Life* in 1862 requesting a governing body that had sparked those Freemason's Tavern meetings. He became the FA's first secretary and was rewarded with the second Presidency in 1867. Cobb played in both those initial games as well as scoring in that first inter-association match against Sheffield FC in 1866.

Other Alcock firsts include: being the first man to be officially caught offside when the FA played Sheffield in the world's first representational fixture in 1866, playing for Middlesex in the first inter-county football game when they drew 0-0 with Surrey, at Battersea Park, in 1867; and ensuring that the world's first inter-association match went ahead in Sheffield on December 2nd (his birthday) 1871 – he was also captain that

Life's a ball

day. In addition, he organized and played in the first North-South game (0-1) at The Oval in 1870. With impeccable taste, he turned out for the North. Oh, and he organized the world's first international football match.

He had originally called for a match between England and Scotland in early 1870 but it would be two years before the first official match took place, largely because Scotland was yet to form its own FA. Undeterred, the irrepressible Alcock organised five unofficial games against them (often referred to as the Alcock Internationals) and captained England each time.

The first official match took place at Hamilton Crescent Cricket Ground, Glasgow on St Andrew's Day (November 30th) 1872 in front of a crowd of 4,000 and finished 0-0. Alcock selected himself for the England side, picking himself as captain again, but an injury kept him out – so he umpired for England instead.

Though apparently chosen for the next two internationals, injuries twice more prevented him from turning out and it seemed as if his international playing days were over but, in 1875, he played his one and only official England game, a 2-2 draw with Scotland at The Oval.

In typical audacious style, not only was Alcock captain, he also scored from Von Donop's corner assist. The outlandishly named George Pelham Von Donop played his club football for the Royal Engineers and was in their 1875 FA Cup Final winning side the week following the Scotland game. He is one of only four English internationals to have three 'O's in their surname; he's the toughest to get, do you know the other three? The Royal Engineers had been formed in 1863 by Major Marindin and were to have a rich FA Cup pedigree.

By 1874, Marindin had already played in two FA Cup Final defeats and was club captain. He played in all '74–75 Cup games but when he realised the final was against his alma mater, Old Etonians, for whom he could also have played, he elected not to take the field for either side. When the game ended in a draw he also refused to play in the replay so although the Royal Engineers finally won the cup he never got a cup-winners medal.

Incidentally, both cup final and replay were refereed by... CW Alcock. Marindin himself went on to referee a record seven FA Cup Finals in addition to a long tenure as president of the FA (1874–90).

Flawless in his timing, Alcock retired the year of his official international appearance. He continued his administrative duties in football and cricket while also finding time to be the first president of the Referees Association, chairman of the Richmond Athletic Association and vice-president of Royal Mid-Surrey Golf Club. He also took the England football team on their first international tour, in 1899, when they visited Germany and Bohemia. After a busy retirement, Charles W Alcock passed away peacefully at his home in Brighton on February 26th, 1907, aged 64. The father of association football was buried in West Norwood Cemetery, where his headstone still stands. The cemetery is a delight, a Victorian gem – London's Montparnasse. His grave was recently rededicated and there is an engraving of the 'little tin idol' on his tombstone. It is unlikely to be coincidence that the Crystal Palace was in the neighbouring suburb, still staging the FA Cup the year he died. In death, as in life, he wanted to be near to the thick of the action and his beloved cup.

Chapter Eight

SWEET FA

'I said I've shit better referees'
'I see,' said Clegg. 'All right, I'll tell you what I'll do. I'll
give you a week to prove you can do just that. But if
you can't, I'm afraid you'll have to pay a £1 fine.'

JC Clegg to unknown player at an SFA disciplinary hearing.

WHEN THE SHEFFIELD Football Association was founded in March 1867 it created a sense of autonomy and detachment from the London-based FA. While there was covert competition, it does not appear, on the surface, to have been in direct competition with the FA and, though the SFA played exhibition matches nationwide, there were no direct raids south of the Watford Gap to entice clubs to turn to the North side. Cordial relations were maintained between the two and the stronger SFA actually maintained the viability of the FA during the late 1860s when it was seriously under the hammer and in danger of collapsing. In a sense they like were two bookends, and each probably recognized the other's necessity.

That it was to be a decade before the two merged exemplifies their divergent views on rules but both made the appropriate noises and courtship concessions, commencing with Sheffield removing its law on rouges and widening the goalmouth to eight yards.

The FA's remit appears to have been crystal clear: to introduce a unified code to which all clubs would adhere, and if that meant changing the rules (including absorbing certain Sheffield clauses) to make it more acceptable then so be it. That of the SFA is more opaque.

Did it intend to challenge and overcome the FA to become the national organisation, centralised in Sheffield? Did it intend to continue as separate autonomous entity and if so, how large or small did it envisage it would become: an ever-decreasing boutique association slowly haemorrhaging clubs to the FA or an association on an equal footing, perhaps administering teams across the north of England? Or did it know its days were numbered and intend to get as many of its rules as possible absorbed into the code before it was too late? Evidence is scant and unclear but while all these options may have been entertained at one time or another, minutes of, and letters between, the two organisations suggest nothing more than courteous and respectful relations, notwithstanding the era's restrained formality.

The Association was a robust, proficiently run organisation with JC Shaw at the helm during its late '60s heyday. At the time Sheffield was the world-leader in innovative football-firsts and was responsible for introducing referees, corner kicks, the one-man offside rule, heading, the use of a crossbar (initially rope or tape then wooden and fixed), penalty kicks, indirect free kicks, and free kicks for hand ball – catching of the ball was rescinded in '69–70. Indeed, it was probably the ban on catching the ball that led Sheffield to introduce free kicks for handball and to allow them to first develop the skill of heading the ball as an alternative to catching it.

It also seems likely that they were the first to introduce goalkeepers but again, corroborative written evidence is lacking. As can be seen below, by October 1871 the SFA's 'Laws of the Game' began to approximate to the modern game; in fact most of the following had been in place since 1866 showing the rapid evolution achieved in just eight years:

1. *The maximum length of the ground shall be 200 yards, and the maximum breadth 100 yards. The length and breadth shall be marked off with flags, and the goals shall be upright posts, eight yards apart with a bar across them, nine feet from the ground.*

2. *The winners of the toss shall have the choice of goals. The game shall be commenced by a place kick from the centre of*

the ground, by the side losing the toss; the other side shall not approach within ten yards of the ball until it is kicked off.

3. *After a goal is won, the losing side shall kick off, and goals shall be changed; but if, in playing a match, half the specified time shall expire without a goal being obtained, the sides shall change goals, the kick-off being from the middle, in the same direction as at the commencement of the game.*

4. *A goal shall be won when the ball passes between the goal posts, under the tape, not being thrown, knocked on, or carried.*

5. *When the ball is in touch, a player of the opposite side to that which kicked it out, shall kick it in from where it went out, and no player be allowed within six yards of the ball, until kicked. The player who thus kicks the ball, shall not kick it again until it has been kicked by another player.*

6. *Any player between an opponent's goal and goalkeeper (unless he has followed the ball there), is off-side and out of play. The goalkeeper is that player on the defending side who, for the time being, is nearest to his own goal.*

7. *When the ball is kicked over the bar of the goal, it must be kicked off by the side behind whose goal it went, within six yards from the limit of their goal. The side who thus kick the ball are entitled to a fair kick-off in whatever way they please; the opposite side not being allowed to approach within six yards of the ball. When the ball is kicked behind the goal line, a player of the opposite side to that which kicked it out, shall kick it in from the nearest corner flag. No player to be allowed within six yards of the ball until kicked.*

8. *No player shall stop the ball with his hand or arm extended from the body. The side breaking this rule forfeits a free kick to the opposite side, and the offending side shall not approach within six yards of the kicker; but nothing in this rule shall extend to drive them to stand behind their goal line. The defending side shall be exempt from this rule, within three yards of the goal.*

9. *No goal shall be obtained by a free kick.*

10. *Neither tripping nor hacking shall be allowed, and no player shall use his hands to hold or push his adversary, nor charge him from behind. Any player so offending shall forfeit a free kick to the opposite side.*

11. *No player shall wear spikes, projecting nails, or iron plates on the soles or heels of his boots.*

12. *An umpire shall be appointed by each side, at the commencement of the game, to enforce the preceding rules, whose decision on all points during the game shall be final. And they shall be the sole judges of fair and unfair play, and have power to give a penalty for foul play of any kind. Each umpire to be referee in that half of the field nearest the goal defended by the party nominating him.*

Note. Rule 7 introduced the corner kick into the game and, under encouragement from the SFA, it was incorporated into FA Laws in 1872.

Certainly a goalkeeper was now clearly delineated in the rules. Despite it being whosoever was nearest to the goal at any one time, he now became the only player on the pitch allowed to handle the ball and then only within three yards of the goal. Sheffield had slowly been trying to remove handling from the game completely and, in January 1871, had tried limiting handling to any player within the three-yard limit.

By October, they had obviously seen an opportunity to limit this further and they had seized it, albeit by a slender margin, voting 44 to 36. Around the same time the FA declared that a designated goalkeeper could handle the ball anywhere on the pitch. After all their stinginess about offside laws, this unusual generosity on the part of the FA presented Sheffield with a dilemma. On the one hand they wanted to limit handling as much as possible, removing the last vestiges of the carrying game and making it a purely dribbling game, but on the other they did not want FA concessions to make the Sheffield game look more boring.

Sweet FA

They did the right thing and fudged, expanding the area a goalkeeper could handle up to the halfway line. It worked. A few years later the FA followed suit. Goalkeepers then continued to roam their half till they were made to retreat to their penalty areas in 1911.

Unfortunately, by 1871 the SFA had been hoisted on its own petard. Following the popularity of the Youdan and Cromwell Cups, it had not seized the initiative, failing to introduce another cup inviting all-comers nationwide. The FA did, and the fight for supremacy was ended with one crushing blow. FA Laws, which by now had incorporated most of the Sheffield clauses and become acceptable to a wider audience, had gained dominance and Sheffield FC had a bitter pill to swallow when they entered the FA Cup for the first time in '73–74, with no choice but to abide by the rules. Still the SFA held out despite the first England internationals being played, with Sheffield players selected to play under FA Laws. Rather than looking like the cool older brother who was into it first, they suddenly began looking more like a parochial cousin who doesn't quite get it; grim, gritty, determined Yorkshiremen with a point to prove.

The SFA had also hindered rather than helped their cause when they became affiliated to the FA in 1871, as this gave a clear impression of subjugation. They only made things worse for themselves when, faced with a deluge of new clubs scrambling to join, rather than seeing it as the perfect opportunity to consolidate an expansionist policy they began to turn them away. In 1873 there was a failed attempt to institute a rival local association but despite reading the signals, the SFA still refused smaller clubs admittance.

Finally, in 1877, a rival Sheffield organisation, The New Association, was formed to oversee the minor clubs hitherto excluded. It was a considerable success, immediately admitting more than twenty clubs and, the following year, establishing its own challenge cup. By 1880, it represented more than forty clubs and, within a few years, had its own representative team travelling to Edinburgh, where it took a pasting from a combined Hearts, Hibernian and Edinburgh side. It later challenged counties including Staffordshire, Lincolnshire and Cheshire all the while – ironically – spreading the Sheffield gospel[1]. Tragedy struck during the 1883 Cheshire game, when a spectator, a Mr Turner, got overexcited, keeled over and died from a heart attack.

However, just as Bill Shankly later quipped 'some people believe football is a matter of life and death... I can assure you it is much, much more important than that', after a brief delay, presumably to remove the offending corpse, play resumed.

And so a crucial chance to challenge what was becoming an irresistible shift in the balance of powers was missed. From the mid-1870s many cities and counties followed Sheffield's lead and created their own local associations, and things briefly looked up in 1876 when both the Birmingham and District FA (a sizeable organisation) and the Derbyshire FA accepted Sheffield Rules and became affiliated to the SFA. Even the *Athletic News* was trilling:

> *We firmly believe there is a much greater vitality in the cutlery town's society than there is in the so-called national one of the London Association.*

Despite their sphere of influence now extending over much of the midlands, the SFA had, it seemed, seen the writing on the wall and were negotiating terms with the FA regarding throw-ins and offside. Sheffield were prepared to accept a three man offside if the FA agreed to a throw-in in any direction, not just at right angles, a pity really since Sheffield's lax offside law had allowed the local development of the fluid passing play first championed by the Royal Engineers – and much in evidence north of the border.

In 1877 they finally gave up the ghost and accepted FA Laws, though, as mentioned many elements of the Sheffield game had been incorporated. In an underwhelming gesture that had more than a whiff of tokenism about it, the FA elected the SFA's unfortunately named William Pierce-Dix to its committee. Amongst all this is another feather in Alcock's cap. His decision to establish a nationwide Challenge Cup provided vital grassroots support and a major morale boost for the FA at a pivotal point in its history. If there was a moment that led to the ultimate supremacy of the FA, this was it.

A short note on other rules: the SFA had lowered the bar from nine to eight feet in 1874, in line with the FA. They also appear to have been the first to suggest the introduction of a penalty goal:

> *...if a player fouls the ball within 2 yards of his own goal and in the umpire's opinion a goal would have been obtained but for such a foul, a goal shall be given against the defending side.*

This is recorded at an SFA meeting in 1879, pointing to a continued, albeit attenuated, autonomy.

The rules of the game were further developed at the Manchester conference of 1882, when the associations of England, Scotland (c: 1873), Wales (c: 1876) and Ireland (c: 1880) met to agree a unified code. They also formed the International Football Association Board (IFAB), with the portfolio of deciding all future rule changes and established the annual British Home Championship, the world's first international football tournament (won by Scotland in 1884). The Federation Internationale de Football Association (FIFA) was formed in 1904, though the IFAB retained a monopoly on rule changes.

England joined FIFA in April 1905, possibly wooed by the previous month's Parisian invitation to, and visit by, Sheffield FC. The other three home countries joined in 1910; FIFA, however, was not admitted to IFAB until 1913 such that all prior decisions on international rules were British sworn. The IFAB today retains these five members, though FIFA has four votes on any one motion while each country gets a vote apiece. A minimum of six are needed to secure a motion so while nothing can be passed without FIFA's approval, neither can they pass a law alone.

The SFA continued to exist as an effective body, administrating the leading clubs in, around and beyond Sheffield and, in addition to Sheffield FC playing nationwide, an SFA side was formed using selected players from member clubs. In red tops, white knickerbockers (and, originally, nightcaps), they regularly played other composite teams throughout the 1870s and 1880s, until the Football League began.

From Sheffield with Love

Most noteworthy were the regular inter-association games against London and Glasgow, organized by JC Shaw. The annual Glasgow game had its heyday from 1874–87 but was played (with a few interruptions) until the 1950s. Like the London games it was similarly played under alternate SFA and Scottish FA Laws depending on the venue and attracted big crowds, both in Sheffield and Glasgow. The first fixture in March, 1874 ended 2-2 which pleased Sheffield no end as the Glasgow team was essentially the Scotland side that had beaten England the week before. The lineups were as follows:

Sheffield: J Marsh (captain), JC Clegg, J Houseley, HE Dixon, WH Carr, JRB Owen, WH Stacey, R Gregory, J Hunter, T Buttery, W Wilkinson.

Glasgow: JJ Thompson (captain), Charles Campbell, James B Weir, W M'Kinnon, Harry McNiel, Joseph Taylor, D Wotherspoon, JH Wilson, F Anderson, R Gardiner.

Umpires: Mr Archibald Rae (Scottish FA) and Mr RH Dickinson (vice-president, Sheffield FA).

This was the cream of the Sheffield crop and four players (Clegg, Carr, Hunter and Owen) had won, or would win, international caps. Note the lack of a referee. They were first introduced as off-field mediators in 1871; any dispute the two umpires could not settle was referred to them; hence the name. They were not to make an appearance on the pitch until 1891.

After the first Sheffield–Glasgow game the teams repaired to a local hostelry (probably the Adelphi or the Maunch Hotel) for 'jollifications' which ended in a hootenanny, a contemporary report reading:

> *A particularly pleasant evening was spent, the visitors not only being the best football players, but decidedly the best singers that have yet visited Sheffield with a football club.*

James Lang, England's first professional (paid) footballer, played for Glasgow against Sheffield in February, 1876 prior to being recruited by the Wednesday, who had seen him at closer quarters when they played his club, Clydesdale, in April 1876.

Sweet FA

He represented Sheffield six times in SFA matches though never against Glasgow; he did however play for Glasgow against the SFA in February 1878, at which point he was principally playing for Third Lanark with the occasional foray south of the border to represent the Wednesday in cup games. Similarly, Peter Andrews, England's first 'foreign' player represented Glasgow against Sheffield in 1875 and 1876 matches before moving from the Eastern Club to Sheffield's Heeley FC. He played for the SFA team on one occasion – against Manchester.

Games were also regularly arranged against Birmingham, North Wales, Staffordshire and The Royal Engineers. Other teams played included Cambridge University, Cleveland, Lancashire, Derbyshire, Nottinghamshire, Edinburgh, Manchester, Surrey, Berkshire and Buckinghamshire, Combined Universities, the Swifts, and the North of England. Attendances dwindled with the entrance of local teams into the FA Cup (1873–74 onwards) though the Glasgow games remained popular throughout. The last significant SFA match appears to have been played in 1892 at Bramall Lane, when they beat London 4-1 in front of a crowd of 10,000.

The Association was also instrumental in setting up North v South trials, which were used to select squads for England internationals. These annual games were played between teams selected from the north of England (including the midlands) and the London area. Alcock had first suggested the idea for a North–South game and arranged a match in 1870 with himself representing the North by dint of birthplace; one of the few occasions he did not appear as captain. No further matches took place till the SFA organized one in '79–80 and, over the first few years, they were alternately held in Sheffield and London. Sheffield players featured heavily in that '79–80 team – seven – reflecting local superiority; the other four coming from the early professional Lancastrian teams Darwen, Blackburn Olympic and Blackburn Rovers.

But standards were slipping: by 1882 just two Sheffield players, John Hudson and Tom Cawley – of the Wednesday – were included and by 1886 there were none. Incidentally, one of the first times a trial was undertaken was during the 1891 North-South game.

Finally, two key SFA figures cannot go unmentioned: the Clegg brothers. John Charles Clegg ('JC'; 1850–1937), played for England in that world-first official international in 1872 and was Sheffield's answer to Alcock. Son of three-time Sheffield Lord Mayor, William Johnson Clegg, who laid the foundation stone of Sheffield's town hall, JC was another footballing great. As well as playing for Sheffield FC, Broomhall, Albion, Norfolk and Perseverance, he was player, director and president of the Wednesday.

Alcock's *Football Annual* described him (in true cigarette card style) as 'very fast with the ball, passing it with great judgment and, when within sight of the enemy's goal-posts, an unerring kick.' Ever-present in the early days of the SFA, as well as administrating he played regularly in Association matches and was responsible for the merging of the two Sheffield associations. He refereed and umpired many SFA matches including the more important Challenge Cup and Wharncliffe Cup fixtures and also became an international, cup and league referee, officiating in the FA Cup finals of 1882 and 1892. He was central to the foundation of Sheffield United in 1889 and served as chairman and president of the club. In 1889 he became chairman of the FA (a post he held for nearly fifty years!) and in 1923, at the age of 73, he also became president of the Football Association following the death of Lord Kinnaird; in so doing he became the only person to ever hold both positions.

He was knighted four years later: the first football knighthood. It would be another thirty-eight years before the second title was bestowed – on Stanley Matthews. JC Clegg died in office in 1937, having served the Football Association for more than fifty-one years, affectionately known as 'the Napoleon of Football'.

His younger brother, William Edwin (1852–1932) was a lawyer and another prominent Sheffield player who turned out for the same clubs as JC. Among other things, he played in the 1873 England fixture against Scotland and the first international against Wales in 1879; his appearances making the Cleggs the first brothers to win England caps. His cap against Wales came while he was defending notorious Sheffield criminal Charlie Peace[2]. During the same trial he called an adjournment so he could play football up the road in Leeds, scoring two goals. Both brothers played in Sheffield's first inter-association match in 1871, Sheffield FC's first FA Cup tie, the first Sheffield Challenge Cup final in 1877 and the world's first floodlit match in 1878. Furthermore, JC refereed the first United v Wednesday derby in 1890 while William umpired. Testament to their legacy, the home of the Sheffield and Hallamshire Football Association is Clegg House.

William Clegg started his playing career at Sheffield FC and finished it at Sheffield Albion, retiring early (in 1880) following an arm injury sustained in a game against Scottish side, Vale of Leven. He became a leading member of the SFA, regularly refereeing and umpiring Sheffield Association games. In 1899 he became Mayor of Sheffield, introducing the city's first tramway system and was knighted in 1906 – though not for services to football. While his brother may have been Napoleon, William was locally known as 'the uncrowned king of Sheffield'.

Footnotes

[1]The name was changed to the Hallamshire Association in 1883 and they finally amalgamated with the SFA in 1887, creating the Sheffield and Hallamshire Football Association. In 1888, to accommodate both associations' cups, there was a new Senior Cup, with sixteen nominated teams, and a Minor Cup with sixty-six entrants.

[2]The criminal, Charlie Peace, whom William Clegg defended, makes for interesting reading. Born in 1832, he was raised in Sheffield, the son a one-legged lion-tamer-turned-shoemaker (who had lost his leg in a colliery accident not in a lion's jaw; he subsequently married the daughter of a Navy surgeon). At 14, while working in the steel mills, a chunk of red-hot steel impaled Peace's leg, requiring an eighteen-month stint in hospital and rendering him permanently crippled.
He turned to a life of burglary punctuated by periods of penal servitude, ultimately ending in murder, firstly of a policeman and later the American husband of his alleged mistress, with whom he often consorted at the Grand Theatre, West Bar. On the run he was a master of disguise, able to contort

From Sheffield with Love

his face beyond recognition. He even wore a false arm to cover the fact he was missing a finger on one hand. (The arm was made of gutta percha, a natural latex. This material was banned under rule 13 of the FA's 1863 Laws of the Game, along with projecting nails and iron plates from player's boots – cf. rule 11 of the '71–72 Sheffield Rules.) He limped it to London where he incongruously interspersed his felonious pursuits with developing and patenting a contraption for raising sunken vessels and inventing a smoke helmet for firemen, a brush for cleaning train carriages and a modified hydraulic tank. After countless daring burglaries he was apprehended, tried and sentenced to death. He was executed in 1879 by William Marwood, inventor of the 'long drop' which ensured a broken neck and swifter death than previously, when it would take several minutes of agonising asphyxiation. A pun about Marwood at the time quipped: 'If pa killed ma, who'd kill pa? Marwood'.

In 1930, over fifty years after Peace's death, William Clegg was invited to Cromwell's old Theatre Royal to see a stage play of the villain's life, including a re-enactment of the trial. Nineteen years later a film *The Case of Charles Peace* was made with a largely unknown cast, save for a bit-part by Arthur Mullard. Earlier, in 1905, two English films about Peace had been made; one was directed in Sheffield by Frank Mottershaw of the Sheffield Photographic Company and has been lost. The other, by William Haggar, is cited as one of the most important films of the decade by the British Film Institute.

Its significance is eclipsed by another Mottershaw film, *Daring Daylight Burglary* (1903): a phenomenal success in America it was a major influence on Edwin S Porter's legendary 'The Great Train Robbery' (1903), the first narrative American film and the one that launched the American action movie. Like most films in those days it was a one-reeler lasting about ten minutes; the first feature length film was the Australian *The Story of the Kelly Gang* in 1906. Ned Kelly (who, like Peace, had killed police, and was hung the year after him) had only been dead 26 years when it was filmed in, and around, Melbourne. Another early Sheffield filmmaker, H Jasper Redfern, followed Sheffield United on their many FA Cup exploits, photographing and filming their 1899 run and their 1902 victory.

Chapter Nine

FOOTBALL! FOOTBALL!

*Away with all fouling and partisan howling,
and strive with good humour forever;
That fairly contented each game may be ended,
befitting the knights of the leather*

Music hall song, JA Parkin and WH Draycott: 1880s

BY 1871, WHEN the FA Cup began and the nation awoke, football was already well-established both in, and around, Sheffield. It was like a cottage industry with scores of local clubs created. So much so that in 1865 the *Sheffield and Rotherham Independent* included a fixture list for the coming season, in 1867 charabancs were laid on to take supporters to local away matches and in 1871 The *Sheffield Daily Telegraph* began publishing tables of results. While some had more serious aspirations, most of the teams that sprang up were just out for a good game.

The social fabric of the game was changing too; football was rapidly becoming a working class sport. Most of the earlier clubs had originated from cricket clubs (including Attercliffe, Exchange, Mackenzie, Mechanics, Pitsmoor, York and the Wednesday) with middle and upper class patronage but by the 1870s there was an explosion of teams from works or pub sides or those affiliated to a church or temperance society.

There were some wonderfully named teams: the players of Chesterfield's Spital United worked for Masons and Sons, tobacco manufacturers, and St. Jude's (named after the patron saint of lost or hopeless causes) never won a cup game. There were All Saints Ramblers and Killamarsh Red Rose, Zion Wanderers and Perseverance Temperance, and my two favourites: the Dickensian Ebenezer Wesleyan and the stunning Wild Myrtle. Yet still there were Halfway Rovers and Pomona, Kilnhurst Old Oak and

Rising Star, Bethel Reds and Park Friendly, Old Whittington Revolution and Stumperlowe. The hamlet of Stumperlowe was a neighbour of Hallam, and Hallam FC had originally been called Hallam and Stumperlowe FC. Old Whittington Revolution took their name from Revolution House in their home village of Old Whittington in Derbyshire. Formally a pub, 'The Cock and Pynot' (pynot was local dialect for magpie), it was there in 1688 that the Earl of Devonshire from nearby Chatsworth House met the Earl of Danby and John D'Arcy to plot the successful overthrow of James II in favour of William of Orange.

The FA Cup was the only national competition in which Sheffield was eager to be involved but for the first two seasons they refused to play under FA Laws. By 1873 the SFA conceded it would have to play the FA way and submitted a composite side but their application was rejected on the grounds that only individual sides could enter.

Sheffield FC subsequently applied, were accepted and played Shropshire Wanderers in the first round. After two draws Sheffield won on the toss of a coin: the only time this has happened in FA Cup history. They went on to lose to then-huge Clapham Rovers 2-1 in the quarter-finals, not bad for a first attempt and the start of a reasonably successful early FA Cup history. Although they did not take part in '74–75 (they scratched their round one tie with Shropshire Wanderers because they didn't want to travel to Shropshire and Wanderers – who had become the country's preeminent exponents of the passing style – were awarded the game), they reached the quarter finals in the '75–76 and '77–78 seasons, losing on both occasions to eventual winners, Wanderers. In the first of these JG Wylie is reported as playing for Sheffield FC. He later played for Wanderers and was in their 1878 Cup-winning side, presumably appearing against Sheffield FC in the quarter-finals; he gained his only England cap three weeks before the final.

In the intervening season, the Club had lost in the third round to the mighty Royal Engineers, recording a 7-0 thrashing of South Norwood along the way. In '78–79 they went out to Nottingham Forest in the second round and in '79–80 lost to them again when they reached the fourth round and refused to play extra-time after the game had ended one-all. The game was awarded to Forest.

These two victories must have been sweet revenge for the people of Nottingham. In their first ever FA Cup in '77–78 Notts County were knocked out in the first round by Sheffield FC with the help of Arthur Cursham – a Notts County player! Cursham was famous in his day, earning six England caps, both captaining and scoring twice for his country. It remains unclear what tempted him to turncoat but he turned out several times for the Sheffield club, certainly money does not appear to have been the motivation.

His brother, Harry, another Notts County player, remains well known to this day by dint of holding the record for the most goals ever scored in FA Cup games. His record is 48 (though he scored once in a preliminary round, so it is sometimes cited as 49). He was a prolific scorer, netting five times in eight full appearances for England.

For Notts County he scored one double hat-trick (in football this refers to six goals in one match whereas in cricket it refers to four consecutively bowled wickets), twice netted five goals in one match, scored four goals in a match on six occasions and put away ten hat-tricks.

Both brothers also played for another Sheffield club, Thursday Wanderers, the Sheffield FC breakaway team (q.v.), which in this case was probably for cup glory since Sheffield commenced its own annual Challenge Cup (they won it in '78–79). As if to make up for his brother's misdemeanour, Harry slotted five goals past Sheffield FC in one game and three in another for Notts County. Arthur did subsequently play for Notts County in two games against Sheffield FC scoring a hat-trick in one but, perhaps filled with remorse for his earlier perfidy, emigrated to Florida in 1884. He died of Yellow Fever the following Christmas Eve aged just 31.

Sheffield and Nottingham football have rich, overlapping early histories (for all we know Robin Hood had kickabouts with Little John, Alan a Dale and Will Scarlet in Sherwood Forest, completing their five-a-side team with Rotherham signing Much the Miller's son), sharing plenty of footballing firsts. Sheffield FC is the oldest football club in the world and Notts County, who formed in 1862 (before the FA even existed), is the oldest professional football club in the world – inspiring AC Milan and Juventus to copy their strip.

The first match played by a current professional team was Notts County (then called Nottingham) v Sheffield FC (0-1) at the Meadows Cricket Ground, Nottingham on January 2nd 1865. It was also Sheffield FC's first out of town match and was a three-hour, eighteen-a-side affair played under Nottingham rules. The Club fielded such luminaries as the Creswick brothers, JC Shaw, AA Dixon, Harry Chambers and William Chesterman.

It must have been love at first sight; Sheffield and Nottingham just could not stop meeting each other from that point on, recording twenty-four assignations over the next thirteen seasons. Interestingly, Notts County originally played within the grounds of Nottingham Castle, backdrop for Robin Hood's legendary away clashes with the Sheriff of Nottingham.

The first use of shin pads was recorded in an 1874 match between a Sheffield team and Nottingham Forest; they were worn by the Forest captain, the Dickensian named Sam Weller Widdowson, who cut back his cricket pads. He later patented his design though, curiously, the FA banned the use of shin pads until the mid-1880s, despite their endorsement by the SFA. Incidentally, Widdowson later refereed a trial game between Nottingham and Everton in January, 1891, when goal nets were used for the first time.

Everton's first great centre forward, Fred Geary (no relation to Sheffield United's Derek Geary), who won two caps for England – scoring three times – put the first ever goal in the onion bag that day. The net was designed by Liverpudlian engineer John Brodie, not to be confused with either John Brodie the Wolverhampton Wanderers centre forward who gained three England caps (1889–91; skippered and scored once), or John Brody, co-author of *The Wednesday Boys: a Definitive Guide to Sheffield Wednesday Football Club* (2005).

Football! Football!

Additionally, in 1878, Nottingham Forest played Sheffield Norfolk in the first game in which an umpire is reputed to have used a whistle. As mentioned, two umpires, one from each side, originally managed games; in 1871 an off-field referee was introduced with each umpire appealing to him on behalf of his own team. Another Sheffield innovation, the off-field referee had actually first been used in the Youdan Cup in 1867.

The idea was developed by the committee which ran the cup, comprising two members from each of the twelve entry teams, the rules allowing referees to award free kicks for infringements. In 1891 referees took centre-stage on the pitch, umpires were banished to the sidelines and renamed linesmen. The idea for linesmen wielding flags actually came from JC Clegg, who proposed that umpires should carry them; at the same 1874 meeting he proposed that umpires make the call on deliberate handball and that the three-yard limit for goalies to handle the ball be imposed.

There is no apparent documentation of the Forest–Norfolk game; in fact, although the two teams began to meet annually, after Forest joined the SFA in 1872, the last time they played is believed to be 1874. Records have survived, however, to show that Forest's secretary-treasurer purchased an 'umpire's whistle' in December 1872, so it may be that the 1878 date is erroneous and a whistle was blown in earnest for the first time in a much earlier match between the two.

Further support for this comes from the minutes of the SFA meeting that followed the first game between the two in March 1872. A motion by Forest that umpires should be allowed to use whistles to attract the referee's attention in the event of a foul was raised but not voted on. It looks like Forest went ahead and began to use them anyway, they may have tried it in the March game or possibly they used one for the first time in the return fixture in 1873.

Incidentally, Hudson's the makers of the 1875 'Acme City' brass whistle still make the whistles used in Premiership, FA Cup, Champion's League and World Cup games today. They also made the first police whistle in 1883, which had an astounding

117

From Sheffield with Love

one-mile range and replaced the wooden hand rattle. Legend has it that company founder, Joseph Hudson, dropped his violin at home, which, as it broke, made the perfect note required.

Following the Club's fit of pique in refusing to play extra time against Forest in the FA Cup, it was downhill all the way. In '80–81 they were knocked out in the second round by Darwen – who made the semis – though they did beat Blackburn Olympic (who would win the cup two seasons later) in the first round. The Darwen match was played on ice, a feature of that winter which allowed a cricket game to be played on ice between the Sheffield Skating Club and Worksop Cricket Club at Welbeck Abbey. Incidentally, Darwen were the first team to openly use professional players, causing apoplexy amongst FA mandarins when they first fielded Glaswegians Fergie Suter and Jimmy Love in the '78–79 FA Cup.

In '81–82 and '83–84, Sheffield FC also lost in round two: to local teams Heeley and Lockwood respectively (they did not enter in '82–83). In '85–86 and '86–87, they made the third round but were heavily defeated on both occasions by Notts County (9-0 and 8-0). After this they were condemned to qualifying rounds: trounced 13-0 by Rotherham Town (first qualifying round) in 1891 and making their last appearance of the era in 1896, losing out 2-1 to Barnsley St Peter's in the fourth qualifying round. They were not to reappear in the FA Cup till the 1946–47 season.

The seeds of their downfall had been sown many years before. Since playing Norton in 1866, Sheffield FC played only one other Sheffield team – Sheffield United Gymnasium in 1870 and 1871 – complaining that they always played the same players no matter which team they faced. It is true that players often did rotate between sides, but it is also true that as early as 1863 the Club began losing heavily. In his annual report in September 1863, Chesterman was complaining that the Club had lost all six matches that season.

Rather than blame the opposition (whom he admits had improved) he pointed the finger squarely at the Club's own players for regularly not showing up. His report inferred that the same problem had arisen, translating into the same poor results on the pitch, the previous season. He also surmised that Sheffield FC players themselves had previously turned out for other clubs by his mention of them not having done so during the current season.

By refusing to play other local teams they denied themselves the competitive spirit of fiery derbies and a true match atmosphere in which to excel. Instead, since they were under pressure to spread their rules, they played numerous exhibition matches in many other British cities. Both factors led to a lack of match fitness. Furthermore, fierce local rivalries were being fuelled by games between the other Sheffield teams leading to a dwindling fan base for the Club. The refusal to play local sides was ironically punished when they were thrown up against, and knocked out by, Heeley in the '81–82 FA Cup. Their star was on the wane.

By the 1880s the big Sheffield teams were now the Wednesday, Heeley, Lockwood Brothers, and Attercliffe (previously called Christ Church). At the time Attercliffe was the spiritual heart of industrial Sheffield but had once been an Anglo-Saxon settlement and merited a mention in the Domesday Book, as a manor separate from Sheffield. My mother, Ursula, was raised in the suburb as was Tom Crawshaw, hero of the Wednesday and captain for their FA Cup triumph in 1906–07; he remains fifth in the list of appearances for the club with 465. Another Atterclevian was John Stringfellow, the man responsible for the first powered aeronautical flight in 1848, fifty-five years before the Wright brothers were wrongly credited with it.

He was born in Attercliffe in 1799, which means that the man who invented powered flight shared the same century as the diarist Samuel Pepys and the incomparable Samuel Johnson. Huzzah! Not only that, he was born the century after the one in which Henry the Eighth's daughter, Queen Elizabeth the First died. Zounds!

Starting as a local toolmaker he moved to Somerset and became an apprentice lacemaker at Henson's lace mill. He developed an interest in balloons and soon teamed up with William Henson who shared his vision of powered flight. In 1842, they designed a 20-foot wing prototype aircraft, the 'Aerial Steam Carriage', intending it to be built to a much bigger scale to carry passengers. They set up the Aerial Transit Company in 1843 and lobbied Parliament for funds to design and construct a fleet of aircraft and to develop an international airline. They used scale models and pictures of the craft flying over London, the Channel, the pyramids, India and China to get their point across, but were met with deafening laughter and a resounding no. Unfortunately, the prototype failed anyway due to a combination of faulty wing design and insufficient power. Henson gave up, but Stringfellow continued undeterred and two years later constructed a ten-foot span monoplane consisting of wood and silk, with a single-cylinder steam engine.

He flew the craft on several test runs in a disused lace mill, to avoid air perturbation, and it managed to travel forty yards at twelve miles an hour, unaided, proving that a heavier-than-air machine could fly. Its success was attributed to the fact that Stringfellow curved the wings; a suggestion of Da Vinci's of which no one had previously taken heed.

Curiously, Stringfellow then went deep cover until the Aeronautical Society of Great Britain was founded in 1866. With their encouragement he developed a model for a triplane, exhibited at the Crystal Palace in 1868, but it never really took off. He retired from his passion and flew away in 1883, just as the internal combustion engine was coming in to land.

Other amateur Sheffield clubs entered the FA Cup but with little success, until the Wednesday reached the semi-finals at their second attempt, in '81–82, losing to then giants Blackburn Rovers. After beating Lockwood Brothers 5-1 in round one and Sheffield FC 4-0 in round two, Heeley FC made the fourth round of the same year only to be knocked out by their *bête-noire*, the Wednesday, who regularly beat them in important local matches. For the following four consecutive seasons ('82–83 to '86–87) they were knocked out of the FA Cup by Nottingham Forest, Notts County, Notts Wanderers and Notts Rangers respectively.

Heeley had Jack Hunter and Peter Andrews in their squad. Hunter was an England international while Andrews, a Scottish

Football! Football!

international (and goalscorer), was the first Scottish player in England; when he went to Heeley he became the first player imported from another country in football history.

Derbyshire side and SFA members, Staveley, now a suburb of Chesterfield, did make the fifth round in '86–87, losing in a replay to eventual winners Blackburn Rovers, while Lockwood Brothers, a local works side, enjoyed modest cup runs in the mid '80s. Their progress in '86–87 benefited from a late Cup application from the Wednesday, who were not entered that season; five Wednesday players (including two future England internationals) volunteered their services rather than miss out on cup capers. For a brief period in those mid '80s years, the Lockwoodites were the preeminent Sheffield side, twice winners (and once losing finalists) of the Sheffield Challenge Cup[1].

That competition had been initiated by the SFA in 1876, following growing concerns about the lack of national match practice for local teams playing its rules and the poor results the SFA team was starting to achieve. It was open to all member clubs, though Sheffield FC, those champions of isolation, declined to participate. In fact, they actually withdrew their membership of the SFA soon after. The cup was not actually a challenge cup as such as the winners had to start from scratch the following year.

The trophy itself was chosen from designs submitted by students of the Sheffield School of Art; the winner Mr Fidler received £5, though the deciding panel were so impressed by the design of the runner-up, Mr Archer, that they awarded him a guinea. The cup was made locally by Martin, Hall and Co, makers of the FA Cup. The Wednesday beat Heeley 2-0 in the first of many finals at Bramall Lane, the Cup running until the '99–00 season.

The match drew a crowd of about 8,000, twice the number that witnessed that year's FA Cup final and a record attendance at any football game till the FA Cup final of 1883; indeed, SFA Cup finals drew larger crowds than their FA counterpart for many years. There is an obvious explanation for this. Interest in the Sheffield Cup was spread over a far wider geographical plane than would first be supposed. With all member clubs being eligible, this meant that non-Sheffield clubs from affiliated FA's also took part, and these included Wednesbury Old Athletic (the team from Birmingham that Harry Cursham knocked six past in Notts County's 11-1 FA Cup rout in 1881), Hunslet and Leeds Oulton (both Leeds sides), Derby, Chesterfield, Notts Trent, Redcar and Middlesbrough.

The cup, then, was far more appealing to the sentiments of the nation's working classes than the Southern-dominated Old Boys-heavy FA Cup. It is surely no coincidence that FA Cup attendances finally overcame those of the Sheffield Cup when Blackburn Olympic became the first northern team to win the FA Cup in 1883. Overnight it became a nationwide cup while the Sheffield Cup suddenly became a distinctly provincial affair eschewed by all but Sheffield and her satellite towns. The FA Cup had come of age. Game on.

Sheffield FC's refusal to take part in the Challenge Cup caused chagrin amongst its players who sniffed local cup glory and it prompted them to form another club in 1877. Thursday Wanderers – so called because they played on Thursdays to avoid their Sheffield FC commitments – went on to win the cup in '78–79. The team were short-lived and are believed to have played their last match in 1882 when they took on an all-star side featuring Fergie Suter and James Douglas, both of Blackburn Rovers and Scotland, and England internationals Billy Mosforth (the Wednesday), EH Greenhalgh (Notts County) and CP Wilson (Hendon).

The assembled cast was captained by PH Morton, ex- of Trinity College, Cambridge, and one of only five to have ever gained a hat-trick in a University Match (cricket's equivalent of the Boat Race); he also included his Trinity chum JR Napier, who had played first-class cricket for Lancashire, in the lineup. Why Wanderers did not simply show up for this exhibition game as Sheffield FC may be a question of remuneration: the Club were strictly amateur and this game may well have attracted emoluments over and above necessary expenses. Certainly Suter, one of the country's first three professional players, was happy

Football! Football!

to be paid for his pains and Mosforth, despite the Wednesday still being amateur, was not above a payday. The Club's players also pulled a crafty one in '80–81 when they entered the local Challenge Cup as Endcliffe but were embarrassingly bundled out 5-0 in the first round by a frisky Heeley side; the entertaining crowd-pleaser watched by 2,000 at Bramall Lane. They had also entered the local Wharncliffe Cup the previous season, when they were also knocked out by Heeley in the first round, this time by a more respectable 2-0 following two 1-1 draws. In other words, Sheffield FC, in all but name, had entered local cups for four seasons in a row: the tricksters.

It was the Wednesday, however, who dominated the Challenge Cup winning seven times; though the newly-formed Sheffield United (c1889) would win it four times from 1892–99. Sheffield FC finally officially entered in '88–89 but never went on to win it, though they did settle a score with Heeley by dumping them (6-1) out of the first round of the 89–90 cup. For the roll call it is worth mentioning that in the cup's early years, Lockwood Brothers and Rotherham Town both won twice and Mexborough won on three occasions.

Rotherham Town had the fanciful early name of Lunar Rovers, so called because the shop assistants who started the club were unable to play during the day and so were confined to moonlit nights and holidays. For similar reasons Everton were, for a brief period in the 1880s, dubbed the 'Moonlight Dribblers'. Everton had started out in 1878 as St Domingo, a Methodist church side that grew out of the church's cricket club of 1876; they changed their name the following year.

This was Liverpool's first association football club, the city previously having a monogamous affair with rugby; indeed St Domingo Everton were not formed till 21 years after the city's first rugby club, Liverpool FC (c: December, 1857; no relation), the world's second oldest club in any code. St Domingo originally played at Stanley Park before moving (as Everton) to a field at Priory Road for a season and then to Anfield Road, adjacent to Stanley Park, in 1884. They came full circle (having described a very small arc) in 1892 when they returned to

Stanley Park, settling at the northern end by Goodison Road; they named their new ground Goodison Park and Lord Kinnaird and Ebenezer Cobb Morley came north to celebrate the opening. Anfield Road now vacant, Everton's usurped boss, John Houlding, quickly gained his revenge by forming a new club, Liverpool FC, in May 1892.

Four months later, playing in the blue and white quarters they would sport till they saw red in 1896, they won their first game 7-1 against... Lunar Rovers. Liverpool FC has now commenced building the new stadium it will move into in 2009. No prizes for guessing where; it will even be called Stanley Park. This pivotal turf even sported another football team in the 1880s, called Liverpool Stanley; the name Liverpool City Rugby League Club also went by during the 1930s and '40s.

Lunar Rovers were not Rotherham's only exotically named team: Phoenix Bessemer were a local works side that had a minor FA cup run in 1882–83 – beating Grimsby Town by a huge 9-1 in round two and losing 4-1 to semi-finalists Notts County in the next round. Another club, Rotherham Swifts, enjoyed a brief summer during the 1880s before folding in 1891. Three of their players, Rab Howell, Arthur Watson and Mick Whitham were snapped up by a grateful Sheffield United in early 1890, a few months after they had formed; they were to make a crucial contribution with 527 appearances between them.

The small town of Mexborough in South Yorkshire must have something in the water – it produces such special people. Former poet laureate Ted Hughes was raised there, and it is the birthplace of: the actors Roger Livesey (the sublime lead in Powell and Pressburger's compelling *The Life and Death of Colonel Blimp*), Brian Blessed (Shakespearean lovely and part-time soccer pundit) and Keith Barron ('60s Angry Young Man-cum-sitcomster); former BDO and PDC world darts champion Dennis Priestly; William 'Iron' Hague, the British heavyweight champion from 1908–11; Donald Watson who coined the term 'vegan' and founded the Vegan Society in 1944; and my first sweetheart, Sylvia Emmett (not Plath!). William 'Iron' Hague is not to be confused with William Hague, Conservative

Football! Football!

MP, shadow foreign secretary, and one time party leader who was born five miles away, in Rotherham.

Britain's first Formula One champion, Mike Hawthorn, also hailed from Mexborough. During his victorious 1958 tour his two other Ferrari teammates, Peter Collins (his close friend) and Luigi Musso, died in Grand Prix crashes and not surprisingly Hawthorn retired that same season. Tragically and ironically he was killed in a car crash a few months later.

The '87–88 season proved a defining moment for the Club. As we know their woeful displays in the FA Cup, culminating in resounding thumpings at the hands of Notts County the previous two seasons, had condemned them to qualifying rounds. There were a number of reasons for their decline. As well as their refusal to play other local teams for nigh on two decades or to take part in the local cup competitions of the previous decade they had not, unlike other local clubs, secured a permanent home.

They were a nomadic side, wandering from ground to ground, variously putting down at East Bank Road, Strawberry Hall Lane Park, Newhall Athletic Ground, the Old Forge Ground, Hunters Bar and Bramall Lane. They finally rocked up at Abbeydale Park in 1921, which they shared with their comrades, Collegiate Cricket Club (who play there to this day), and where they remained for many years before alighting once more to travel around various stadiums.

The park is opposite Abbeydale Hall, once occupied by Ebenezer Hall, whose company made the original FA Cup. In 1946 Derbyshire County Cricket Club also used the Abbeydale Park for two first class games and when Bramall Lane turned the tables and shut its doors to cricket in 1974, the park welcomed it with open arms, hosting 41 first class games for Yorkshire, including a visit by a triumphant West Indies (by 19 runs) in 1976. Surprisingly, in a 60-overs limited match against the Zimbabweans at Abbeydale Park in 1982, Geoff Boycott managed to score 98 to secure a three wicket victory for Yorkshire; somewhat surprising given his reputation for slow play and record of one century and five half centuries in 36 one-day internationals. Less surprisingly he was opening batsman and ended the innings not out.

The final first-class match in 1996 fittingly pitted Yorkshire against Derbyshire. *Wisden* cricketer of the year, Dominic Cork bowled for Derbyshire, while Tykes, Michael Vaughan and Martyn Moxon, batted out the draw.

After 144 years Sheffield FC finally secured its very own ground – formerly the Coach and Horses Ground, now the Bright Finance Stadium – in Dronfield.

The Club's inconstancy did them no favours in securing a loyal, local following. Also, as we shall see, professionalism had recently entered the equation, the Football League was just around the corner and the footballing landscape was soon to change beyond all recognition. Times were getting harder for the amateurs. Sheffield FC had vehemently opposed the introduction of professionalism in 1885, had been the country's most vocal advocate for maintaining the amateur status of the game and they had lost.

At the Club's annual general meeting in October 1887, disgruntlement sat heavy in the air. They realised that they had realised too late. They had painted themselves into a corner with their continued opposition to professionalism and there seemed no way out. Although they could finally see the writing on the wall, they would need a Rosetta stone to decipher it. They had lost. Still, they had a go at stopping the rot. Collegiate School, which had enjoyed such close ties with Sheffield FC in its early years, providing it with many of its players, had formed an old boys cricket club in 1881, and this had since been extended to include a football team.

There had been a Collegiate football club formed back in 1861, but it had rarely played, though it is of great historical importance since it took on Hallam in March 1861 in what was possibly the world's second oldest inter-club football match. The establishment of the new football section within the cricket club allowed many pupils to turn out for either sport but it denuded Sheffield FC of players who had historically played for them, further aggravating the situation. By 1885, the school had closed

Football! Football!

after merging with a local grammar school, so the needs of the pupils were no longer a consideration.

It was proposed that Collegiate's football section be absorbed into Sheffield FC and an extraordinary meeting was called, chaired by Harry Chambers, to ratify the motion. (They had already informally combined the teams the previous season. In the '86–87 season Collegiate had reached the final of the Sheffield Challenge Cup, losing 2-1 to Wednesday in the final at Bramall Lane. Once again, in their search for cup glory, several Sheffield FC players had sidestepped their club's non-participatory clause and pulled a swifty by fielding for Collegiate.)

Several other radical measures were adopted at the meeting including playing local teams, entering local cup competitions and seeking readmittance to the SFA. They also managed to secure the Ecclesall ground of current big-hitters, Lockwood Brothers, for some fixtures, a move that they anticipated would attract many new members.

The Collegiate Cricket Club continued as a separate body but, as the school had closed, old boys dried up. The last old boy, Doctor Edward Bramley, who had played for the cricket club as a pupil in the 1880s made it well into the next century, passing away in 1968, a centenarian. Luckily the club began to invite outsiders to play, and it continues to thrive today, recently producing its most famous old boy England's Ashes-winning captain, Michael Vaughan.

Late in 1887, the Club at last relented and voluntarily played a local team (the Wednesday) for the first time in sixteen years. The following year they entered the Sheffield Challenge Cup for the first time, but it was too late, they had become victims of their own isolationist policy and were beaten 4-0 by Staveley in the semi-finals.

They would finally win it, their first silverware, in 1893 but by then the game had turned professional and clubs were looking to the new leagues and the FA Cup for trophies.

From Sheffield with Love

Footnotes

[1] The firm of Lockwood Brothers later became Lockwood and Carlisle's. My father, Paddy, worked there for 25 years, along with his brother, Jack, and brother-in-law, Dennis. My brother Joe and I worked there the summers before we went to University, cousins too. It was a marine engineering business, which specialised in the manufacture of piston rings for ship's engines and is believed to have supplied the rings for the Titanic. It is comforting to know that, like my fellow Northerner, CW Alcock (whose birthday falls the day before mine), I was also briefly in the shipbuilding business.

Chapter Ten

THE PLAY'S THE THING

Am I so round with you, as you with me,
That like a foot-ball you do spurn me thus:
You spurn me hence, and he will spurn me hither,
if I last in this service, you must case me in leather.

Comedy of Errors, Act II, Scene I, by William Shakespeare

BEFORE TURNING AWAY from the amateur game it is worth mentioning that following the Youdan and Cromwell Cups the local relationship between stage and pitch continued to flourish. In 1885, veterans of the Garrick Club played a charity match against The Pantomimists, a team made up of actors from two local venues, Cromwell's Theatre Royal and Youdan's old enterprise, the Alexandra Theatre and Opera House. The Pantomimists played in the costumes from the two productions they were appearing in, Aladdin and Sinbad. The term pantomime was first coined as 'ballet-pantomime' in 1717 by John Rich to describe the show The Loves of Venus and Mars, which was performed at his theatre in Lincoln's Inn Fields, the London area that was also home to the Freemason's Tavern, where the FA had founded in 1863.

Panto's cousin, the circus, began its modern day incarnation with Philip Astley in London, 1768. Three years later he opened Astley's Amphitheatre, the world's biggest circus, upon which Youdan's Adelphi Circus was based. In 1824 it was taken over by the flamboyant Andrew Ducrow and he, in turn, took the greatest show on earth on the road for the first time when it travelled to Sheffield for a season in 1831.

So excited was the city at the prospect of beholding such wonderment that the Master Cutler rode out to the assembled arena with all his civic dignitaries in a cavalcade of fifty carriages.

From Sheffield with Love

On receiving his card, the uppity Ducrow commented that he received only crowned heads not 'a set of dirty knife grinders'. The seething cortege slinked back to town and in a fit of sour grapes spent the evening at a hastily arranged ball.

Needless to say, the circus bombed and had to be bailed out by another proprietor, as Ducrow hastily exited stage left, to the sound of hissing tongues and sharpened blades. Coincidentally, the first recorded dramatic performance in Sheffield was at Sheffield Castle in April 1581. Mary Queen of Scots was still imprisoned there and was presumably in the audience. The performance was staged by the Earl of Shrewsbury, who was married to Bess of Hardwick Hall ('more glass than wall') and whose son, Gilbert, provided Sheffield with its first hospital – Shrewsbury Hospital – in 1616. Sheffield's first theatre proper was not to be till 1700 when the Pepper Alley Playhouse opened.

The Garrick–Pantomimists match proved so popular that it was repeated at Bramall Lane the following year in front of an impressive 20,000 spectators (approximately the average gate for Sheffield United during the 2004–05 season) with monies going to the Children's Hospital and the Totley Orphanage. Repeated pitch invasions reduced playing time and rendered the pitch a mud bath, nevertheless the crowd seemed to enjoy the spectacle as Garrick laboured to a 1-0 victory.

The Pantomimists, who always played in their costumes, went on to play other charity matches to large attendances, including a game against Derby County, while a me–too team of professionals, calling themselves Sheffield Clowns, plied similar entertainment, though with less success. The following are details of an 1886 charity match between the Pantomimists and the Licensed Victuallers:

The two teams left for the match from the Wharncliffe Hotel, both in dress: the Victuallers in aprons and the Pantomimists in costume. They stopped at Barker's Pool in the city centre for photos then proceeded to Sheaf House, a ground next to Bramall Lane, which hosted some important fixtures including inter-association games. The sponsors had wanted to use Bramall Lane but the ground committee declined, presumably because of

The play's the thing

the repeated pitch invasions at the Garrick–Pantomimist match. Ladies from the Pantomimists, dressed as Little Bo Peep, Lillie Taylor, Little Boy Blue and Miss Moffatt, wandered through the crowd of 5-6,000 selling flowers, cigarettes, matches and toffees. Admission had been doubled from the previous year 'to exclude the rough element' with the money raised from the event going to the Licensed Victualler's Almshouses.

Players entered from the Cherry Street entrance with the following being fielded for the Pantomimists: Dame Durden, Clown, Johnny Green, Demon Wolf, Mrs. Crusoe, Johnny Stout, King Tum-tum, Policeman, Friday, Monkey, Flipper and Flapper. The match was umpired by JH Saville and Billy Mosforth and refereed by E Brayshaw, and the final score (oh yes it…) was Pantomimists 2, Licensed Victuallers 2.

Billy Mosforth was a Sheffield journeyman who was capped nine times for England, gaining his first cap at only 19. He originally turned out for Sheffield Albion but, much to the chagrin of his teammates, jumped ship to the Wednesday on the eve of Albion's first round Challenge Cup tie against Exchange in 1880; by so doing he avoided being cup-tied. Five of his Albion teammates angrily refused to play the fixture which was awarded to Exchange without a kick being taken. He spent most of his career with the Wednesday, becoming one of their early heroes, before settling at Sheffield United in their inaugural season.

Known as 'the Little Wonder' he specialised in the 'screw shot', a Sheffield invention commonly used today, allowing the player to bend the trajectory of the ball. He represented Lockwood Brothers in their 1886–87 FA Cup run, when the Wednesday applied too late to gain entry. He was also instrumental in forming Sheffield Rovers when the Wednesday initially refused to embrace professionalism. Never one to accept Sheffield's censure on pay-to-play, there are numerous instances of him accepting gifts for his turf-work. The referee Brayshaw was then an England international who played his club football with the Wednesday.

A group of big-name Sheffield players, from the local teams, including Mosforth, also dressed up for charity under the guidance of a Mr Brewer of Fargate. The Zulus, as they were collectively called, donned African tribal costume and played an unbeaten series of novelty matches in the midlands, the north of England and Scotland from '79–82. Proceeds went to widows and orphans of soldiers killed in the Boer War, but the Zulus fell foul of the SFA in 1881 when it was revealed that they were pocketing some of the entrance fee. The players were accused of professionalism, a dirty word in those days, and banned from further Zulu matches.

Those that went on to defy the ban were suspended from SFA matches by the scandalised Association, and a crisis was avoided only by the players relenting. One defiant was Jack Hunter, of the Heeley, who would later captain England. He and his teammate, George Wilson, defected to Blackburn Olympic (who played at the charmingly named Hole-in-the-Wall ground), lured by lolly. They went on to win the FA Cup in 1883 when Blackburn Olympic became the first northern team to succeed; ironically Sheffield's ultra-orthodox pro-amateur Pierce-Dix was one of the umpires. Hunter, who essentially acted as player-coach, introduced a new brand of professionalism into training including special diets and an intensive fitness regime a week before the final.

The repercussions from the Zulu affair were grave. Firstly, at the objections of Heeley, the SFA threw Providence out of the local Wharncliffe Charity Cup in 1881, for fielding Zulu players. Things snowballed with claims and counter-claims, accusations and denials from clubs and players thick in the air. In the end, the embattled SFA, glowing red in equal portions of rage, humiliation and embarrassment, had little choice but to scratch the cup final.

This annual knockout cup had started in 1879, sponsored by the Earl of Wharncliffe. It was introduced to provide more regular support for local charities and proved highly popular, with other charity cup competitions following. Each year, eight teams were chosen by the SFA to take part, with most matches being held at Bramall Lane to boost the takings. The Wednesday again dominated the proceedings (victors six times), though Staveley (thrice), Heeley (twice) and Lockwood Brothers (once) had their names engraved on the trophy. The most notable match was the '89–90 Cup final replay between Staveley and Rotherham Town. Normal time ended 1-1, but when the referee called for extra-time, the Staveley players walked off. Rotherham kicked off against no opposition but for some unrecorded reason were unable to score, one can only assume because the referee immediately called off the game. Staveley won the second replay 3-0.

The Wharncliffe Cup was second only to the SFA Challenge Cup in local importance and the final's cancellation was serious business. It also appears to be the first time in history a whole team was paid to play football and undoubtedly helped pave the way for the game to turn professional. The world's first professional player, incidentally, was reputed to be James Lang, a Scottish international recruited by the Wednesday in 1876. While they kept quiet to the authorities about paying him, he kept quiet to them about his accident at a Clydebank shipyard in 1869, when he had lost sight in one eye. He played out his career Government-listed as blind!

The world's first charity match between two football clubs – Sheffield FC and Hallam FC – ushered in a rich era of philanthropic games to support local and national causes, including testimonial matches for retiring players and benefit games for the families of players who had been injured or had died prematurely – not uncommon at the time. One such match was played in 1877 for John Marsh who had skippered Sheffield in the first inter-association games against London and Glasgow and had also fulfilled administrative duties for the SFA.

He was both original captain and secretary for the Wednesday and had led them to triumph in the Cromwell Cup in 1867. He was a spectator at the world's first international between Scotland and England in 1870 but by 1874 had returned to his native village of Thurlstone, which like its spitting-distance neighbour Penistone, was one of the few historical strongholds of football in the country. He managed the Crystal Palace Inn and created a local football team; so respected was he that the

Wednesday agreed to play Thurlstone's opening match and 500 people turned out to see the game (25/10/74; Wednesday won 4-0). Tragedy struck during a fixture in 1875 when he fell and broke his arm; the significant injury was insufficiently dealt with and ultimately he had to go to St Bart's in London to have his arm treated. It was only bound, presumably because it was too late to reset it and monies from his benefit match helped pay for the trip. It is unclear why he died in 1880, there is some evidence that it was as a consequence of the injury that a chronic bone infection had set in.

But there is also evidence that he developed depression as a result and, keeping a pub, may have succumbed to alcohol, which as we will see, was not uncommon in ex-footballers of the time. Either way he left a widow and four children. His death may have been the prompt for William Clegg to retire from football in 1880 following his own dislocated elbow that had set poorly.

In the late 1860s Sheffield had also created the world's first health scheme for footballers – The Sheffield Players Accident Society – in response to the growing number of accidents, some fatal, related to the sport. One such accident at Walkley in 1877, involved a Broomhall player, James Beaumont, running off the pitch to retrieve the ball only to fall down a quarry and perish. The society was principally dependent on charitable donations and bequests; among his many benevolent ventures (which included donating prizes for both Norfolk and Mackenzie's athletics days), Tommy Youdan organised a benefit night as well as theatrical performances for the society.

Chapter Eleven

THE PAY'S THE THING

To say that these men paid their shillings to watch twenty-two hirelings kick a ball is merely to say that a violin is wood and catgut, that Hamlet is so much paper and ink. For a shilling the Bruddersford United AFC offered you Conflict and Art

The Good Companions by JB Priestley, 1929.

SHEFFIELD IN GENERAL strongly opposed professionalism; it was the Lancashire teams that flagrantly flouted the law. From about 1876 onwards, a steady stream of Scottish guns-for-hire drifted down and to the right and the grateful teams began to regularly pay players.

The SFA adopted a position of staunch resistance and its member clubs concurred, Heeley proposing at an 1883 SFA meeting that 'that no player shall be allowed to receive any money or remuneration whatever beyond his actual travelling or hotel expenses'. Such sentiments were reflected in the actions of Lockwood Brothers who refused to play any Lancashire clubs during the '84–85 season, so strongly did they feel about professionalism.

There was more than a whiff of Victorian hypocrisy emanating from the SFA: it was outrageous that working class men should be remunerated for playing football, but it was wholly appropriate that Pierce-Dix, who regarded professionalism as 'an evil which must be repressed', should receive an 'honorarium' of £25 for his role as secretary to the SFA. The Wednesday meanwhile were keeping very mum about James Lang's financial position.

The majority of the FA were also against payments, other than for necessary expenses, though there was a significant and potentially vocal minority, who could be moved to a pro-professional position. This included Alcock, who ever the pragmatist thought that if it was an evil then it was an unavoidable and perhaps necessary one, saying:

> *Furthermore, I object to the argument that it is immoral to work for a living, and I cannot see why men should not, with that object, labour at football as at cricket*

Mirroring Sheffield's double standards, the FA did not seem to mind the 'expenses' that the gentlemen amateur clubs collected, which often amounted to more than the 'illegal' new professional wages. With the SFA now effectively in feudal submission to the FA, the new threat came from the powerful Lancastrian axis. Ever since Darwen had openly used professional players in the '78–79 FA Cup, the Lancashire clubs had been a thorn in the FA's side, yet once again, true to their colours, the FA vacillated. Paralysed into indecision by their own perceived weakness they dithered for five years – though they probably span it as a watching brief.

In 1884, when they finally complained, the Lancashire clubs felt sufficiently confident to hold the FA to ransom, threatening a breakaway organisation unless the FA legalised professionalism. This was regarded as the most despicable act of sedition by the FA who demurred, though their decisive refusal carried a nuance of bluff-calling. True to their word the northern clubs immediately coined and pressed into action the British Football Association (BFA) at a meeting in Blackburn. How much of this was audacious sabre rattling is unclear but the issue picked up momentum like a runaway train.

Sheffield FC and the SFA were incandescent. As the national champions of the amateur game they were immoveable, yet the FA, to whom they had sworn allegiance, was not and now saw the future as unstoppable. World's were colliding, the ground was heaving beneath the SFA's feet; everything was about to change. All appeared lost, yet still the FA fiddled.

For years the SFA had complained to the FA, but had had to stand idly by as the impotent central administration did nothing. WF Beardshaw, a former Corinthian and member of the SFA, who had called for the first FA investigation into illegal payments more than two years before, captured the frustrated Sheffield mood in his open letter dated November 21st 1884:

> *As the game of Association football is at present passing through a crisis it would be well if the question of professionalism now being introduced into our justly popular winter pastime was ventilated before the general meeting is held to decide this all important point. It is well known to a large number of followers of Association football that the payment of players gradually crept in by the introduction into Lancashire of proficient exponents of the game from Scotland and elsewhere. Unfortunately the Football Association did not take any steps to stamp out the disease in its infancy and it was not until many English districts suffered by the abstraction of several of their best men that any outcry was made and the committee were almost unanimously instructed by a general meeting to suppress what was generally regarded as a growing evil.*
>
> *A great outcry was raised in Lancashire against any effort to suppress professionalism, and many tainted clubs immediately banded together to form, if possible, a rival association to the Football Association. Two or three powerful Lancashire clubs assisted this movement and they were joined principally by small clubs in that district who saw a chance of getting a match and, consequently, a 'gate' from a visit of well-known clubs. This slight opposition appears to have alarmed the Football Association Committee and they decided to suspend the rules objected to until a sub-committee should meet and report as to the best means of dealing with the situation. I had the honour of being selected on this sub-committee, which met in Manchester, but I found after some discussion that although every member, except one, condemned professionalism they did not consider the Football Association sufficiently strong to deal with this question as it should be dealt with, namely the stamping out of the evil entirely.*
>
> *My amendment that 'the legislation of professionalism will tend to lower the game of Association Football and that the committee shall have full powers to suppress the evil entirely'*

was seconded by Mr T Lawrie, Vice-President of the Scottish Association, who had supported us loyally throughout, but this was negatived by a large majority...

Strong words indeed, but hollow-sounding and destined to fall on stony ground. Common sense won the day (in no small part due to Alcock) and despite strenuous protests from the SFA, the FA capitulated in January 1885. Retrospectively, one cannot see it that it could end any other way, and the FA's weakness helped rather than hindered events by accelerating the inevitable and preventing a much more serious conflict, perhaps civil war. With passions in the two camps running at fever pitch it is no surprise that the decisive FA meeting was their largest to date with hundreds in attendance. Players, club officials and delegates all packed into the Freemason's Tavern from where, almost 21 years ago to the day, the first FA Laws of The Game had been issued.

The BFA immediately dissolved, spirited away as swiftly as it had been conjured up, and the way was paved for the world's first football league in 1888. In January 1884, anticipating the FA's decision by a year, Preston hosted the first representative match between amateur and professional players; the amateurs won 1-0. The following match, in March of 1885, was a 2-1 reverse and the Players were once again triumphant over the Gentleman (3-2) in 1886.

Sheffield FC adamantly refused to turn professional, instead they girded their loins and launched a campaign of home and away exhibition matches against teams around the country; to what end is unclear. Perhaps it was to develop the amateur game such that it could compete with the professionals or to try to keep as many teams amateur as possible; maybe it was simply a case of manic defence, a flurry of denial. A more pragmatic explanation is that they needed the money.

They had recently built a new wooden stand at their Old Forge Ground on Brightside Lane in Attercliffe but with membership at a low ebb treasury funds were meagre. When the builders demanded the balance of payment in 1885, the Club desperately

The pay's the thing

tried to come up with the cash, requesting overdue membership fees, organising a musical evening and requesting a share of gate receipts from away matches. Between February and May 1885, they organised fixtures against Derby School FC, Retford, Middlesbrough, Redcar, Newcastle, Darlington, Lincoln City, Long Eaton Rangers and Liverpool Ramblers. By the end of the season they were still in the red and had to arrange even more games for the following period. Heartbreakingly, just when they seemed to be getting on top of things, they turned up for a home game to find that the new stand had been blown over by a gale.

Being unable to pay for it to be rebuilt, nor with sufficient funds to pay the constructors, in October 1886 they humbly asked if J Smith and Son would take back the stand's timber in part payment. The builders declined their bartering gambit and the Gentlemen were forced to cough up the residual. Sadly it appears that the Club could not even afford to have the wreckage removed, a Club minutes entry from two years later reading:

> *The Secretary should have the wood of the grandstand in the Old Forge ground carted away and stored for next season. (June 4th 1888)*

Heaven knows what happened to it after that.

Sheffield's first fully professional team, Wednesday Club, had existed as a cricket club since 1820. Members of the Wednesday Cricket Club played on the eponymous day since this was when they were allowed a regular half-day off work. Of the founders, William H Woolhouse had represented Yorkshire in 17 first-class matches while George Dawson had done so eight times. One of their future players, Tom Armitage, would play in the world's first two tests against Australia in 1877 and had a career of 57 first-class matches for Yorkshire before heading west to America where he turned out for Players of USA.

On September 4th 1867 (a Wednesday) the club was extended to include football at a meeting at the Adelphi Hotel, Sheffield. By so doing, this makes them the Football League's third oldest club after Notts County and Nottingham Forest; Chesterfield FC was formed the following month. The Adelphi, which stood next to Cromwell's Theatre Royal, has a remarkably rich sporting history. As well as being the birthplace of Sheffield Wednesday, it was the regular venue for SFA meetings and knees-ups after major games; Alcock and his London team had been entertained there when they played the SFA team in December 1871.

It was also where the decision to build the Bramall Lane ground took place in 1854... and was the birthplace of the Yorkshire County Cricket Club (YCCC) in 1863. Its legacy lives on despite being long demolished – it is now the site of the Crucible Theatre, home to the World Snooker Championship and squash's equivalent of Wimbledon – the English Open Championship. The Adelphi must have had a bohemian air about it, positioned as it was, in the heart of the central theatre district, next to the Theatre Royal (c: 1763) and a stone's throw from both the Surrey Street Music Hall (c: 1824) and Hangler's Circus (c:1879) – and later the Lyceum Theatre (c: 1897).

It was regularly patronised by theatregoers, theatre staff and visiting actors, poets, musicians and singers; the addition of cricketers, footballers and Sheffield luminaries would have made for some heady evenings.

The Surrey Street Music Hall, not to be confused with Youdan's West Bar Surrey Theatre, was the city's 'highbrow' venue with literature and poetry readings, philosophical debates and choral and classical music recitals. It hosted Dickens, Thackeray, Montgomery, Paganini and Jenny Lind – the 'Swedish Nightingale', whose frumpy looks inspired Hans Christian Anderson to write *The Ugly Duckling* but whose divine voice inspired him to *The Angel and The Nightingale*. The sexually ambiguous Anderson appears to have been in love with Lind, she, in turn, with Felix Mendelssohn and him, in turn, with his wife.

The Surrey, incidentally, hosted two of Mendelssohn's friends: Ignaz Moscheles, who succeeded Mendelssohn as head of the London Conservatoire, rivalled Liszt in his advocacy of the pianoforte and was the man responsible for Beethoven almost completing his unfinished tenth symphony; and Sir Walter

The pay's the thing

Sterndale Bennett, Sheffield-born composer and Principal of the Royal Academy of Music.

At the time when the Wednesday came into being the landlord was Harry Sampson, an ex-cricketer who had played 38 first-class games from 1840–57. He has the novel record of recording the highest cricket score on ice (162) – ice cricket was a boutique sport in those colder Victorian climes – during a match for Wednesday Club against Sheffield Town. In 1832, aged 28 he defeated Thomas Marsden, the former champion of England, in a single-wicket cricket match. Marsden, another Sheffielder, suffered a further defeat the following year, this time at the hands of Fuller Pilch, arguably the greatest batsman before WG Grace. Marsden, whose star was on the wane, rather rashly challenged all-comers to a game of single-wicket cricket and Pilch (who had learnt his craft in Sheffield) accepted.

Two games were played, Pilch winning both convincingly. Such was the popularity of the venture that more than 20,000 spectators witnessed the second game, held in Sheffield. Marsden turned out for the Wednesday in addition to his appearances for Sheffield Cricket Club and its later reincarnation Yorkshire, which in turn became Yorkshire County Cricket Club. In 1840, during a match between the Wednesday and Denton, Marsden (who was to die less than three years later at the age of 37) is recorded as bowling a 'new fashioned overhand twist' though he subsequently 'reverted to underhand'.

The new technique was roundarm bowling, developed in the 1790s by Tom Walker of the Hambledon Club, illegally in vogue since the 1820s and finally legalised by the MCC in 1835. William the 'nonpareil' and patriarch of the Lillywhites, was a pioneer of the technique, which was subsequently championed by WG Grace and ultimately superseded by overarm bowling in 1864.

Several of the of the original board members merit a mention: John Marsh, who was honorary secretary and, as mentioned went on to captain the Wednesday, before meeting an untimely death; Charles Stokes, a dentist, who had played for Heeley and would be central to the formation of Sheffield United; and William Fuller

Pilch. Pilch is interesting because it is possible he is a relative of Fuller Pilch. Fuller (b: 1804), like his older brothers Nathaniel (b: 1793) and William (b: 1794) – who were also first-class cricketers – was born in Norfolk, but he moved to Sheffield, in 1820, to play cricket and work as a tailor. Coincidentally Nathaniel's birthday is the same date Wednesday Club was formed, September 4th – and on a Wednesday!

More eerily, William Pilch died in Sheffield on the very same day, the year before the club was formed, in 1866. This also suggests that William may have settled in Sheffield, and it is not beyond the bounds of possibility that he had a son whom he named William, after himself, and Fuller, after his illustrious brother.

The Wednesday Club played their first game at Norfolk Park on October 19th, 1867, beating Mechanics by 4 goals and 3 rouges to nil. Their home ground for the first two years was a pitch at Highfield. It was opposite the Cremorne Gardens, which were home to the Mackenzie club and were named after the Chelsea leisure gardens to which they aspired (Melbourne was the only other location in the world to open its own Cremorne amusement gardens).

The club then enjoyed stints at Myrtle Road (1869–77) and Sheaf House (1877–87), which was next door to Bramall Lane. They played some lesser matches at Hunters Bar in addition to hiring out the pricey Bramall Lane ground for their bigger games and by the mid-1880's they were at the Lane so often it was essentially their home ground. In those early days many of Sheffield's football pitches were densely situated within a mile of Sheffield FC's birthplace: Strawberry Hall Lane, East Bank Road, Bramall Lane, Sheaf House, Highfield, Myrtle Road, Olive Grove, Cremorne, Machon Bank, Ecclesall and Hunters Bar.

From the off the Wednesday were an immediate local success, winning the Cromwell Cup in 1868, the first professional football club in the world to win a trophy. They would go on to win the Challenge Cup seven times and the Wharncliffe Charity Cup four times but exclusively played local clubs during their first four years. It was not till the '70–71 season (when they

The pay's the thing

also recruited the Clegg brothers) that they met their first non-Sheffield competition, Derby St Andrews, winning home and away. By now they were the lords of the city and attracting big crowds.

When a Derbyshire FA side visited Sheffield, 3,400 turned out to see them take on the Wednesday but only 2,000 to see them against Sheffield FC. Interestingly, the River Sheaf was still the border between Yorkshire and Derbyshire. The Derbyshire side was therefore selected from players whose clubs lay south of the Sheaf and these included Norton, Gleadless and Heeley despite them falling within the city of Sheffield. In 1883, with steely coldheartedness and a sense of dynamic purpose the Wednesday football club separated from its illustrious and historic twin, the Wednesday Cricket Club, which wilted, withered and went to the wall. Sentiment must not get in the way of progress.

When professionalism broke through in 1885, the Wednesday were initially happy to maintain the Sheffield position of amateurism and did not turn professional till two years later; even then it was only after a breakaway professional club, Sheffield Rovers, was formed in early 1887 by disenchanted Wednesday players who wanted pay dirt. The nucleus of the rebels was those players who had briefly switched allegiance to Lockwood Brothers for their FA Cup run – including the nine-time capped Billy Mosforth, current darling of Sheffield football. Rovers played only three games: the first two against Eckington enabled eligibility to compete in the 1887 FA Cup, the third and final game was a benefit match against Heeley for the widow and children of JE Deans, a long-time player and committee member of Heeley, who had recently died of TB at the age of 38. His death was also marked at Heeley FC's end of season sports day, by players wearing black armbands during the two matches of the Heeley FC Sports Cup. The cup, played against the Wednesday, is the world's earliest recorded two-legged match. Predictably, Heeley's bogey team won 2-0 on aggregate.

The Wednesday–Rovers crisis was a microcosm of the FA–BFA skirmish and, alarmed at haemorrhaging star players, the

From Sheffield with Love

Wednesday quickly moved to embrace professionalism, accepting it at a meeting at the Garrick Hotel in April 1887; Sheffield Rovers immediately collapsed and the players returned to the fold. In need of more salubrious surroundings the Wednesday searched for a ground more in keeping with their new status and installed themselves at Olive Grove (also near Bramall Lane), remaining there for their first dozen years of professionalism.

It was pretty snazzy. There was a north stand for 1,000 fans (and plans for another – covered – stand), a six-foot wide cinder path encircling the iron railing encircling the pitch and 'entrance facilities' at both ends of the ground. Although called Wednesday Club till 1929, the Olive Grove ground had 'Sheffield Wednesday Football Ground' painted on the stand roof in large letters; furthermore the FA Cup was inscribed with 'Sheffield Wednesday' when they won in 1896 and 1907. Their opening match was a friendly against current FA Cup winners Blackburn Rovers; it was refereed, of course, by JC Clegg and Billy Mosforth just had to score the ground's first goal. The most historically significant match held there was against Aston Villa in the '98–99 season. When the match was abandoned after eighty minutes due to bad light with the Wednesday 3-1 up, the League decided that either the result stood or that Villa should return to play out the extra ten minutes. A farcical fifteen weeks later the Villa went back to play out a bizarre goalless ten minutes and ever since abandoned matches have always been fully replayed.

The result hardly mattered: Villa went on to win the league (for the fourth time) and the Wednesday were relegated. There had been a recent local precedent to this refereeing decision. In 1886, a game between Melville and Bethel Reds was abandoned with eleven minutes to go due to the crowd encroaching on the pitch with Melville 1-0 up. The referee ordered the final minutes to be replayed at a later date, though there was no further score; neither side is recorded as having kicked up a fuss at the decision.

In 1899 the Wednesday were visited by the twinned ill-fates of eviction from their ground and ejection from the First Division. They were turfed from their turf by an unsporting

The pay's the thing

and unsympathetic landlord – the Midland Railway Company – who wanted to lay tracks across the pitch. Things looked bleak and United even offered Bramall Lane as a temporary spot to ensure they could fulfil their remaining relegation-laden fixture list. After frantic stadium-hunting they finally turned up across the city at Owlerton in 1899.

Known as 'Grovites' during their Olive Grove tenure, their new home gave them their charming nickname the 'Owls'[1]. They briefly and unfortunately flirted with a monkey as a mascot after a new signing had been given a chimp called Jacko as a present in 1908 but they soon wised up and opted for the obvious owl. The stadium's name was changed to Hillsborough in 1913. The change of location did Wednesday the world of good. On the day the stadium was opened by William Clegg they beat Chesterfield 5-1 and never looked back; they raced to promotion not dropping a single home point.

Sheffield United also began as a cricket club. They were founded at the Adelphi Hotel in 1854 as a management consultancy team to facilitate the building of a top of the range cricket ground intended to ensure Sheffield's position as the home of Yorkshire cricket. Cricket in Yorkshire can be traced as far back as 1751 when the Duke of Cleveland's XI took on the Earl of Northumberland's XI at Stanwich, near Richmond; the same year Sheffield Cricket Club is believed to have formed. Six years later the new Sheffield club travelled to Derbyshire to take on a local team.

On Shrove Tuesday of the same year, Sheffield authorities hired professional cricketers to entertain the public at free exhibition matches in a bid to prevent the popular but cruel game of throwing at cocks. This ancient national pastime consisted of tying a cockerel to a post and pelting it with cudgels and other projectiles till it perished. Mentioned by Pepys and painted by Hogarth, it was customarily played on Shrove Tuesday and the cock was supposed to represent the invasion-happy Frenchman, the Latin for cock being 'gallo'.

By 1771, the Sheffield Cricket Club, which was now synonymous with Yorkshire cricket, had visited Nottingham;

it is likely that both teams were precursors of their respective county sides. Sheffield defeated Nottingham in a return home match the following year and began playing first-class games against other northern opposition increasing the public's exposure to the game.

By 1802 it was a popular enough pursuit for a match to have been recorded between two Sheffield works sides on Intake Common, one of whom was from a firm part owned by one of Nathaniel Creswick's older relatives, James Creswick. Soon after, broadsheets advertising and covering fixtures were sold on the streets of the city.

When the Sheffield Cricket Club finally became Yorkshire County Cricket Club is unclear; the first match recorded where the team was called 'Yorkshire' was in 1833. Curiously, the Sheffield club continued to play matches after this, often fielding virtually the same side as the county cricket club, which continued to exist informally until coming into official being at the Adelphi Hotel in 1863.

The problem with the Sheffield/Yorkshire club was that it had never had a permanent base. There had been a large cricket ground with seating for 2,000 in the Darnall area of Sheffield, built in 1821 by a Mr Steer. Tragedy struck the following year, during the first major match – Sheffield v Nottingham – when the grandstand collapsed killing two spectators and injuring fifty. Steer then built another ground nearby with a terrace for 8,000 spectators, which came under the stewardship of William H Woolhouse, one of the founder members of the Wednesday Cricket Club. It opened in 1825 and soon after held a five-day cricket game between the All England XI and The Rest of Yorkshire.

Crowds of up to 20,000 each day were reported (though the official capacity was only 8,000) and the local roads were reported as being crowded with 'pedestrians, gigs, waterloos and horses'. All England were reported to have won by 28 notches; in those days runs were tallied by making notches in wooden sticks, with every tenth run having a deeper notch. Individual scores were not kept so only total scores were reported.

The pay's the thing

The Darnall New Ground hosted six first-class cricket games between 1826 and 1829 making it something of a big hitter. In those early days of cricket very few first-class games were played annually: there were 46 matches nationwide in the period 1826–29, which means it hosted about one in eight of them. The ground's main claim to fame was that it hosted the first of the three 'Experimental' matches between Sussex and the All England XI that looked at the possibility of legalising roundarm bowling.

A stadium built in 1830 in Hyde Park, Sheffield, superseded the Darnall ground, principally by dint of its closeness to the city centre but this fell into a state of disrepair by the mid-'50s. Although shabby round the edges it still hosted the world's first charity football match – Hallam FC v Sheffield FC – in 1861 and continued to host football games during the '60s and '70s. All in, it hosted twenty first-class cricket matches, a tidy sum – including Yorkshire's inaugural titular match in 1833, when Tom Marsden and teammates beat Fuller Pilch's Norfolk (featuring 'the Three Pilches').

Furthermore, although Sheffield and Manchester had previously met, the ground hosted the first official Roses match when Yorkshire defeated Lancashire in 1849. Hyde Park's greatest claim to fame is as the source of the term 'hat-trick'. In 1858 Heathfield Harman (HH) Stephenson took three wickets in three consecutive balls for the all-England XI against the twenty-two of Hallam and the phrase was coined.

Its origin is unclear: it has been suggested that a new hat was awarded by a club to a player achieving a hat-trick or, more believably, that the player was allowed to take his hat round the spectators for a collection. My guess is that it was originally called a Heath-trick and that the phrase was quickly whittled down.

A new ground at Newhall, which was to become the athletic ground, was used briefly for cricket but it was too far from town with limited seating and a poor wicket, though it did stage a United England XI v Sheffield XV match. A new ground was needed. The site was chosen by Michael Ellison, the Duke of Norfolk's agent, the Duke being the direct descendant of the traitor, Norfolk, who had plotted with Mary Queen of Scots to overthrow Elizabeth I.

He selected a plot of his land in Highfield – the suburb where Sheffield FC was founded – away from the pollution of the city's east end. It is alleged that the eponymous lane was originally called Whitehouse Lane but was renamed in honour of David Bramhall whose factory and house lay at the end of the approach to the ground. Early publications refer to it as Bramhall Lane though Bramall also appears to have been used relatively soon after it opened in 1855.

A grand affair, capable of hosting three simultaneous cricket matches (later expansion increased this to five), it was completely enclosed with perimeter walls and kitted out with a pavilion, refreshment booths and a raised private enclosure. It was managed by a committee of local cricket clubs, known as the Sheffield United Cricket Club – the first sporting body in the world to use the word 'united' – who were responsible for organising sporting events.

William Prest, who was not to found Sheffield FC for another two years, appeared for a Sheffield XI in the very first cricket game at Bramall Lane that April and Michael Ellison, the Duke of Norfolk's agent and a man who was to figure centrally in Sheffield United's birth, turned out for the ground's first county cricket game on August 27th, when Yorkshire hosted Sussex; he was caught out in the second innings by John Wisden and Yorkshire lost by an innings and 117 runs.

Bramall Lane was to become the home of the Yorkshire CCC for forty years, from its inception in 1863, the resident club's name changing from the Sheffield United Cricket Club to the Yorkshire County and Sheffield United Cricket Club. It hosted various county cricket games during those early football years of the '60s and '70s – with Prest turning out for the earlier games until his football commitments kept him away – as well as North versus South cricket matches. In 1868 it hosted one of the games of the Indigenous Australian Cricket Tour – a draw with Sheffield – and a decade later Australia met Yorkshire there, two years before Australia first played England away: the Bramall

The pay's the thing

Lane clash became a regular fixture on their touring calendar. Later, in 1902, it became the seventh Test ground when it hosted the Ashes Third Test (the other six, of course, being Lords, The Oval, Old Trafford, Trent Bridge, Headingley and Edgbaston). The Australians won by 143 runs and had six of their team mentioned in Joyce's *Finnegan's Wake*. Interestingly, Joyce's fellow writer and countryman Samuel Beckett is the only first-class cricketer to win the Nobel Prize having played two first-class games for Dublin University.

The 1902 Test was the only test match played at Bramall Lane though touring national sides still took on Yorkshire there until 1969, and it continued to host county cricket until 1973, when Yorkshire and Lancashire met there for the last time. It remained the youngest Test ground for over century until England played Zimbabwe in Chester-Le-Street, Durham in 2003.

The legendary WG Grace also made a number of appearances at Bramall Lane. He first played there in a North v South match in 1869; as opening batsman he clocked up an impressive 122 runs in his first innings to guide The South of England to victory by 66 runs. The 'Doctor' also paid annual visits to Bramall Lane with Gloucestershire from 1872–86. Although he continued in first-class cricket till 1908 he made his last appearance at Bramall Lane – again for Gloucestershire – in 1891. Incidentally Grace, a firm friend of CW Alcock's, occasionally turned out for Wanderers.

Football had an uneasy start at Bramall Lane: the cricket-loving ground committee viewed it with disdain and did not want it played there. This caused some consternation among football clubs who were led to believe that the ground would be available for all sports except greyhound racing and clay pigeon shooting. From its inception the Club attempted to hold matches there but was repeatedly turned down by the Bramall Lane committee resulting in severely strained relations between the two.

The first match was not granted till five years later, in 1862, and then only under sufferance since it was for charity. As mentioned, the Sheffield–Hallam game finished in a brawl and was nicknamed 'The Battle of Bramall Lane', doing the nascent sport no favours with the ground committee. Only two more games were played there in the 1860s, the Youdan and Cromwell cup finals; those first two football cup finals in history. The ground was happier to host other sporting events including the Wednesday's second athletic sports day in 1869, which attracted 2,000 spectators – bigger than any football gate for the Wednesday thus far.

By the 1870s football was becoming too popular to ignore and the gate receipts from football crowds were badly needed to cover the ground rent, which cricket alone could not do. Bramall Lane slowly opened up to football and hosted the inter-association match between Sheffield and London in 1871. Its success prompted the ground committee to sanction further SFA games.

The Royal Engineers visited in 1873 and could not believe that Sheffield headed the ball but beat them 4-1 all the same, overpowering the locals with their pioneering, military tactics-inspired silky 'combination' (passing) and positional play. From 1874 there was also an annual game between the Sheffield and Glasgow Associations, initially played alternate years at Bramall Lane. In the same year, in a bid to clear debts, the ground committee also endorsed exhibition matches of baseball with visiting teams from Boston and Philadelphia and in 1876 it hosted lacrosse when Sheffield played Glasgow. The Sheffield lacrosse team was composed of local football players, including the Clegg brothers and JC Shaw.

Later that year there was a North v South lacrosse game at The Oval, London, with four Sheffield footballers fielding for the north in scarlet jerseys and black knickers. The game was refereed by... CW Alcock.

Another world first had occurred in 1872 when Bramall Lane became the first ground to install turnstiles, and a further one was to follow in 1878 when it hosted the world's first floodlit game. Two teams made up of Sheffield stars and skippered by the Clegg brothers, played under four corner lamps thirty feet high, to an estimated crowd of 20,000.

The pay's the thing

Almost twenty-one years to the day since the Club had formed it was Sheffield football's coming of age party. It was also a world premiere, a dazzling event and Sheffield's glitterati were out in force, complemented by the biggest names in Sheffield football. The Clegg, Stacey and Buttery brothers, Mosforth, Marples, Malpas, Hunter, Gregory and Tomlinson all played, while William Pierce Dix refereed and W Skinner and RH Dickinson (both prominent SFA members) umpired. The world had never seen such brilliant illumination, it was the acme of sports technology and a reporter for the *Sheffield Independent* trilled:

The Sheffield public were last evening introduced to a decided novelty in football – a match with the assistance of the electric light. The contest, which took place at Bramall Lane Ground between two teams selected by the Sheffield Football Association, was the first ever played in this country – or anywhere else, we believe – with the aid of artificial illumination, especially that which is derived from the powerful currents of electricity.

…It would have been difficult to select a ground more suitable than Bramall Lane for a display of the illuminator. Those who have seen the enclosure under the blaze of a midsummer sun, with thousands of excited spectators witnessing the performances of Yorkshire's favourite cricketers, can hardly possess a complete idea of the black wilderness it presents by night when there is no moon or the heavens are overcast. To walk there is literally like wandering over a bleak moor…

The match was announced to commence at half-past seven o'clock and considerably before that hour the roads to Bramall Lane were completely besieged. The wonder was where all the people came from. There seemed no end to the ever-coming stream, and the crowd of excited people outside the gates struggling to pass in at the turnstiles created a scene of great animation. The vast enclosure – extensive as it is – appeared quite crowded, so large was the assembly, and there must have been a considerable number who failed to get a fair view of the play…

…at each corner of the ground marked off for the players a wooden stage was erected some ten yards high for carrying the

lamp and the reflector. Behind each goal was placed a portable engine, each of which drove two Siemen's dynamo machines – one for each light. The illuminating power equalled 8,000 standard candles, and the cost per hour for each light was about 3 ½ d... As if endeavouring to rival the artificial illuminator the lunar orb stood high and bright in the heavens; the atmosphere was pure and pleasant, and it was generally admitted that... everything indeed appeared favourable for the occasion...

At first the light was certainly too powerful to be looked at with comfort, but... everyone seemed highly pleased with the result of the experiment, the light being most brilliant and effective. It may be stated here that the experiment turned out a great financial success, the novelty of the thing drawing together an immense attendance, reaching, in our estimation, nearly twenty thousand people. When everything was in readiness, at 7.30 the distinguished colours of the two sides were clearly visible... spectators could distinguish with ease the faces and figures of football players at a distance of perhaps two hundred yards.

Meanwhile, the rival *Sheffield Telegraph* opined that 'many of the ladies, once within the rays, shot up umbrellas as they would parasols to shield them from the sun at midday'. Strangely, Bramall Lane, like all other English grounds, did not go on to install a permanent floodlight system till the 1950s – more than seventy years after the event – finally allowing evening games to take place midweek; the Belgians (if French read 'French') meanwhile had had floodlights at Heysel Stadium for years.

By the 1880s the ground was getting big attendances at Association games and at Challenge Cup and Wharncliffe Charity Cup finals, bringing in much needed revenue during the winter months. After The Oval it was arguably the country's most important football ground and hosted two football internationals in the 1880s: England's first home tie not played at The Oval – England v Scotland (2-3) in 1883 – and England v Ireland (7-0) in 1887. Bramall Lane and The Oval share the unique record of hosting a Test match, an FA Cup Final and an England football international.

The pay's the thing

It was the hosting of an FA Cup semi-final in 1889, however, that proved the turning point. Receipts of £700 from the match between Preston and West Bromwich Albion (refereed by JC Clegg in front of a then-record Sheffield attendance of 22,688) proved so attractive to the club that Charles Stokes convinced the committee to form a football team to consolidate revenue during winter. Stokes, a member of the ground committee, was passionate about local sport.

He was a former cricketer and footballer of Heeley FC and the Wednesday and a founder member of the Wednesday, winning the Cromwell Cup in 1868. United would be the first official club in Sheffield to be a professional outfit from the off, although the original intention was for it to be a mixture of amateur and professional, thus allowing Club and other local players to join. The motion had the full backing of Michael Ellison. A true Blade to the last, he died a happy man in 1898, aged 81, having seen them secure the championship a few months earlier.

Six days after the FA Cup semi-final, on Friday March 22nd 1889, the Sheffield United Football Club was born at a meeting in JB Wostinholm's offices in Norfolk Row, yards from the Adelphi Hotel. As Alcock had been born on a Norfolk Street, so United were born on Norfolk Row. (The actor Sean Bean, a lifelong fan and now a director of the club, unveiled a commemorative plaque at the site in 2004.) They were also the first professional football team in the world to call themselves United.

There were robust early connections to Sheffield FC with as many as eleven of the members also belonging to the Club, including HB Willey and WF Beardshaw, who had so opposed 'wicked' professionalism less than five years before. Just as Wednesday Cricket Club had set up a football section, one can argue that Sheffield United were the football arm of the YCCC.

For one they shared the same stadium, and for another they shared the same core administration, with JB Wostinholm (secretary of the Yorkshire CCC since its inception in 1863), Harry H Stones, Charles Stokes, David Haigh (who was also the SFA secretary) and Michael Ellison leading figures on both committees/executives. At the time Sheffield Wednesday had seceded from the SFA who, in turn, extended a benevolent hand to the new club.

With WF Beardshaw and J Tomlinson (an SFA official and former Heeley player) also on board and JC Clegg oozing goodwill, Sheffield United Football Club was commencing on a very solid wicket.

The main difference was that Wednesday Club had originated to keep Wednesday cricketers together during the winter and, originally at least, the same people had turned out for both sides. Football had evolved since 1867 and cricketers could not now be relied upon to be footballers of the standard required by the professional game; neither, of course, could county cricketers give of their time to such a degree.

Unfortunately, other Sheffield clubs did not share the administrators' enthusiasm, not least the Wednesday, who rightly divined a direct threat to their status. When it came to providing players, even the Club, who had pledged their support, withdrew, followed in short order by Heeley and Owlerton. They were a club with no players. Needs must, they advertised in the Sheffield papers:

SHEFFIELD UNITED CRICKET CLUB
The Committee have decided to form a FOOTBALL CLUB for next season for Bramall Lane Ground. Professionals may send testimonials and particulars on or before March 30th to Mr JB Wostinholm, 10 Norfolk Row.

Despite only three suitable candidates, United were united and undeterred; they knew that players had to be recruited from elsewhere and the board turned squarely to north of the border.

The origins of football in Sheffield (and therefore in the world at large) owe much to the local steel and silver industries. Philanthropic magnates helped create, fund, play for and manage the amateur and professional clubs while their workers both played for and supported them. This legacy lives on in Sheffield United's nickname; it is poetic economy, striking symbolism and sublime synecdoche: they are the Blades. The name was pre-loved and had been around for a while; between 1873 and 1907,

The pay's the thing

any team from Sheffield was referred to as the Blades or, to a lesser extent, the Cutlers, by non-Sheffielders. This included the Sheffield Association side, Sheffield FC and Sheffield Wednesday, who did not become known as the Owls till 1907.

The new club played the old Club in a practice match on August 1st 1889, winning 3-1. The fixture was smothered in secrecy, the players being taken on a magical mystery tour till their brake pulled up at Sandygate. They were not as smart as they thought though, being followed, cloak and dagger style by Brayshaw of the Wednesday and a newspaper reporter, who rapidly spilled the beans.

Their first official game was a 4-1 loss at Notts Rangers on September 7th 1889, with Nottingham once again contributing to a Sheffield first. William Robertson, a Scottish import, scored the Blades first official goal that day – he also scored their first hat-trick (against Exchange) the following month, was their first man sent off and was the first player to score in a United–Wednesday derby. Local legend Billy Mosforth and Jack Hudson, both formerly of the Wednesday (Mosforth was formerly of every major local club!), also turned out for United in that first official game. Later that September, United played their first competitive game in Sheffield, a 2-1 win over Heeley as well as their first match at Bramall Lane, a 4-0 loss to Birmingham St George's.

Their first truly competitive game was a 1-0 win over Heeley in that season's FA Cup. From the off they signalled their intention to challenge the supremacy of the Wednesday and with one club in red and the other in blue, memories of those early Sheffield FC–Hallam encounters were rekindled. Wednesday Club appear to have chosen blue from the off, though there is no documented evidence for this. Throughout the 1870s and 1880s they wore blue and white hoops, briefly switching to blue and white halves and then blue butcher's stripes (both for a season) before settling on the classic blue and white strip in 1891. With economy of style Sheffield United opted for red and white stripes from the off and never changed.

The first derby took place at Olive Grove in December 1890, thirty years to the month since the world's first inter-club football match and derby between Sheffield and Hallam. Wednesday, understandably feeling threatened by the arrival of a rival, insisted on a home berth and 10,000 were sardined into the ground. Being stuck at the foot of the Alliance League while United were flying high in the Midland League did not help their confidence but derbies are a breed apart from other games, played on a different (mythic) dimension. Anyway they needed only to look back a few months to an FA Cup final and an Alliance victory to inspire them.

They packed their side with cup final experience and topped it off with their new signing Harry Brandon, making his debut and playing alongside his brother Bob. Amongst United's new side were the Rotherham Swifts trio, Whitham, Watson and Howell (all Ecclesfield born), future England international Harry Lilley and Bernard Shaw – not the Irish man of letters but son of the great JC Shaw. Talking of local legends, JC Clegg refereed the game while his brother, William, umpired. The atmosphere was electric and the crowd was in for a real humdinger. The Blades cut through first, with Robertson scoring, but the Wednesday dug deep equalizing late through 'Toddles' Woolhouse with Winterbottom grabbing the winner with a few minutes to go.

A return match at Bramall Lane less than a month later produced a similar storyline: the away team going 2-0 up before the home team rallied to equalize and then snatch the winner with minutes to go. Ingram and Brandon scored for the Wednesday and then Watson, Howell and Calder for United. The following October the Blades whipped the Wednesday 5-0 again at Bramall Lane, but three weeks later at Olive Grove the Owls got their revenge, licking the Blades 4-1.

Although the two teams have never met in a cup final, they nearly did, way back in '95–96. Both teams reached the semi-finals of the Birmingham Cup (the west midlands equivalent of the Sheffield Challenge Cup), however the Wednesday were unluckily knocked out 1-0 after Aston Villa were ordered to retake their missed penalty. United beat Walsall and, progressed to the final, but lost to Villa. They got even closer in the Wharncliffe Charity Cup of '91–92. Both reached the final but the Wednesday

The pay's the thing

– with memories of five goals to nil still fresh – quite reasonably, refused to play at the usual venue, Bramall Lane.

The SFA in turn would not relocate the fixture and the final was cancelled with the Cup shared between the two sides. The first time they ever met in the FA Cup was in the second round in February 1900, a fixture the fans of Sheffield had long anticipated. Frustratingly, snow caused the first match to be abandoned and the replay to be cancelled. Such was the passion for the match that, two days later, scores of people helped clear Bramall Lane of snow allowing another replay to take place.

If they wanted passion they were not disappointed but skill was lacking in a dirty game played out on a sludgy pitch. Cup-holders, United were the main culprits in the 1-1 draw, to the extent that, for the replay two days later, three of the Wednesday were incapacitated, including the goalkeeper and the first and second choice centre forwards, one of whom was their main goalscorer, Spiksley.

The replay at Owlerton was never going to be a handbags-at-dawn affair and quickly deteriorated into a modern version of the Sheffield–Hallam match of 1860. Thickett's clumsy, crunching, career-ending tackle on Lee broke the third-choice centre forward's leg, an injury from which he never recovered, dying six years later, a broken man. An incandescent Wednesday began hitting out, rapidly conceding a penalty, tucked away by a grateful Needham. They then had two men sent off for injuring two United players, neither of whom could play on and, with eight playing nine, the Owls lost 2-0.

A shocking day for Sheffield football had its karma when a limping United went out five days later to Bury, who went on to win the cup.

Footnotes

[1]There was another team, also founded in 1867, called the Owls (though it was their full name, not nickname). They were a London-based club that played the Marlborough College football code, a variant of rugby.

Chapter Twelve

LA BELLE ÉPOQUE

*Football is all very well a good game for rough
girls, but not for delicate boys.*

Oscar Wilde.

THE FOOTBALL LEAGUE had its first season in '88–89 and consisted of twelve teams: (in order of finish) Preston North End (PNE), Aston Villa, Wolverhampton Wanderers, Blackburn Rovers, Bolton Wanderers, West Bromwich Albion, Accrington, Everton, Burnley, Derby County, Notts County and Stoke. In this first professional league season, PNE went on to clinch the world's first League and Cup double. In his 1901 book, *Association Football*, Ernest 'Nudger' Needham of Sheffield United, wrote of those original league teams:

> *Their vitality was so stimulated by alliance (transfers) that one only of them has passed from existence – the Accrington club; the others having, in almost every case, maintained their position in the First Division or the Second.*

More than a century later, all except Notts County (League Two) and Accrington (disbanded 1896) still play in the Premiership (old First Division) or Championship (old Second).

It may seem bizarre that the two cities who had exercised most influence in establishing association football, London and Sheffield, had no teams accepted into the new league but London had no professional teams at that point and Sheffield only the one. Furthermore, from the off, the League was only intended to cater to teams from the north and the midlands so southern teams did not get a look in; once again the north had stolen a march on the FA. The Wednesday were Sheffield's only professional club but when William McGregor convened a series

La Bell Époque

of meetings for clubs interested in forming a new league they refused to attend for fear of incurring the wrath of the FA. They were then offered a place in the poorly-organised Combination League but declined this poor imitation, happier to continue with friendlies and cup games. They chose wisely as the League quickly folded.

By the following season Sheffield United had formed and the Wednesday had a professional rival in the city. Eager to show their superiority they now applied to join the Football League but were unsuccessful. Many applied and all failed for the simple reason that the four teams finishing at the bottom of the League were not expelled as anticipated; neither was the league expanded, or another league added.

In response, John Holmes, president of the Wednesday, went ahead with his plans to organise the rival Football Alliance League, along with eleven other clubs including Nottingham Forest and Newton Heath – whose name was to change in 1901 to Manchester United. Newton Heath FC was founded in 1878 as the works side of the Lancashire and Yorkshire Railway engineering works Newton Heath depot; nicknamed 'the Heathens', they consisted of wagon and carriage workers and played in green and gold jerseys.

London teams were also excluded from the Alliance League. London would have to wait until the '93–94 season to see its first team in the Football League when Arsenal was admitted to the Second Division along with Liverpool and Newcastle United. Arsenal had started as southeast outfit Dial Square in 1886 changing their name to Royal Arsenal on Christmas Day the same year.

The cash-strapped club included two former Nottingham Forest players who wrote to their old club for support and were provided with Forest jerseys, which explains why they wear red. They turned professional and changed their name to Woolwich Arsenal in 1891 (playing a friendly with Sheffield United soon after), moved to Highbury in 1913 and dropped the prefix in 1914. They were the first London club to compete in the First Division – in the '04–05 season.

From Sheffield with Love

Their future manager Herbert Chapman, one of the country's all-time great coaches, was from Sheffield and played for Sheffield United, though he was upstaged on the pitch by his brother, Harry, who fielded for the Wednesday. At Huddersfield, Herbert won the FA Cup (1922–23) and two League titles ('23–24 and '24–25; the triple followed after he had left for Arsenal).

He mirrored his success with the Gunners winning the FA Cup in '29–30 (beating Huddersfield) and two league titles in '30–31 and '32–33. In 1933, while still with Arsenal, he became England's first professional manager but died suddenly in 1934, aged fifty-five. His team went on to do the triple (with League titles in '33–34 and '34–35) just as his Huddersfield side had. This feat was not repeated till Liverpool managed it half a century later. His bust now guards the entrance hall of the Emirates Stadium.

In the first Alliance season ('89–90), the Wednesday not only won the title but became the first non-league team in history to reach the final of the FA Cup, and in so doing gave the Football League the finger, skittling out three League teams in the process. Accrington was first and Bolton last; sandwiched between was Notts County, who took three matches to knock out: Notts County complained about the state of the pitch in the first match at Olive Grove and then the Owls complained about three County players in the return fixture. They were hammered 6-1 by Blackburn Rovers (of the Football League) in the FA Cup final at The Oval.

The Wednesday had also made the semi-finals as amateurs in '81–02 and the quarter-finals in their first two seasons as (non-league) professionals in '87–08 and '88–09. Incidentally, the only non-league team to ever win the FA Cup is Tottenham Hotspur (c: 1882), who beat Sheffield United in 1901 (2-2 at Crystal Palace, attendance 114,815, 3-1 at Burnden Park, Bolton; the replay earning the nickname 'Pie Saturday' on account of the excess food prepared for the vastly reduced crowd of 28,000). Although non-league they were no amateurs and the team contained a number of gifted players, including four internationals, lured to the Southern League by high wages. Spurs joined the Football

Top: 1883. Blackburn Olympic beat Old Etonians in the FA Cup final and the trophy goes north for the first time.
Below: Sheffield United's FA Cup winning team in 1899 at the Bramall Lane ground. Legendary goalkeeper William 'Fatty' Foulke is front centre while Ernest 'Nudger' Needham is holding the cup.

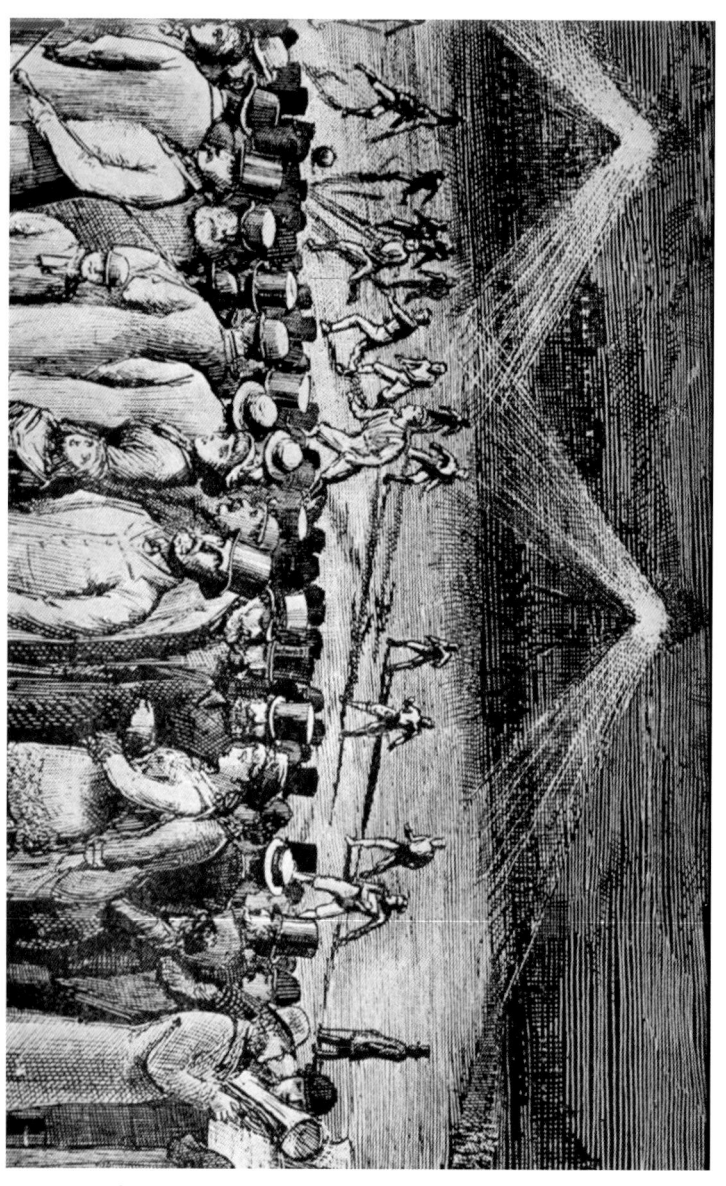

Wanderers v Clapham Rovers in the first floodlit match at Kennington Oval. There is debate whether this engraving was of a match at the Oval or at Bramall Lane.

Top: The Corinthians on tour in 1896/7.
Below: (from left). Three legends. RE Foster, the only man to captain England at football and cricket; CB Fry and GO Smith.

Top: Sheffield FC prepare to tour in 1893. (Picture Sheffield)
Bottom: Bramall Lane 1905. (Picture Sheffield)

*Top: The original FA Cup – 'The Little Tin Idol'.
Bottom: A jug to commemorate Sheffield Wednesday's 1896
FA Cup victory. (Picture Sheffield)*

Top: Sheffield Wednesday on March 11 1890 the day they lost 6-1 in the FA Cup final to Blackburn Rovers. (left to right) back: Holmes, Smith, Nixon, Waller, Woolhouse, Pearson, Mumford, Muscroft, middle: Cawley, Brayshaw, Winterbottom, Bennet, Betts, front: Dungworth, Ingram, Morley. (Picture Sheffield)

Bottom: Thomas Youdan (seated front-centre), sponsor of the first trophy in Sheffield, and his Surrey theatre company the morning after his theatre had burned to the ground. (Picture Sheffield)

Sheffield United stalwart and captain, Ernest 'Nudger' Needham.

Sheffield United (1895) (left to right) back row, George Waller, Mick Whitham, William Foulke, John Docherty, Bob Cain; middle row, Jimmy Yates, Harry Hammond, Ernest Needham, Walter Hill, Arthur Watson; front row: Harry Thickett, Rab Howell.

La Belle Époque

League in the '08–09 season immediately winning promotion to the First Division with a Second Division second-placed berth.

The Football League refused to expand for the next season ('90–91) and the Wednesday, disconsolate at the rejection, lifelessly played out the Alliance season, finishing last; firmly rooted to the bottom spot all season. Come the following season, it was more of the same from the Football League, despite being wined and dined by a hopeful Wednesday and other Alliance members at a Sheffield hotel on April 20th, 1891.

The meeting was to vote on a visionary plan to expand the League into three divisions of twelve each, the business prefaced by a one-off League v Alliance match (1-1) at Olive Grove. Predictably this brilliant idea was rejected, leaving the dyspeptic Alliance hopefuls out in the cold again. Despite being spurned, and this time after a good deal of grovelling and schmoozing, the Wednesday conducted themselves with dignity, finishing fourth in the Alliance in '91–92 and, in the process, averaging a home gate of around 9,000. In May 1892, the Football League finally relented and added a second division incorporating much of the Alliance; the First Division was also expanded – to sixteen teams – and Wednesday Club was elected to it, finishing twelfth in their inaugural season.

Sheffield United had played in the Midland League during its second season ('90–91), finishing fifth. They were hopeful of moving up a grade to the Alliance but when they applied were not elected, Stokes convinced of Wednesday skulduggery. Chins probably a little higher than usual, they instead switched to the Northern League for the following season (91–92), hoping for stiffer competition and finishing third.

The league was based in the north-east and included Newcastle East and Newcastle West End (who would pull together at the end of the season to form Newcastle United), Middlesbrough (founded 1876 from a local cricket side), Middlesbrough Ironopolis (who, in their five-year existence, won three-in-a-row league titles and made the FA Cup quarter-finals twice) and Sunderland Albion (city rivals to Division One club Sunderland).

From Sheffield with Love

Come 1892, United were elected to the new Second Division of the Football League and in its first season ('92–93) were runners-up. After being defeated in their first three away games they did not lose again that season and, along the way, recorded a 10-0 win against Burslem Port Vale (Port Vale), still the highest ever away win in League history. They did not get automatic promotion, however. The top three, Small Heath (Birmingham City), United and third-placed Darwen had to play a 'Test' match – or play-off – against the bottom three in the First.

Small Heath played bottom-placed Newton Heath (Manchester United) at Bramall Lane and lost 5-2 in a replay so, rather unfairly, stayed down. United played Accrington (who had finished fifteenth) at Trent Bridge and won 1-0, courtesy of a heavenly forty-yard solo run and finish from Jack Drummond that left even Needham breathless, maintaining to the end it was the best goal he had ever seen. In so doing they became the first team in the world to be promoted. Finally, Darwen (who had been relegated the previous season) beat Notts County, who had finished fourteenth, and were also promoted.

Although the Wednesday finished twelfth, they went into their last game of the season in fourteenth, avoiding a Test match only by winning 3-2, after coming from behind. United meanwhile were clearly keen not to have to fight to get into the top flight again and remained in the First Division for a staggering forty-one years. Accrington sniffily refused to play in the Second Division and seceded, believing there was not enough money to be had. It was to be their downfall, a few seasons later, in 1896, faced with crippling financial problems they collapsed.

At last the two Sheffield clubs could lock horns in earnest. The Blades promotion heralded Sheffield's professional golden years including a twelve-season run during which one or other side won either the First Division or the FA Cup, or were runners-up in the division or losing finalists or semi-finalists in the Cup. The roll of honour is as follows:

'92–93 Sheffield United: runners-up Second Division (promoted)
'93-94 The Wednesday: semi-finalists FA Cup

La Belle Époque

'94–95 The Wednesday: semi-finalists FA Cup
'95–96 The Wednesday: winners FA Cup
'96–97 Sheffield United: runners-up First Division
'97–98 Sheffield United: winners First Division, Charity Shield winners
'98–99 Sheffield United: winners FA Cup
'99–00 Sheffield United: runners-up First Division
   The Wednesday: winners Second Division (promoted)
'00–01 Sheffield United: finalists FA Cup
'01–02 Sheffield United: winners FA Cup
'02–03 The Wednesday: winners First Division
'03–04 The Wednesday: winners First Division, semi-finalists FA Cup
'14–05 The Wednesday: semi-finalists FA Cup, Charity Shield winners

If you include quarter-final FA Cup appearances (Wednesday six; United two) then the record stretches all the way back to the '87–88 season and forward to '06–907 – when the Wednesday won the FA Cup for the second time. That's twenty years! It took another century to match these statistics. If you include top six finishes then the stats stretch forward to '14–15 (or 28 seasons) when the record was abruptly stopped by the Great War. The record could not have been broken on a higher note, with Sheffield United winning the FA Cup for the fourth time, beating Chelsea 3-0 in the 'Khaki' Cup final, so called because of the number of servicemen in the 50,000 crowd, many destined never to see a game again. With the cup suspended till after the war, United held the trophy for the duration; longer than any other club till Portsmouth FC had the dubious honour during World War Two.

There are several points worth mentioning about the roll of honour. Firstly, in 1897–98, United were crowned 'Champions of Great Britain' after beating Scottish League champions Celtic over two legs. (With a touch of hyperbole, Scottish side Renton FC had been proclaimed 'Champions of the World' after their success in the previous year's fixture against West Brom.) They

163

also played Corinthians FC in the Sheriff of London Cup (as did the Wednesday, beating them 2-1 in 1905). Between 1898 and 1907 the two teams considered the best amateur and professional outfits that year played each other for the Sheriff of London (Dewar) Charity Shield. The idea was suggested by Sir Thomas Dewar, the whisky distiller, who also provided the six-by-three-foot shield – the largest trophy ever competed for in football. In its inaugural year it was shared between Sheffield United and the Corinthians following two drawn matches at Crystal Palace; in the replay United had refused to play extra-time following a disagreement over refereeing decisions – something that would never happen today.

CB Fry and Charles Wreford Brown played for the Corinthians in the match against United. Wreford Brown (who captained England twice and also played for the other great amateur side, the Old Carthusians – old boys of Charterhouse School) was reputed to have coined the term 'soccer' as abbreviation of association. He actually signed on as an amateur for United towards the end of their championship campaign in response to the perceived ungentlemanly behaviour of title rivals Sunderland. He was manager of the British Olympic Team in 1936 in Berlin and ordered them not to give the Nazi salute.

In 1907, the amateur teams fell out with the FA after the latter produced an edict demanding amateur football associations admit professional clubs. The amateurs refused and, following FA sanctions, they formed the Amateur Football Alliance. The following year the competition was replaced by the FA Charity Shield; it still pitted amateur and professional teams but gradually morphed into today's fixture of FA Cup and League winners, played at the start of the new season rather than at the end of the last.

The Corinthians were one of the great amateur teams of the day and like their cricketing brothers, I Zingari, were nomadic playing at various London venues. They were founded in 1882 by Nick Lane 'Pa' Jackson, founder member and assistant secretary of the FA. He also founded Finchley Football club in 1874 and Finchley Rugby Club in 1875 before opening up

La Belle Époque

Stoke Poges Golf Club in 1908, which has acted as the backdrop for several film scenes, notably Oddjob's statue beheading golf scene in *Goldfinger* (starring classic 007, Sean Connery) and the final death scene in *Layer Cake* (starring his natural heir, Daniel Craig). The Corinthians pooh-poohed professionalism, electing only to play other amateur sides. They spurned the Football League and, unlike other amateur sides, refused to play FA Cup or other competitive matches including the FA Amateur Cup though they often played the winners of the FA Cup, hammering Blackburn Rovers 8-1 in 1884. They relaxed their rules in 1898, competing in the Sheriff of London Charity Shield. They then competed in all but one Dewar Shield game – in 1899, when Queen's Park replaced them – until the FA Charity Shield superseded it in 1908.

Their gentlemanliness – now known as 'Corinthian spirit' – stretched to refusing to defend a penalty awarded against them, their goalkeeper walking away from his goal line before it was taken. They played the original amateur's Sheffield FC on occasions, including a game at The Oval in 1889, when they fielded Tinsley Lindley, whose record of scoring in nine consecutive England internationals still stands. In 1892 they played the (still great) amateur rugby club Barbarians, beating them at football, rugby and athletics, though losing the cricket.

The legendary CB Fry played for England in the 1902 Oval test. Fry, an all-round athlete became world long jump champion in 1892, the record standing an astounding 21 years. He played in 26 tests and under his 17 captaincies England never lost. He also gained an international football cap against Ireland in 1901 and played for Southampton in their FA Cup Final loss to Sheffield United in 1902. He also managed to pack a lot into his life off the pitch: he was the founding vice-president of Chelsea in 1905, was offered the throne of Albania in 1919 (they settled for Zog who worked his way up from prime minister to president to king) and dabbled with the ultra-right, meeting Hitler in 1934. There are, in addition to Jackson and Fry, many other Corinthian luminaries of the era including RE 'Tip' Foster, the only man to have captained England at cricket and football[1]. *Wisden* Cricketer of the Year in 1901, he was followed two years later by Corinthian, Cuthbert Burnup who played in 228 first-class cricket matches, principally for Kent, for whom he scored their first double-century. He also claimed an England football cap though my favourite piece of trivia about him is that he Coincidentally appears for the Corinthians in the Bible (Corinthians 3:12-15): 'and the purifying fire of God will burn up everything that was not of Him.'

There was William Neville 'Nuts' Cobbold who, as one the finest dribblers of the age, regarded passing and heading as new-fangled and spurned them. He was a great centre forward as well as a jinking trickster and scored six goals in nine games for his country. Of course mention must be made of Gilbert Oswald 'GO' Smith, Corinthian's master striker who put away 113 goals in 131 appearances for the club. He also scored eleven times in twenty games for England, including the only English hat-trick of the nineteenth century.

The Corinthians played and regularly beat the top professional teams (employing their trademark tactic of five forwards in a line) until banned from doing so when they joined the Amateur Football Association in 1907. They then began touring abroad, influencing overseas development of the game: Real Madrid's white strip was inspired by the Corinthian's jersey. They toured Europe and as far afield as South Africa, Canada, USA and Brazil. In 1902, with more than a touch of 'From the Corinthians to Saint Paul' about it, the newly-formed Sports Club Corinthians Paulista (of Sao Paulo) were named after them following a six-match undefeated Corinthian tour of Brazil.

In 1988 the chain-smoking, medically-trained former captain of the Brazilian team, Sócrates fielded for the Corinthians when they repeated their tour. Many England players turned out for Corinthians FC in addition to their primary professional club, though 17 players who considered Corinthians as their primary club (including CB Fry) have won 52 England caps between them. They finally entered the FA Cup in 1922 (knocking First Division Blackburn Rovers out the following year), merged with the Casuals to form Corinthian-Casuals FC in 1939, acquired a

La Belle Époque

home ground in 1988 and currently play in Division One South of the Isthmian League. They are responsible for Manchester United's biggest loss, an 11-3 drubbing in 1903.

The second point to draw from the roll of honour is that in the '99–00 season not only did United finish runners-up and the Wednesday finish victors of the Second Division, but United also equalled Preston's impressive record (set in '88–89) of going twenty-two matches unbeaten. Bury, United's bogey team that season, ended the run, also dumping them out of the FA Cup (after the Blades–Owls brawl). United ultimately lost out in the League to the Villa, who had visited Bramall Lane for a top of the table clash on October 28th 1899. Amongst the crowd, one figure in particular – belatedly attending his first ever League game – must have been glowing with pride as he watched the Blades win 2-1: CW Alcock.

If Sheffield was the home of football during the Victorian era, then Aston Villa was *the* club, winning the championship six times (five times in seven seasons between '93–94 and '99–00!) and the FA Cup five times before World War One. They were another team to form from a cricket club, the members of Villa Cross Wesleyan Chapel forming a football section in the winter of '73–74.

They won their first match 1-0; a game at Aston Park against Aston Brook St Mary's Rugby Club which, in the spirit of egalitarianism, was played with one first half under rugby rules, the other under association. In 1876 they recruited the great Glaswegian, George Ramsay, who moved them to Perry Bar (they landed at Villa Park in 1897) and turned them into a crack outfit, skippering them to the Birmingham Cup in '80–81. Incredibly he went on to manage them for more than forty years (1884–1926) overseeing their triumphant era, including reclaiming the FA Cup in the first post-war final in '19–20. Only after he had died, in 1935, did the Villa dare pause for breath and take it easy; they were immediately relegated.

Third and finally during Wednesday's heady '03–04 back-to-back titles season, there was only one week during which either Sheffield club were not at the top of the table. United also equalled

Preston's '88–89 season record of winning their first eight league games, a record not matched for another sixty years till Hull City accomplished it in the Third Division. Furthermore, it was during this season that United famously had a record twelve internationals in their squad: Foulke, Thickett, Boyle, Johnson, Morren, Wilkinson, Needham, Brown, Common, Bennett, Priest and Lipsham.

Footnote

[1] *A History of the Corinthian Football Club,* FNS Creek (1993).

Chapter Thirteen

SHEFFIELD, ENGLAND

Nor tripped neither, you base foot ball player

King Lear, Act I, Scene IV, by William Shakespeare.

SHEFFIELD PLAYERS FEATURED prominently in early internationals, a reflection of national respect for their ability. The first five England internationals were those unofficial ones against Scotland, organised through the energies of Alcock. They all took place at the London Oval between March 1870 and February 1872. While no Sheffield player took part in the first four, a Sheffield-born player did. Reverend Arnold Kirke-Smith of Oxford University, whose family was from Ecclesfield, now a suburb of Sheffield, played for Scotland in the third and fourth matches[1]. He later became a Sheffield FC player, making his debut in 1872, just after the last official international.

This did not stop him playing for Oxford University in their '72–73 FA Cup run, becoming a losing finalist when they went down after 'challenging' Wanderers. Another Reverend – Francis W Pawson – gained two England caps while playing for Cambridge University and later joined Sheffield FC. He scored on his England debut in the 7-0 drubbing of Ireland in 1883.

At the time of these unofficial 'Alcock' internationals, Scotland was yet to form an FA and the Scotland teams were made up of London-based players who were Scots or had a Scottish connection, plus 'all-comers', who were usually English players selected to make up the team: Kirke-Smith was one of the latter. For the record, William Henry Gladstone, eldest son of the then-current Prime Minister, William Ewart Gladstone, represented Scotland in the first unofficial game. Gladstone senior was born in Scotland of Scottish parents and raised in Liverpool; his son,

William Henry, while also raised in England, was actually born in Wales.

Morton Peto Betts, the Wanderer's striker and scorer of the first FA Cup Final goal, played as goalkeeper for England in the third unofficial match and as a forward in the fourth. Curiously, he also played in goal in his only official game for England in 1875. Betts was also a cricketer with three first-class caps for Middlesex and Kent. The great JC Clegg, then of the Wednesday, represented England in the fifth and final unofficial game and scored the only goal.

Clegg also played in the world's first official international in 1872. Contested between Scotland and England – as were all the early internationals until Scotland and Wales first met in 1876 – this goalless draw was played in Glasgow in November 1872. Kirke-Smith played again, though this time for England and WH Stacey of the Wednesday was on the England bench. While Alcock handpicked the England team, the mighty Queen's Park Football Club of Glasgow selected the Scottish side (all their own players!) and the game was played under the Scottish rules they had created.

Although Kirke-Smith played against England in two unofficial games and for them in one official game, only two players have played both for and against England in official matches. The first, John Reynolds, was born in Blackburn, England but moved to Ireland as a child. He played five matches for Ireland from 1890–91 including two against England; he scored Ireland's only goal in the first England game, a 9-1 reverse.

He subsequently made eight appearances for England from 1892–97, scoring in three games and remains the only player to have scored both for and against England. Unfortunately, he did not replicate his unique record, failing to score in either of his two England games against Ireland.

The second player, Robert Evans, was born in Chester, England, of Welsh parentage and represented Wales ten times from 1906–10. He played against England on four occasions, never scoring. He then made four appearances for England from

Sheffield, England

'11–12 while playing club football with Sheffield United, scoring on his debut against Ireland.

Clegg had unpleasant memories of playing for England as the only Northerner in that first official team, claiming the 'snobs' neither passed nor spoke to him. It seems that teammate Kirke-Smith, whose family seat was in Ecclesfield, did not consider himself a Northerner. England played this game in matching white tops (emblazoned with three lions) but differently coloured knickerbockers denoting which public school they had attended: no wonder Clegg felt alienated. The Scots played in their dark blue Queen's Park jerseys and while the club changed their strip to black and white hoops in 1873, the national side still continue to play in these colours.

JC Clegg's brother, William, also of the Wednesday, played in the second official international in 1873 and John RB Owen of Sheffield FC played in the 1874 fixture. William H Carr of Owlerton played the fourth the following year (when Alcock won his only official cap) though he arrived fifteen minutes late and became the first England international to play less than ninety minutes. In those early amateur years, from 1872–87, nine Sheffield players made twenty-four appearances for England, some going given that only a few matches were played each year. In the first ten years alone, eight players made twenty-two appearances in fifteen internationals.

They played for a variety of Sheffield teams: Heeley and Sheffield FC (with both teams having a player representing England as captain), Owlerton, Albion, the Wednesday and Thursday Wanderers. Both Hunter, of Heeley, and Mosforth, of Sheffield Albion, had the dubious pleasure of playing in the only two England games to field the unfortunately named Bastard. Segar Richard Bastard (of Upton Park FC) played in the 1880 games against Scotland and Wales and also refereed the 1887 FA Cup final between Wanderers and Royal Engineers.

He is not the only fruitily named referee of a Victorian FA Cup final; it almost seems to have been a cryptic Masonic joke. Sheffield's own William Pierce Dix, brother-in-law of JC Clegg, a leading member of the SFA and an international referee oversaw the '80–81 final when the Old Carthusians beat the Royal Engineers 3-0. There was also (if one takes the vernacular slang) Clegg, himself in 1882 and 1892 and, of course, the legendary Alcock who refereed in 1875 and 1879. Even the chronological list of FA Cup final referees holds a joke with Wright preceding Bastard in 1886. While the monocle-sporting Charles Crump (1883 final) misses out, his delicious name nevertheless merits a mention as does Major Marindin (1880 and 1884–90 finals).

In the first years of professional football, from 1888–91, when neither Sheffield team was in the Football League only one Wednesday player got an England call-up, but in the glory years, from 1892–1904, twenty-one players (15 United, 6 Wednesday) made sixty appearances in forty internationals, scoring eleven goals and captaining three times (Jack Hunter of Heeley, John Hudson of the Wednesday and United's legendary captain, 'Nudger' Needham).

During this era, Sheffield clubs also had Scottish internationals including James Lang, of the Wednesday, who scored twice for Scotland, and Peter Andrews, of Heeley, who scored once. There appears to be only a matter of weeks between the two players first playing for their respective Sheffield sides (in 1876) and, while still a matter of some contention, it appears that Andrew's pipped Lang in becoming the first 'foreign' player in English football though Lang was the first to be paid.

Both players gained their caps while playing for Scottish clubs. The Scottish Football Association, who deplored professionalism and refused to acknowledge it till 1893, spitefully refused to select English-based (paid) players till as late as 1896.

Additionally, United had Peter Boyle of Ireland, who won two FA Cups with the Blades, while his son went on to win one in 1925, and John Leonard Jones of Wales, who jumped ship to Spurs in 1898, captaining them to their FA Cup victory over the Blades in 1901. In that final, all but two United players had international caps and, by '03–04 they had a full set with twelve internationals on their books.

After Sheffield's football epoch, the following sixteen years (1905–20) were fallow ones for international appearances (9 players, 17 appearances, 41 internationals) reflecting poorer club performances, though EH Milnes of Sheffield FC did represent the England amateur team in France in 1907. Better times were to follow: from 1921–27, ten players (5 United, 5 Wednesday) made forty appearances in thirty-five England matches, scoring once and captaining on seven occasions (Wilson and Kean, both of the Wednesday). In the period from 1928–33 Wednesday dominated caps; thirteen players (10 Wednesday, 3 United) made sixty-seven appearances in thirty-two internationals, scoring seven and captaining seven games.

The great amateur era was also coming to an end with fewer and fewer amateurs appearing in the England side. Bernard Joy of the Casuals was the last amateur player to earn an England cap, though this came as late as May 1936.

Footnotes

[1] Ecclesfield had a decent football club, Ecclesfield FC, who supplied several players to the early Sheffield United side.

Chapter 14

A CLUTTER OF SPIDERS

Some drive the jolly bowl about
with dice and draughts some chas'd the day
and some, with many a merry shout,
in riot revelry, and rout, pursued the foot-ball play

Excerpt from Lay of the Last Minstrel, Canto 5, Verse 6, by Sir Walter Scott, 1805.

QUEEN'S PARK, AS mentioned, selected themselves as the Scotland team to play England in what was to be the first official football international in the world. They were the wonder team of Scotland, created in 1857, ten years after the Club, and nicknamed the Hoops or the Spiders. Incidentally, there is actually a spider 'Neosparassus patellatus', found only in Tasmania, Australia, which is known as the football spider, on account of its red and white striped body and legs. It is not to be confused with 'Phryganoporus candidus' (otherwise known as the foliage webbing spider) an Australian communal spider that lives in football-sized nests housing up to 700.

There are several parallels between Sheffield FC and Queen's Park FC; those two grand dames of British football. Sheffield FC was England's oldest association football team, Queen's Park was Scotland's, though the country's oldest football team in any code is Edinburgh Academicals Football Club founded either in late 1857 or early 1858.

They were formed prior to the schism between the two sports so did not have rugby in their name but were a rugby team from the off, always playing the carrying game; they still retain their original name. Both the Club and the Spiders were pioneering teams who were initially successful: Queen's Park were twice runners-up in the English FA Cup and won

A clutter of spiders

the Scottish Cup ten times! Both drew local teams together to form their own football association; both developed their own set of rules which they promulgated widely; both refused to turn professional and both were ultimately overshadowed by their city's two new professional teams – in Queen's Park's case, Rangers (c1872) and Celtic (c1888). It was only natural that the two teams should cross swords at some point and evidence for this is provided in Fred Walter's centenary history of Sheffield FC; in fact Queen's Park were guests of honour at the centenary celebrations, playing a match against an England Amateur XI at Bramall Lane on October 24th 1957.

The players of both sides also regularly met when the Sheffield and Glasgow Associations played each other, except in 1874 that is, when piqued Queen's Park players vetoed the game after the Scottish FA had the gall to offer the captaincy to a non-Queen's Park player. Queen's Park also came south to play the Wednesday on at least one occasion (October 21st 1880). Despite annihilating the Wednesday 5-0 in this friendly, they mysteriously failed to show for their first round FA Cup match against them the following month and Wednesday were given a bye.

Queen's Park were in a different class to any other team in Britain. Amazingly, from first being formed they did not concede a single goal for seven years, finally succumbing to Vale of Leven in a 1-1 Scottish Cup semi-final replay in 1875! More astounding still, it took another two seasons for them to record their first loss despite playing regular games in England and Scotland in the Scottish Cup. Vale of Leven were the culprits again and went on to win the cup, having established themselves as the second big Scottish club of the day, despite their relative minnow status in hailing from the small town of Alexandria, near Loch Lomond.

Not just content with stealing Queen's Park's glory, Vale of Leven swiped their previous team strip of dark blue jerseys, earning their nickname the Dark Blues. Queen's Park got their revenge in '83–84 when they lifted the Scottish Cup without having to play, Vale of Leven not showing for the final due to injuries and a family bereavement. This mirrored Vale's behaviour in that 1875 1-1 draw, when Queen's Park first conceded a goal.

From Sheffield with Love

When Queen's Park equalised, Vale of Leven walked off and refused to play further; the game was awarded to Queen's Park. It is worth mentioning that a first round match in the '85–86 Scottish Cup (won that year by Queen's Park) is famous as being the highest scoring game ever recorded in Britain: Arbroath beat Bon Accord by a ridiculous 36-0. Amazingly the same day lays claim to the second highest ever score when Dundee Harp knocked 35 past a stunned Aberdeen Rovers!

Queen's Park had an enviable cup record. They drew with Wanderers in the semi-finals of the first ever FA Cup, in 1872 but, being unable to afford to stay for the replay, Wanderers were awarded the game and went on to win the Cup. In 1884 they lost 2-1 in the FA Cup final, at The Oval, to Blackburn Rovers, having scored 32 goals (and conceded only one) en route. The following year they again lost to Rovers (2-0) in the final; it was to be the last time an amateur club would get that far. They won the first of their ten Scottish Cups in 1873, the inaugural year (the Scottish FA formed that year) and their last appearance in the cup final was in 1900 when they lost 4-3 to Celtic.

Queen's Park also has the proud record of fielding Britain's first black footballer. British Guiana-born Andrew Watson played for them from 1880–87. Regarded as one of the best players of his day, he was capped three times for Scotland (his father was Scottish) – and was the world's first black international player and captain, commanding the 6-1 drubbing of England in 1881. He also became the first black player in FA Cup history when he briefly turned out for the famous London Swifts in 1882 as well as playing for amateur über-nobs the Corinthians. High-jump wizard Watson was held in such high esteem he ended up as Queen's Park's club secretary. He later went to India before ending his days in Sydney, Australia, where he is buried.

The amateur club was ultimately allowed to join the Scottish League in 1900 and today still proudly remains the only amateur team in this league. Their home ground is Hampden Park, the national stadium and their most famous old boy, Alex Ferguson.

Chapter Fifteen

AND THERE WERE GODS

Who ate all the pies?
Who ate all the pies?
You fat bastard, you fat bastard
You ate all the pies!

English football chant

I CANNOT WRITE about *fin-de-siécle* Sheffield football and go past William Henry 'Fatty' Foulke (1874–1916), one of England's most colourful football characters and described in his day as 'perhaps the most talked of player in the world'. He is, of course, Sheffield United's legendary goalkeeper and not to be confused with William Anthony Foulkes (b: 1932), one of the Busby babes who survived the Munich air disaster in February 1958, in which eight Manchester United players (and another fifteen passengers, mostly journalists) died. Manager Matt Busby was seriously injured and a threadbare United went on to complete the season under Jimmy Murphy, winning their first game 3-1 against Sheffield Wednesday.

Foulkes, who had already won two championship medals with United took over as captain and went on to win another two as well as the FA Cup and the European Cup, playing in 679 games– only Sir Bobby Charlton (752) and Ryan Giggs (716 and counting) have made more appearances. As a centre-half Foulkes netted only nine times but he did score the all-important goal against Real Madrid that sent United to the European Cup Final in 1968.

'Fatty' Foulke, who in his day was more commonly nicknamed 'Little Willie' or, occasionally, 'Tiny' was born in 1876 in Dawley, Shropshire. The year after Foulke's birth, Dawley's most famous son, Captain Matthew Webb, became the first person to swim the English Channel. Although, a Shropshire lad, Foulke was raised in Blackwell, Derbyshire; the terraced family home facing one side of the cricket ground at which he would later play, and which hosted Derbyshire for seven first-class cricket games from 1909–13. The town produced a number of decent players over the years. Another Blackwell colliery worker, Willie Layton, joined Sheffield Wednesday in 1895. When he took the night off work before his trial, seven of his colleagues died in an explosion. At the time of the tragedy, despite playing for Sheffield United, Foulke was still living at his Blackwell home and commuting to work by train (till 1899): two of his neighbours died. One of Foulke's greatest friends, United winger Walter 'Cocky' Bennett (whose brother was the Wednesday forward, 'Mickey' Bennett), was later to die in a colliery accident aged 34. He was another Mexborough gem, helping the Blades to one League title and two FA Cups and himself to two England caps.

As well as with Foulke, Blackwell (which appears in the Magna Carta) is associated with another larger-than-life character: Percy Toplis (1896–1920), otherwise known as 'the Monocled Mutineer'. Toplis was a career criminal whose offences included theft, rape, black market fraud, forgery, and murder. Born in Chesterfield he worked for a while in Blackwell. He was incorrectly credited with having been a key figure in the heroic mutiny at the appalling Etaples training ground in France during World War One. He did serve in the army but deserted in 1918; he was also an impostor, at times sporting a monocle, so perhaps the 'Monocled Deserter' is more apt. He was shot dead by police during his manhunt.

Foulke played in goal for the local colliery side before signing for Sheffield United as a twenty-year old in 1894. His older brother, Tommy, was an outfield player, though he ended up between the sticks for Wellington Town, while his younger brother, Jack, went on to keep goal for Blackburn Rovers. There is a story of Willie as a sixteen-year-old, playing in a friendly between Blackwell and Derby County, missing in his attempt to punch clear a ball and connecting instead with the attacker's teeth, taking out two in the process. The striker was no less

And there were Gods

than John Goodall, previous star of the Invincibles, the double-winning Preston North End side of 1888–89, who never lost a league game nor conceded an FA Cup goal. So excited were Preston fans on securing the double that they are reputed to have kicked the FA trophy about the streets of Preston, necessitating extensive silversmith repairs before it was handed back to the FA, still bearing clear 'scars of war'.

Nicknamed 'Johnny Allgood', Goodall scored fifty goals in fifty-six games for them before moving to Derby County in 1889, to score seventy-six in 211 appearances. Born in Westminster of Scottish parents, he won fifteen England caps, scoring twelve times, though his brother played for Ireland, having been born there; as a result they became the first brothers to play for different countries, though they both played for Derby County. Goodall went on to play for Glossop FC, a small-town club that spent one glorious season in the First Division, before drifting back into obscurity, the countryside no doubt encouraging him to continue his eccentric lifelong pursuit of walking foxes.

He became player-manager for Watford, hanging up his boots at 44 years of age, having also squeezed into his sporting career two first-class cricket games with Derbyshire; in addition he enjoyed curling, fishing, golf and pigeon shooting. Sadly the former England skipper fell on hard times in his later years, walking his foxes up to his allotment in Watford where he grew vegetables to feed himself; he died in 1944 in penury and was buried in an unmarked grave.

Six feet two and twelve stone as a teenager, Foulke grew to a gargantuan twenty-five stone by the end of his career, his robust frame conferring distinct goalkeeping advantages as he was difficult to circumnavigate and left little of the goal to aim at. Doubtless he would have been impossible to beat in the days of rouges and the four-yard goalmouth.

He may have been a behemoth, but he was no lumbering lummox; he possessed speed and agility and was one of the biggest punchers of the ball in history, capable of sending it over the halfway line. He was also an expert penalty saver. In those days goalies did not have to stay on their line and could advance toward the kicker. Using his bulk to his advantage Foulke would storm out towards the penalty spot, simultaneously worrying the penalty taker and shrinking the target. The penalty area was the entire length of the pitch so that a penalty could be conceded by an infringement at the sidelines. Curiously, the goal area in those days was two adjacent six-yard semi-circles meeting to form an 'M' or upturned 'B' shape, with the central prong pointing to the centre of the goal-line; the modern design was not introduced till the '01–02 season.

The origins of this kidney-shaped area go back to 1872 and a story illustrates its introduction. Just as the FA were flummoxed when they played the SFA under their rules by the offside rule so the SFA were irritated when they visited London and played under FA Laws. What got the goat of the Tykes was that whenever an opposing defender was put under pressure he could kick the ball over his own goal line, which allowed his own team to then kick it back out of touch. Unlike the last match in London in March, 1866, when they insisted on keeping touchdowns despite having erased them from the rule book the previous month, this time they got rid of the ridiculous rule the following month, though a tad ham-fistedly.

The amended laws stated that if the ball rolled over the goal line the opponents of the offender were awarded a corner kick. However, if the ball was kicked over the crossbar by the attacking team (only) then the defending side was awarded a free kick from within six-yards, hence the need to mark out two six-yard semicircles. Why they chose semicircles and not a rectangle eludes me.

Foulke's professional career as a goalkeeper at Bramall Lane began just as another intriguing player's was drawing to a close: that of Arthur Wharton (1865–1930). Wharton was born in Accra, his father a West Indian (Grenadian) Methodist minister, his mother of royal Ghanaian blood. Both parents had Scottish heritage. After commencing his education in Ghana, he schooled in London for four years before completing two years at the Wesleyan High School in Ghana.

He returned to England to study divinities for three years in

And there were Gods

Cannock, Staffordshire (birthplace to footballers Stan Collymore and Steve Bull), enjoying cycling, rugby, football and cricket. In 1885 he moved his studies to Darlington where his interest in athletics was kindled. Notwithstanding his natural talent, he must have trained hard because the following year he became the fastest man in England when he won the Amateur Athletics Association 100 yards Sprint Championships at Stamford Bridge; his time of 10 seconds was unbeaten for, astonishingly, thirty years. He retained the title the following year but then drifted away from athletics, strangely to the relatively static profession of goalkeeping.

Between 1886 and 1887 he kept goal for Darlington, Newcastle, Durham and PNE. In truth, the job of a goalie was somewhat different in the days of Wharton and Foulke, less immobile and more involved with the general play. Although goalkeepers had long been recognised, it was not a fixed position and whosoever was nearest to goal acted as keeper, or in other words they played 'goalie wag'. Before 1869, under FA Laws, any player could handle the ball anywhere on the pitch but in 1870 a new rule stated that only a designated goalkeeper could do so.

Sheffield rules restricted goalkeepers to their own half from 1874 onwards, and London later followed suit though they were not restricted to their own penalty area till 1911; this despite JC Clegg having proposed a three-yard limit way back in 1874. In 1875 Sheffield determined that goalkeepers should continue to be goalie-wag i.e. they could be changed at any time, though they added that goalkeepers could not carry the ball. Furthermore, until 1895, goalkeepers could be charged down with or without the ball by oncoming forwards and keepers holding the ball were often bustled into their own nets for a goal. The very evident potential for injury resulted in keepers punching the ball away more often than today, a skill both Wharton and Foulke excelled at. The position also doubtless appealed to their innate sense of showmanship.

During his time at PNE, Wharton – who was nominated, but not selected, for England – played in their FA Cup semi-final loss to West Bromwich Albion. In 1888 he moved to Sheffield to train with other black athletes winning the September Handicap at the Queen's ground. Initially he still turned out for PNE but switched to Rotherham Town the following year. He retired completely from running in 1890 to keep a pub as well as keep goal. He made 34 League appearances for Rotherham Town in the '93–94 season and, in so doing, became the Football League's first black player. He discharged his duties with some aplomb; an old supporter recalling some years later:

> *In a match between Rotherham and Sheffield Wednesday at Olive Grove I saw Wharton jump, take hold of the cross bar, catch the ball between his legs and cause three onrushing forwards... to fall into the net. I have never seen a similar save since, and I have been watching football for over fifty years.*[1]

In August 1894, Wharton switched to Sheffield United under the lure of both Tom Bott, his former running manager, and the chance to run another pub. Bott was now the current United director, though he essentially acted as manager to the team, second only to coach George Waller – the man largely responsible for United's quarter century of success – in influence. Waller was an all-round Sheffield sportsman who had originally played football for his home suburb of Pitsmoor before switching to play for the Wednesday, helping them to reach the 1890 FA Cup Final and to their Alliance victory.

He then moved across the city to the Blades, playing football and cricket for them before turning trainer, all the while playing first-class cricket for Yorkshire. In those days the coach managed the squad with input from the captain on team selection but Bott's ability to blend and bond with his players enabled him to help at a much more grassroots level than was normal for a director. There is a story of Bott entertaining the team by arranging a race between the lumbering Foulke and Jack Houseley, United's trainer, during a week-long training holiday to Skegness before the '98–99 Cup Final. Bott tried to convince his players Foulke would win but they would have none of it. Foulke and Houseley, no competition boss – and there wasn't. Foulke won.

Wharton's arrival was ill-timed as it coincided with that of the

And there were Gods

young Foulke and he remained a reserve player for two seasons, making only three starts. Ever the journeyman, he returned to Rotherham but lasted only a season before switching to Stalybridge FC as player-coach for two stints, sandwiched by two years at Ashton FC as both centre forward and goalkeeper. He finally joined Stockport County in 1901 making his last League appearance – against Newton Heath – in 1902 and returned to Rotherham to become a publican. He continued to play cricket till about 1915 when he began work in a colliery in Edlington, Yorkshire, and remained there for fifteen years till illness, most likely related to years of excess alcohol, intervened and he passed away, buried in an unmarked grave. A memorial stone was placed on his grave during a special ceremony in 1997 initiated by the national anti-racist football project 'Football Unites, Racism Divides', to whom I am grateful for the information on this pioneering man. Coincidentally the project was initiated by disgruntled Sheffield United fans at Mount Pleasant Community Centre, a stone's throw from where Sheffield FC was born.

The arrival of the promising Foulke's not only dismissed Wharton of any notions of first team football, it also displaced United's current goalkeeper, Charles Henry Howlett (1865–1906). Charlie Howlett may not have been as out there as Wharton or Foulke but in true turn-of-the-century United 'keeper tradition he was an eccentric.

He started his career at Gainsborough Trinity, the Lincolnshire club founded in 1873 that would later join the Midland League with Sheffield United and become champions in '90–91 and runners-up in '91–92. They were elected to the new Football League Second Division in '92–93 but never fared well and were voted out of the League in 1912, replaced by local rivals, Lincoln City. They are currently in the Nationwide Conference North League, two divisions below the Football League Second Division. Fred Spiksley (1870–1948) played for Trinity before moving to the Wednesday (who poached him from Accrington) in 1892. Spiksley was Hillsborough's first hero, scoring over 120 goals for the Owls and helping them to First and Second Division Championships and the 1896 FA Cup, scoring both goals in the final. He went on to score seven times in as many games for England. There is another connection too: Sheffield United's previous manager Neil Warnock began his professional managerial career with Trinity.

Howlett left Gainsborough for newly-formed United in 1889, becoming their first keeper and stopping shots in their very first game against Sheffield FC, though it is worth mentioning that WF Beardshaw, the former Corinthian, acted as occasional deputising 'keeper. The banjo-strumming Howlett was a nervy soul who was easily rattled, once refusing to play Newton Heath, because of their reputation for strong-arming 'keepers. For all that though, the crowd loved his speciality of diving to the ground to fist low shots off the line.

He also wore glasses when playing and, in their 1890 FA Cup tie against Bolton Wanderers, lost his specs in the mud; the resulting 13-0 result remains United's heaviest ever defeat. Myopia aside, Howlett was still able to help United gain promotion from the Second Division in their first season in League football and to a tenth place berth the following season. He then slinked off back to Trinity; no doubt terrified at the prospect of having to compete with Fatty Foulke.

Howlett is not to be confused with his teammate Rab Howell who played for United from 1890–98 and was the first full-blooded Roma (gypsy) to play League football. Howell was born and brought up in a caravan in Wincobank, Sheffield, and continued to live in one as a player. When precipitously transferred to Liverpool following his own-goal brace in a crucial top-of-the-table, end-of-season six-pointer against Sunderland, he simply hitched his wagon and rode his horse into the sunset.

Howell's howlers were believed by his bosses to have been financially-determined and there was a history of gambling to back up the claim. He was dropped for both the Champions of Great Britain match against Celtic and the inaugural Sheriff of London fixture against the Corinthians but returned to the side for the penultimate game of the season. Liverpool then came in and crossed United's palm with silver (£200) and he was released to play their final game of the season against the mighty Villa.

And there were Gods

A lucky talisman indeed as Liverpool won 4-0 with the usual goal-shy Howell scoring on his debut.

Since Howell, many Roma and Sinti (a closely-related group) have travelled his professional trail; Sir Alf Ramsey is reputed to have been part-Roma. Unfortunately, despite the genocide of up to 500,000 Roma and Sinti during the Nazi regime, sickening, pernicious anti-gypsyism remains rife in Romanian and, to a lesser extent, Bulgarian football.

And then came Foulke. From the off his career was peppered with tall tales (even his understudy was called Biggar) often relating to his strength, his puckishness or his foul temper. When he arrived at the Lane as a nipper he was already able to carry a man under each arm without breaking sweat. Presumably he was not carrying Boyle and Thickett his two hefty full-backs who weighed fourteen stones apiece; more likely two of the three half-backs – Needham, Howell and Morren – who were all five foot five and weighed ten stones.

What a sight that back line would have been: a troll, two giants and three midgets – priceless. During a match in 1898 Foulke dug in his heels and refused to try and save what he believed was a wrongly awarded penalty kick after he allegedly dumped Liverpool's George Allan head-first in the goalmouth mud. He repeated the act in his denouement when, after conceding a penalty for throwing a player into his net, he unwillingly stood on his goalline under captain's orders, but refused to move or watch the shot, instead glowering at the ref.

When United lost to Aston Villa in the 1896 Birmingham Cup Final, Foulke quipped to the Villa that they had better make sure that no one nick this cup, apropos of the FA Cup that had been stolen while in their possession the previous season. It wasn't just Wharton who could swing from the crossbar; during the '96–97 season Foulke did just that. Unfortunately, he bought the United–Wednesday derby to a halt when the bar broke.

The apocryphal story that led to the 'Fat Bastard' poem being coined about him was set during training for United's FA Cup semi-final game against Liverpool in 1899. The match itself ended in a draw and the fixture turned into a campaign, taking four games to separate the two teams. The first at Nottingham ended 2-2 with United twice coming from behind and Needham saving the day. In the replay at Burnley, Liverpool went two up only for United to draw level. Things then swung sharply Liverpool's way courtesy of a United own goal and a penalty but once again United dug deep and again came from two goals down to peg it back to 4-4, thanks largely to captain Needham's crazy 'who dares wins' tactic of resorting to eight strikers with eight minutes to go. The second replay at Fallowfield, Manchester, was abandoned due to crowd invasion and bad light with Liverpool 1-0 up and the final game at Derby was heading for a draw till Beer scored at the death. Rab Howell, only just been rejected by the Blades and transferred to Liverpool, must have been gutted that he had failed in the time-honoured duty of wreaking revenge on your old club.

One-nil down at half-time, Sheffield United came from behind to beat Derby County 4-1 in the final at Crystal Palace, cheered on to victory by the Clegg brothers and having played ten matches in all. Legendary United fullback Henry Thickett played out the final with fractured ribs, but it is doubtful that he played in forty-six yards of bandages or needed a half-time bottle of champagne to keep going, as his club doctor impishly suggested. Thickett's devotion to the cup cause was exemplified two seasons later when he made himself available for his club's semi-final replay against reigning League champions Aston Villa days after his wife had died.

United won 3-0 but went down to Spurs in the final, though Thickett was to see cup success again the following season. That first cup final victory had taken ten games, all away, to achieve; it was the Cup of a Thousand Minutes, a glittering prize seized in a sparkling palace, a happy ending of fairytale proportions for a club less than a decade old. The afternoon's merriment and mirth did not extend to their neighbours. The day United won was the Wednesday's last ever game at Olive Grove. It was not a happy one – they were already down; victims of the new automatic relegation rule that had just replaced Test matches.

On the day of that first semi-final, while his comrades were

And there were Gods

out for their early morning drill, Foulke was excused. In the preceding quarter-final match against Nottingham Forest, Foulke had made a spectacular diving save only to tear a hamstring and need six men to pall-bear him off. With such an important fixture coming up Foulke was rested from league games – to his chagrin, and excused from training – music to the ears of this exercise-shy leviathan. With the Liverpool game only hours away but with the possibilities of such legitimate absolution dancing in his head, the convalescent tippy-toed downstairs, snuck into the hotel dining room and Bunteresquely scoffed all fifteen breakfasts. His 'fifteenses' japery became the stuff of legends and stories of his eating prowess legion; even Foulke saw the funny side. Famously, when a newspaper described him as 'one of the curiosities of football', he replied 'I don't care what they call me, as long as they don't call me late for lunch'.

His very real aversion to training was turned to puckish punning one day when he entered the dressing room with five times capped Irish international, Peter Boyle, across his shoulders. 'I can't train today' he winced, 'I've got a painful boil on me back.'

He was even able to laugh through the tears; when United's record-equalling 22-match unbeaten sequence was broken by Bury (nicknamed the Shakers), he was able to quip: 'We've not only been beaten; we've been badly shaken'. During matches, Foulke would even pick up players who annoyed him and dangle them upside down or sit on them till they apologised. There is another tale of him, after the 1902 FA Cup Final, blancmanging naked through the corridors of Crystal Palace looking to berate the referee, Tom Kirkham, whose extremely questionable late decision had led non-leaguers Southampton into stealing a late draw. Kirkham diplomatically locked himself away till the FA secretary had calmed down the furious Foulke.

He kept goal for United for a decade, amassing a record of 340 league and cup games, one championship, two runners-up, one England cap, an FA Cup final defeat and two FA Cup victories. His were a safe pair of hands, or more correctly, his was a safe hand: he scorned picking up the ball with both. He even scored for United. They played a friendly against the black African touring team, the Kaffirs; when they were 4-0 up a chorus of 'give 'em a goal' rallied from the Kop. Foulke left his goal unattended with the result that he scored two goals himself – one a thirty-yard scorcher – and the visitors pulled two back. The intrigued visitors later visited Foulke in his dressing room, exclaiming 'What a monster – a team in himself', doubtless out of earshot.

During his tenure he also played four first-class cricket games for Derbyshire and remains the world's heaviest ever cricketer; a wag once quipping that when he went to the crease the opposition should appeal for bad light. He additionally took to the crease for Blackwell Colliery for many seasons including 1895, when they won the Derbyshire League.

Coincidentally his Blades skipper, Ernest Needham, played in the same League for Staveley; on the occasion of their meeting that season, each caught the other out. Needham was the greatest United player of his generation, captaining them to one League Championship and two FA Cups in 554 appearances; he remains in their All-time XI. During his 22 years with the Blades (1891–1913) he gathered 16 England caps and ten inter-league caps, earning himself the nickname 'Nudger', on account of his combative, hustling style.

Less fortunately, he was known nationally as 'the Prince of Half-Backs', surely meant to compliment but, as he was a diminutive, 'no neck' sportsman (á la Gladstone Small and Craig Bellamy), I always conjure up an image of Richard III dribbling his way out of defence. His defining moment came in the League Championship winning '97–98 season, in the title decider against Bolton Wanderers.

Amazingly the Blade's centre-forward, George Hedley would not be released to play by his Lincolnshire employers and Needham stepped up to the plate. His career-best goal won the match; he went on a solo run, jinking half the pitch, beating man after man before asking the keeper 'which side will you have it' and then walking the ball in.

When he eventually stopped playing at around forty years of

And there were Gods

age, he scouted for the Blades in his spare time, right up to his death in March 1936, a month before the Blades last FA Cup final appearance, against Arsenal. Needham also played regularly for Derbyshire (186 matches between 1901 and 1912; left hand bat; 6,375 runs; seven centuries; average 20.15) and both he and Foulke were stars in the Sheffield United Cricket Club.

Incidentally, inter-league games were annual fixtures held between representative teams of the Scottish and English (and later Irish) leagues. As well as Needham, Foulke himself appeared twice, as did their colleagues, Harry Thickett (who gained two England caps), Harry Johnson (whose son Harry junior scored over 250 goals in under 400 appearances for the Blades), Tommy Morren (who debuted against the Corinthians and later kept a newsagents at Hunter's Bar), Bert Lipsham (Millwall's first player-manager), George Hedley (who appeared in three FA Cup finals with the Blades and one with Wolves, scoring in their 3-1 victory over Newcastle United) and Harry Hammond. Hammond, who scored more than fifty goals in just over a hundred appearances for the Blades, was their first player to be sent off in a League game.

So incensed were the Crewe fans, who were losing 4-0 at home at the time, that they ran on the pitch to give him a kicking. Hammond, fearing for his life, legged it from the pitch, climbing a wall at one end of the ground and running to the train station where he hid till his mates found him.

Wednesday players of that era who played in inter-league games include Frank Bradshaw (1907 FA Cup winner and later of Everton and Arsenal), Tom Crawshaw (two FA Cups and two League Championships with the Wednesday), Jack Earp (skippered Wednesday to their 2-1 FA Cup victory over Wolves in 1896), Harry Davis (winner of two League Championships with the Owls), Ambrose Langley (FA Cup winning medallist in 1896), and Fred Spiksley (the Owls first superstar).

By 1901, increasing girth and mounting injuries were plaguing Foulke's game and the enforced absences further diminished his fitness. He hated missing the theatre of live games, the audience participation and applause, and he did not take kindly to his understudy stealing his limelight; it was with more than a touch of prima donna haughtiness that he conducted his arguments with the club doctor over the thorny issue of fitness to play – and unfitness to train. Relations were souring.

Still, he continued to take centre-stage for a few more seasons, which included the two FA Cup finals. When he was ultimately dropped from United's first eleven he refused to play second fiddle and, in 1905, was bought by a grateful new club – Chelsea FC. He stayed only for a season despite being made their first ever captain and enjoying great rapport with the fans; 67,000 watched him in the top-of-the-table clash against Manchester United, a staggering, though prescient attendance for a second division fixture. It is alleged that Chelsea was the first ever club to use ball boys, employing them to stand behind the net to exaggerate Foulke's leviathan physique, in a bid to intimidate strikers. Indeed, when the (already legendary) rugby All Blacks played Middlesex at Stamford Bridge, Foulke jokingly offered his enormous bulk.

In a curtain call to Sheffield football's flirtation with the stage, Foulke was offered a place in George Robey's showbiz XI but had to turn it down as the game clashed with a Chelsea fixture. Robey was a famous music hall star, perhaps the first celebrity football fan. Duetting with Violet Loraine, he immortalised the song 'If You Were the Only Girl (In the World)' and went on to play Falstaff in Olivier's classic 1944 film version of *Henry V*. He was actually awarded an amateur contract with Chelsea in 1907 after scoring against them in a friendly (he had founded the nearby Chelsea Lodge for Masonic entertainers in 1905), in addition to playing three reserve games for Millwall. The now defunct Finsbury Park pub named in his honour – the 'Sir George Robey' – was a famous punk rock venue. Arsenal-mad author, Nick Hornby, aptly used it as the inspiration for the venue in his novel *High Fidelity*.

By coincidence, Robey was playing the Empire Palace, Sheffield, the night the city suffered its only Zeppelin raid, in 1915. As the dirigible's engines announced its approach he had been singing a song whose verses ended with the words

And there were Gods

'Aw shurrup'. The terrified audience started to panic but Robey merely gazed upwards, waved his arm disdainfully and shouted a sarcastic 'Aw shurrup', the immediate outburst of relieved laughter instantly dispelling the air of dread.

If Foulke's offer was the curtain call, then Owl's darling, Fred Spiksley, provided the encore. He went one better and actually performed a football revue in Fred Karno's music hall troupe, which included Charlie Chaplin and Arthur Jefferson – later known as Stan Laurel. Hmmm… now if only Foulkes had met Jefferson.

Actually, the entire 1907 FA Cup-winning Wednesday side had their fifteen minutes of variety fame when they were invited on stage by George Robey in London on the night of their victory. Among them were Harry Chapman, brother to the great Arsenal and Huddersfield manager, Herbert, and Attercliffe-born Tom Crawshaw, the only survivor of Wednesday's 1896 FA Cup win, who Robey cajoled into speaking onstage.

One player not in the limelight that evening but destined to outshine them all, for all the wrong reasons, was Walter Holbem (1884–1930). He had made his debut that cup-winning season and would become a regular, famously sent off in the 1910 derby, but he was no great shakes and his career blandly petered out. He took up bookmaking and it was while he was at Tattersalls Ring in Newmarket that he was tragically and lethally struck by lightning.

He is not the only Wednesday player to end his days at the races. Fred Spiksley, who loved the turf more than football, went out rather more sedately at Goodwood, falling asleep forever; unaware he had won on the Stakes. In some ways it was a repeat performance for Crawshaw. The 1896 FA Cup winning team had had to take to the stage of the new Empire Palace of Varieties in Sheffield for similarly embarrassing plaudits, treading the boards graced by Lily Langtry, Anna Pavlova, Charlie Chaplin, Laurel and Hardy, WC Fields, Dan Leno, Harry Lauder and, of course, Robey himself.

The link between stage and pitch forged all those years ago by Tommy Youdan was now renewed annually. After the

'02–03 season a triumphant Wednesday had entered stage right at Sheffield's Empire Theatre, and it appears the norm for a cup-winning side to appear at a London theatre while home theatre appearances awaited either cup or league winners; all this, of course, in addition to the pantomime of the time-honoured victory parade through the city centre. Certainly, United's cup-winning side of 1899 had been invited onto the stage of the Alhambra Theatre on the evening of their victory, much to the delight of the handkerchief-waving ladies of London.

Spiksley, like that 'Invincible', John Goodall, ended his days playing for Glossop FC and, like Goodall, was offered the job as the first manager of Watford FC, but turned it down as his love of horse racing was brought up at the interview. Spiksley then went on to become one of the first English coaches abroad with spells in Spain, Switzerland, Sweden, Mexico and Germany – where he found himself at the outbreak of war in 1914. He was interred in a civilian of war camp on the outskirts of Berlin. Amazingly the Ruhleben camp of 5,000 also contained three fellow former England internationals Samuel Wolstenholme, Fred Pentland and Steve Bloomer, two former Evertonians, John Cameron and John Brearley, and one former German international Edwin Dutton.

Bloomer was a bit of an uncharismatic loner, known for playing for himself; highly respected but not particularly liked by his teammates. He probably hit it off with Spiksley, himself a loner in his playing days, or at least they would have each divined and respected the other's need for solitude. Bloomer was an awesome player though – a true poacher – and the world's first football superstar, bagging 352 League goals in 598 games, making him the second-highest goalscorer (to Dixie Dean) in English top flight history and the fourth in all divisions.

He never won major honours though he set all sorts of records, including knocking six goals in one game past a bewildered Wednesday. His 28 goals in 23 England games created a goals-to-game ratio better than anyone including Lineker, Greaves and Charlton. Except for a brief sojourn at Middlesborough, 'Paleface' spent his career at Derby County and was mentored in his youth by John Goodall. He remains their top scorer and

And there were Gods

is still lionised there, the present team coming on to the anthem 'Steve Bloomer's Watching' at home games. He enjoyed plenty of dogfights with Foulke, often getting the better of him, though he lost out in the 1899 FA Cup Final when Foulke's crucial save of his seemingly unstoppable shot, when County were one-nil up, turned the game's fortunes and United ran out 4-1 winners.

Of the other POW's, Samuel Wolstenholme played for Everton, Blackburn Rovers and Norwich City and was in England's Home Championship winning sides of '03–04 and '04–05, while Fred Pentland was in the winning '08–09 squad. Pentland spent most of his career at Middlesborough where he played with Alf Common, who was the first £1,000 player and the man who scored Sheffield United's winning goal in their 1902 FA Cup victory over Southampton.

After hanging up his boots, Pentland went on to briefly coach Germany (in 1914!), France and Spain before becoming a Spanish club manager and remains Athletico Bilbao's most successful manager with two La Liga's and five Copa Del Reys. John Cameron sandwiched his time at Everton with two notable non-league stints, the first at redoubtables Queen's Park – where he won his only Scottish cap – the other at Tottenham. Joining the Spurs in 1898, he became player-manager the following season, not only guiding them to FA Cup success against Sheffield United in 1902 but scoring in the final to boot.

Edwin Dutton's place of birth is unclear, but his parents made the move from England to Germany, where his father, Paul, helped establish football and cricket as viable sports. Schooled in Berlin he went on to play for two local clubs, gaining his solitary German cap during this period. Probably a bit miffed at being interred during the war, he later joined Newcastle United, ending his football days as manager of Ipswich Town. John Brearley was a journeyman who turned out for ten clubs including Everton and Spurs.

During his time at the Chelsea helm, Foulke refused to budge from his home in Asline Road, Sheffield, where his wife kept a shop. Curiously, his daughter's name, Selina, is an anagram of Asline. The tiny road, close to Bramall Lane holds another gem: Enid Blyton's father, Thomas Carey Blyton, was brought up on Asline Road, during the 1880s, hence her book Five go to Bramall Lane.

Foulke even tried training with United during the week, rather than travel to London, doubtless with half an eye on keeping his non-match exercise to a minimum. Despite a successful first season he was loathe to move to the 'Big Smoke' but ultimately found the commuting too much. In 1906 he exited stage north to Bradford City, comfortably reducing his travel time while entering his denouement. Legend has it that in a match against Accrington Stanley, the away side argued that his red keeper's jersey was too similar to their own strip. Not finding a big enough jersey elsewhere the irrepressible Foulke wrapped himself in a white sheet.

Bradford won with Foulke neither diving nor conceding a goal giving rise to the term keeping a 'clean sheet'. The rather more prosaic truth is that the term was first used by sports reporters in 1930, referring to the notes they kept on the match: no goals = no notes = blank sheet of paper.

What actually happened during that match was that he forgot his kit for the match, so tried to play in his old blue Chelsea top. When the opposition took umbrage, urging the referee to make him wear a lighter colour, he ambled off to change, returning in a huge white bath towel. Further howls of protest prompted him to whip the towel off and reveal his preferred away top – a big white number, fashioned from yards of bandage swathed tightly around his barrel torso. Accrington Stanley FC is not to be confused with Accrington FC, one of the original members of the Football League.

Surprisingly there was another Victorian club from Accrington, Church FC, who appeared in the FA Cup three times. In '82–83 they went out in the fourth round, 2-0, to eventual winners Blackburn Olympic. The following year they reached their pinnacle losing 2-0 in the quarter-finals to Old Carthusians and in '84–85 they lost in the fifth round to the Swifts.

Despite some sound keeping, injuries forced Foulke out of contention and he retired from football in November 1907. He

And there were Gods

had helped Bradford to a Second Division fifth-berth finish in '06–07; the following season they would be promoted and three seasons later win the FA Cup. In 1908 he gave up the shop, briefly moved around the corner onto Bramall Lane – his spiritual home – then relocated to a city centre pub 'The Duke' where he became mine host.

Two years later he drifted off to another corner shop and faded from history. Not the appropriate final bow for such a character, the history books have changed the ending. Common myth has it that, ever the entertainer, his life ended in poignant pathos when he began to earn money in a beat-the-goalie sideshow at Blackpool, a sad has-been eking out a living from past glories. It was believed that this had led to his early demise, succumbing to pneumonia after a day at the seaside, but his death certificate is likely to be more accurate: cirrhosis. Like Wharton, Foulke found keeping a pub was more hazardous to his health than keeping goal and problem drinking appears to have culminated in fatal alcohol dependency. Sad but true that with his weak puns, 'madcap' antics, crowd-pleasing displays and problem drinking, Foulke bears more than a passing resemblance to the legendary Paul Gascoigne.

Little wonder then that United went for the dependable but boring Joseph Lievesley as shot stopper for the ensuing ten years (1903–13) or that his replacement Harold Gough (1913–25) was sacked, despite twelve years good and loyal service, for keeping a pub. Gough, who had won an FA Cup winners medal with the Blades in 1915 was ousted the year they won the cup for the fourth time in 1925. He had originally only got the gig because the first-team goalie Arthur Edward (Ted) Hufton broke his nose before the start of the '13–14 season. Sheffield-born Ted suffered further injury as a Coldstream Guard in the Great War but, as luck would have it, on recuperating in London he was picked up by West Ham, just as Foulke's cover, Billy Biggar, had been in 1902. He was an instant success starring in more than 400 cup and league games including West Ham's first ever Football League game in 1919 and their FA Cup final defeat to Bolton Wanderers in 1923, the first football match to be played at Wembley Stadium. The final was dubbed the White Horse Final after Billy, one of the police horses needed to clear some of the estimated 175,000 crowd who had spilled onto the pitch. Ted also helped the Hammers to promotion to the First Division and was a noted shot-stopper, saving 11 of 18 penalties over two seasons.

Foulke died in Sheffield, in 1916, aged just 42. Yet still there was a fairytale ending of sorts. Less than a year before his demise he had seen his beloved United beat his second love Chelsea 3-0 in the 1915 FA Cup Final. The first goal was scored by man-of-the-match Jimmy Simmons, who had started his career at Blackwell Colliery. He was Foulke's nephew.

'Little Willie' is buried in Burngreave Cemetery, Sheffield where respects can still be paid to the great man. This tale does not end there though, it lives on. William Henry 'Fatty' Foulke was immortalised in celluloid, filmed during a Sheffield United first division game against Bury in September, 1902; the first football legend preserved in the aspic of time. Only a few fleeting moments of him are captured but there he is, alive and kicking. Excerpts of him are included in the wonderful BBC documentary *The Lost World of Mitchell and Kenyon*, available globally online for all to buy, all to see[2]. His audience lives on. He would be pleased as Punch.

Footnotes

[1] T H Smith, *Sheffield Telegraph and Independent*, January 12th 1942.

[2] Similarly, rare footage of a sixty-year old Spiksley in a training film remains. It can be viewed on YouTube: http://www.youtube.com/watch?v=7tMsFmXtN74#GU5U2spHI_4

Chapter 16

VALE

*Unhappy Sheffield Club, whither doth thy destinies lead thee?
Every match is a defeat, every defeat a disaster*

Anonymous.

WITH SHEFFIELD NOW having two professional clubs the importance of its amateur teams slowly faded. Sheffield FC's close affiliation to the SFA ensured their continued status, though that being said, given their years of self-imposed isolation they were a spent force, no longer even one of the better local amateur sides. From the early 1880s onwards they were recording big losses: 14-0 to Aston Villa; 9-1 to Nottingham Forest; 9-0 and 8-0 to Notts County; 13-0 to Rotherham Town.

In 1889 the Midland League was formed. If the Football League was the Premiership, then the Football Alliance was the Championship, the Northern League (also founded in 1889) was Division One and the Midland League, Division Two. The Club joined the new Midland League (puzzlingly, as Sheffield Town) but remained bottom for most of the season and were replaced by Sheffield United the following season. The '90–91 season proved something of a watershed for Sheffield's amateur clubs, it being the last time during this era that any of them competed in the FA Cup, except for Sheffield FC's swansong in 1896.

All went out in the first qualifying round: Sheffield FC recorded their 13-0 drubbing at the hands of Rotherham Town, while Attercliffe went down 5-2 to Rotherham Swifts and Sheffield Walkley suffered a humiliating 19-0 annihilation at the hands of Staveley. Nicknamed 'the Collier Lads', Staveley were a successful SFA club from Derbyshire, who were founder members of the Midland League in 1889 (along with Sheffield FC and Rotherham Town). In the 1880s they made the third round of the FA Cup three times and the fifth round once, on two occasions losing to eventual winners Blackburn Rovers. Known for their hard tackles and straight talking they were referred to by the offended local press as having 'foot and mouth disease'. So intolerable became the reception meted out to timorous visiting teams (especially local ones) by players and fans alike that they were directed by the SFA to play their '83–84 home FA Cup tie against Wednesday Club at the neutral Saltergate ground at Chesterfield.

They still won 3-1, in part due to Wednesday keeper George Ulyett having just retired and his replacement, Haydn A Morley, making his debut. Despite recording the second-highest win in FA Cup history, '90–91 was their last appearance in the FA Cup, going out to Lincoln City 4-1 in the fourth qualifying round. Many of Sheffield United's original players were poached from Staveley, including 'Nudger' Needham (born in nearby in Old Whittington and star of the 19-0 drubbing of Sheffield Walkley) who joined United in 1891.

The loss of talent led to an inevitable decline and they resigned from the Midland League before folding in 1892. Derby Junction was another Derbyshire team who had a surprising FA Cup run. They were an old boy's team from Junction Street School in Derby, and another founder member of the Midlands League. In '87–88, they knocked out Lockwood Brothers in the third round, got a bye in the fourth and beat Chirk in the fifth to set up a quarter-final tie at home to Blackburn Rovers. Home was actually the Arboretum in Derby, England's first public park, donated by Joseph Strutt, the writer who had described football in 1801. They stunned the cup giants of the era with a 2-1 victory, progressing to a semi-final tie at Stoke against West Bromwich Albion. Perhaps if they had not lost 3-0 it would have been they and not West Brom, who held aloft the 'little tin idol'.

By 1891, Sheffield FC, realising that it, and other amateur clubs, could no longer compete with the professional teams, suggested that the FA instigate an Amateur Cup; they even offered to supply the trophy, as recorded in their minutes of September 11th 1891:

Vale

That this meeting of the Sheffield Football Club considers it in the interests of amateur football that a trophy should be offered by the Football Association to be competed for by purely amateur clubs, and this club are prepared to offer such a trophy if the Football Association will undertake the management of the competition.

The FA declined but 18 months later had a change of heart, and the competition began in '93–94. And so is provided a happy ending to this story. The club was finally rewarded for its dogged loyalty to the amateur game when it won the Cup in 1904, beating Ealing 3-1 in the final. Vivian Simpson, the amateur player who also played for the Wednesday, scoring a hat-trick for them in the 6-0 drubbing of Manchester United in the FA Cup of the same season, was the key figure in the Club's cup run but missed out on the final.

His injury was a significant factor in the Wednesday going down in the semi-final to Manchester City, their dreams of a double and Simpson's of appearing in two finals in tatters. With Solomon-like wisdom he was generously awarded a winner's medal by the FA, just as United's 'Cocky' Bennett had been (with JC Clegg's intercession) after missing the '01–02 FA Cup final replay. Simpson was to go on and play in Wednesday's victorious cup run in '06–07 but did not play in the final; it was another Simpson – George – who bagged the winner in the 2-1 defeat of cup-holders Everton.

There were two delicious historical twists to the final, played out at Bradford's Valley Parade Ground. Ernest Chambers, son of Harry Waters Chambers, one of the key figures in the club's early days and the man whose home provided the birthplace for the world's first football club, played for Sheffield FC that day, sublimely linking the club's past and present success. In fact, the Chambers' association with the club lasted for more than a century. But the real jewel in the crown occurs in the closing reels. Can you guess who presented Sheffield FC with their first ever trophy? Why, Alcock of course! The incomparable father of football, who had first played against

From Sheffield with Love

Sheffield FC almost 40 years before was now Vice-President of the FA, a lion in winter.

His speech included the following words:

> *I can only say that it is a personal pleasure to hand the Cup to the Sheffield Club, especially when I recall its long and unique record in association football. When it was formed in 1855, there was no other club existing in England, and when, in 1872, the Football Association Cup was instituted and the 'old pot' was fought for, Sheffield Club, as I can well testify, made up a considerable power in the competition. It has always been actuated by the highest principles in football and in amateurism and has always been intensely loyal to the Football Association. It is with the best wishes of the Football Association that I hand the cup over to Sheffield Club and with that body's appreciation of the good work which the Club has always done in connection with the game.*

His reference to 1855 as the year of inception is in keeping with the misconception of the time discussed in chapter two. Creswick himself moved swiftly to quash the notion once and for all, issuing a statement two days after Alcock's speech, attesting to 1857 as the year of formation.

In October 1907, a ball was held in Sheffield to mark the Club's golden jubilee. Lord Kinnaird, president of the FA, was guest of honour and while wild horses would not have kept CW Alcock away, sadly he had died ten months before. Local luminaries present included the Clegg brothers and HB Willey. HB had played football for the club (and cricket for Collegiate) during the 1880s and 1890s, indeed he had played for so long that he turned out alongside both JC Clegg and his son, Colin.

He later became the administrative face of the club, holding the position of secretary for 35 years. Willey also had tenure as president and so devoted was the bachelor to the club that he poured his own money into it, such that when he died in 1933, the Club's finances once again hit a crisis.

Sadly, William Prest was not present; he had passed away more than two decades before in his early fifties. Not so his friend and undoubtedly man of the moment, Nathaniel Creswick, co-founder of Sheffield FC and still there fifty years on at the grand old age of seventy-six. His (unrecorded) speech, which received a rousing reception, must have been the highlight of the evening, a jewel in time.[1]

The year 1907 also marked the formation of the Amateur Football Alliance, an amateur league attempting to preserve the spirit of amateurism. The organisation still exists, mainly catering to Old Boy's Clubs. It retains it autonomy from the football league system which also now admits amateur teams. One of the original amateur greats, the Old Carthusians – the only team to win the FA Cup (1880–81) and the Amateur Cup (1894 and 1897) – won the amateur Premier League in 2005–06. They are not the only Old Boys mentioned in this story residing in the Premiership. Three teams who played early pivotal roles also reside there: the Old Foresters, Alcock's Old Harrovians and two-times FA Cup winners, the Old Etonians, who won the League in 2004-05. And as we come to the end of our story so we come full circle. We started off with the first description of football in Britain, featuring no less than Merlin: fitting then that the Amateur Football Alliance's league is titled the Arthurian League.

The Club's centenary in 1957 was commemorated by two matches: a Sheffield XI v England B team on October 23rd and an England Amateur XI v Queen's Park on the 24th. A celebratory banquet followed at the Cutler's Hall patronised by Prince Phillip and the FA Secretary, Sir Stanley Rous.

Sheffield FC are, of course, still going, playing at the Bright Finance Stadium (dubbed the 'Stadium of Bright').

They even made the FA Vase final (which had replaced the FA Amateur Cup in 1974–75) at Wembley in 1977, drawing 1-1 with Billericay Town, before losing 2-1 in the replay at Nottingham Forest's City Ground. The Sheffield and Hallamshire County Football Association continues to minister to the needs of the local amateur sides and, in 2006, hosted the popular FA National indoor five-a-side ('futsal') finals for the third time. They still organise the local Challenge Cup in addition to a Junior and

Senior Cup, recently twice won by Sheffield FC: for the first time in 22 years in 2005 and once again in 2006. At the time of writing the Club has just been promoted from the Northern Counties East League Premier Division (where Hallam FC remain) to the Unibond First Division North where they will face another Sheffield rival, Stocksbridge Park Steel FC. Only four leagues below Football League Two and seven below the Premiership; the Club is gathering steam...

In the 21st century Sheffield FC has attracted a host of celebrity and sporting figures as members of the club including Sven Goran Eriksson, Michael Vaughan, Sepp Blatter, Eric Cantona, Sir Bobby Robson, David Blunkett, Kelly Dalglish, Gordon Banks and Def Leppard. Coincidentally, Sheffield-born goalkeeping-legend Gordon Banks is uncle to my friend, Nick Banks, long-time drummer in hibernating ersatz-eccentric combo, Pulp. The band's lead singer, Jarvis Cocker, shares the same first name as the scorer of the first ever goal in the FA Cup, Jarvis Kenrick, who nabbed a brace for Clapham Rovers in their 3-0 win against Upton Park in 1871.

In recognition of Sheffield FC's unique position as the world's oldest football club they were awarded a FIFA Centenary Order of Merit in 2004. Only one other club out of more than 300,000 worldwide received the Order: Real Madrid.

Sadly, most of those other pioneering amateur Sheffield sides have vanished – their place in football legend forgotten. Perhaps it is worthwhile pausing briefly for a roll call of honour, to remember some of those clubs not yet mentioned, to think of the debt of gratitude we owe them and to reflect on those long-dead men who were there at the birth of football, heroes all: Pyebank, Providence, Port Mahon, Burton Star, Brincliffe, White Lane, Cavendish, Sheffield Clinton, Cundy Street; Fir Mount, Barrow Hill, Norton Oaks, Norton Britannia, Attercliffe Reform, Attercliffe Victoria, Reads Rangers and Darnall Rangers; St Barnabas, Princess Street Wesleyan, Ellesmere Wesleyan, Holy Trinity, Broompark Mission, Priory Wanderers and Duke Street Temperance; Eckington Works, Atlas Works, Adalene, Artillery, Pitsmoor Coal Company, Saxon and Saville Street Foundry;

Vale

Wombwell Clarence, Dronfield Exchange, Postal Telegraph, Grimesthorpe Pavilion and Grimesthorpe Wesleyan; Sheffield Wanderers, Hutton Wanderers, Hallcar Wanderers, Highfield Wanderers, Sharrow Rangers, Meersbrook Rangers and Stocksbridge Foresters.

Thank you... thank you... farewell.

Thank you.

Footnotes

[1] Nathaniel Creswick died on Saturday, October 13th 1917; the day the 'Miracle of the Sun' was witnessed by 70,000 in Fatima, Portugal and eleven days short of Sheffield FC's diamond jubilee.

Appendices

Australia rules!

Those sports-mad Aussies were no slackers when it came to developing team games in their new country. Of course cricket came first – and how. In 1835 New South Wales (which included what is now the state of Victoria) was settled as a colony and a ridiculously short three years later the Melbourne Cricket Club (MCC) was formed, playing its first game against a military side on the site of the Old Mint in William Street, Melbourne. A few weeks later they moved to Batman's Hill, stayed till 1846, then moved again, to land close to what is now Melbourne's Crown Casino.

In 1852, Victoria was declared a separate colony and the following year the Melbourne Cricket Ground (MCG) was established. Nine years later the first touring English side (a Surrey XI) had arrived, playing their first ever game on New Year's Day 1862 at the MCG, and by 1868 a team of Indigenous Australians had toured England. In 1877 the world's first Test match took place at the MCG between Australia (who won) and England, the Ashes following in 1882. By 1892 (cf. English Football League) the Sheffield Shield began: the major domestic first-class cricket competition that is still played today. It was originally named after the Earl of Sheffield but now has the less than romantic title of the Pura (that's a brand of milk, folks) Cup. As I am writing this, one hundred and sixty-nine years after the MCC formed, the English are being skittled out of their second innings in the fifth test in Sydney, doomed to a 5-0 drubbing, the first since 1920–21. A week ago I saw Shane Warne get his magical 700th wicket at the MCG in his last home Test match. The country has taken the game it grew up with, that is deeply

Appendices

embedded in its collective psyche and cherished it to the point of ownership. Howzat?!

As if plotting to dominate one sport was not enough for those early pioneers, they also set about inventing their own game: Australian Rules. Essentially, their particular brand of football is as old as association football and there are obvious parallels in the way the two games evolved. Both came from the same generic sport that was being played in England, each crystallizing essential elements of that game to create two very different sports. Undifferentiated football appears to have been bought across by British settlers and had been played in Melbourne since at least 1839. The first recorded game, however, was on July 31st 1858 – in fact there were two games that day: one a practice match on Richmond paddock (next to the MCG), the other a game between Melbourne Grammar School and a group known as the Saint Kilda Club (apparently unrelated to the present day club) which ended in a fight due to frustration over the lack of rules.

The following weekend Melbourne Grammar played a version of the Rugby School rules against Scotch College (another Melbourne boy's school). This game has legendary status in Australia and is the Aussie Rules equivalent of the Sheffield FC v Hallam FC game of 1860, notwithstanding that neither Australian team was a club nor were they playing under codified rules. They did not have to wait long for either. At the Parade Hotel on May 14th 1859 four men (Thomas Wills – one of the umpires in that first legendary match, William Hammersley, James Thompson and Thomas H Smith – the first three eminent cricketers, Smith a teacher at Scotch College) formed the Melbourne Football Club. Amazingly, this was only nineteen months after Prest and Creswick had formed Sheffield FC making it one of the oldest football clubs in the world. Three days later, on the 17th, they drew up the first set of rules for the sport, known then as Melbourne Rules Football. Melbourne FC, now nicknamed the Demons but originally referred to as the Fuschias and later the Redlegs, were originally without competition but two months later, mirroring, though predating, the formation of Hallam FC,

From Sheffield with Love

Geelong FC were created, the sixth oldest football club in the world (probably!). As mentioned in the Birth of the Beautiful, the rules bear a notable resemblance to the Sheffield Rules:

Melbourne Football Club rules of 1859

1. The distance between the Goals and the Goal Posts shall be decided upon by the Captains of the sides playing.

2. The Captains on each side shall toss for choice of Goal; the side losing the toss has the Kick Off from the centre point between the Goals.

3. A Goal must be kicked fairly between the posts, without touching either of them, or a portion of the person of any player of either side.

4. The game shall be played in a space of not more than 200 yards wide, the same to be measured equally on each side of a line drawn through the centres of the two Goals; and two posts to be called the 'Kick Off' posts shall be erected at a distance of 20 yards on each side of the Goal posts at both ends, and in a straight line between them.

5. In case the Ball is kicked behind goal, any one of the side behind whose goal it is kicked may bring it 20 yards in front of any portion of the space between the 'Kick Off' posts, and shall kick it as nearly as possible in a line with the opposite Goal.

6. Any player catching the Ball directly from the foot may call 'mark'. He then has a free kick; no player from the opposite side being allowed to come inside the spot marked.

7. Tripping and pushing are both allowed (but no hacking) when any player is in rapid motion or in possession of the Ball, except in the case provided for in Rule VI.

8. The Ball shall be taken in hand only when caught from the foot, or on the hop. In no case shall it be lifted from the ground.

9. When the Ball goes out of bounds (the same being indicated by a row of posts) it shall be brought back to the point where it crossed the boundary line, and thrown in at right angles with that line.

10. The Ball, while in play, may under no circumstances be thrown.

Appendices

The main similarities are in the use of a clean catch (Fair Catch or Mark) to gain a free kick (cf. Sheffield amended 1858 Rules, number 3 with 6, above), the kick off rule (cf. 1 and 2), the kick out rule (cf. 2 and 5) and the throw in rule (cf. 10 and 9). Also, both sanctioned pushing and outlawed hacking though the Sheffield Rules forbade tripping while the Melbourne Rules endorsed it (cf. 5 and 7). Furthermore, their unique commonality in being the only two football codes in the world without an offside law suggest that their may have been local knowledge of the Sheffield game.

The glaring difference between the rules is, of course, the emphasis on running with the ball: implicitly prescribed in rule 8 of the Melbourne Rules, explicitly proscribed in rule 8 of the Sheffield Rules. Where the rules differed was due in part to prevailing circumstances particular to Australia at the time. One of these may have been the large number of Irish immigrants whose own version of football (which was ultimately codified as Gaelic Football in 1887) bore marked similarities to the Melbourne game and undoubtedly influenced it (Smith was an Irishman). The temporal relationship between the two games is unclear, however, and the influence may have been in the opposite direction, or even bidirectional. Certainly, Archbishop Thomas Croke, of Croke Park fame and one of the founder members of the Gaelic Athletic Association, lived in New Zealand in the early 1880s and saw a game of Australian Rules. The resemblance continues today allowing an International Rules series (which combines elements of both games) to be played annually between Australia and The Republic of Ireland. Another local condition was the presence of a ball game known as Marn Grook, played by indigenous Australian men, that also bore some likeness to the Australian game, especially the jumping and catching element. Additionally, cricket had a bigger influence on football clubs in Melbourne than it did on clubs in England. While Melbourne clubs differed from many Sheffield clubs in not being directly linked to cricket sides their founder members were usually established local cricket players, for example, Thomas Wills was secretary of the MCC and had represented Cambridge University; he played 32 first-class matches in England and Australia in a career spanning over two decades. As such, the clubs were reliant on using the available cricket ovals as pitches, which allowed for a bigger area over which to play, ultimately leading to the large ovals still used today.

Another factor may be important: while Harrow public school, where the kicking game was more favoured, seems to have had a notable influence on the early direction of the English game, Tom Wills (19/08/35–02/05/80), though Australian-born, had been educated as a schoolboy at Rugby in England (he had been captain of the football team), which clearly preferred the carrying game. It is likely that his early experiences on the playing fields of Rugby would have influenced his later take on the perfect game. Contemporary evidence certainly points to the football games played in English public schools having a significant influence on the development of the game, Thompson writing to Wills in 1871:

> I turn now to football, which I am sorry to see has degenerated into horse play riot. You may remember when you, Mr. Hammersley, Mr T. Smith and myself, framed the first code of rules for Victorian use. The Rugby, Eton, Harrow and Winchester rules at that time (I think in 1859) came under our consideration.

This is not necessarily proof that they were used as Creswick and Prest also considered public school codes but elected not to use them. Wills and Hammersley were also students at Trinity College, Cambridge, and would have been exposed to the Cambridge Rules. Though Hammersley may have left just prior to the publication of the 1848 rules and whilst studying only been acquainted with the in-house rules, it is likely that he became *au fait* with the later rules. It is likely that, as with the Sheffield Rules, the Australian Rules were a synthesis of various public school codes and local variations.

Wills possibly had an even earlier experience that forged his love of the carrying game: either playing or watching Marn Grook as a child in Victoria in the 1840s, though whether he did either

Appendices

of these or, indeed, whether Marn Grook had any influence on the game is a subject of hot debate amongst sporting academics in Australia. This indigenous Australian game (which translates as 'game ball') was played by the Djabwurrung and Jardwadjali clans in Victoria's Western Districts – where Wills was raised – and, as mentioned, placed great emphasis on jumping and kicking – essential elements of the Australian form of football. In 1859 Alfred Bonicelli wrote in the *Melbourne Illustrated News* of a drunken Wills arranging a game and displaying the skills he had learnt from his childhood friends:

> *He declared a game of native football would be played forthwith, and to this end, commandeered a settee cushion and organised two teams, the Romans and the Greeks. Of course, no one could better Mr. Wills at the game, which he insisted on playing barefoot. He had an extravagant leap which he would employ to balance himself momentarily on the back or shoulders of an opponent and thereby increase his upward reach.*

Wills' childhood was spent among the Djabwurrung clan and he spoke their language. The family later moved to Queensland essentially squatting on indigenous land but always enjoying good relations with the locals. This changed in 1861 when a number of indigenous men were killed, wrongly accused of rustling sheep; the murderer resembled Wills' father and, while Tom was away, his father and the rest of the party were killed in mistaken retaliation for the murder: it remains the biggest massacre of white settlers in Australian history. This did not change Will's anti-racist stance (he was not involved in the subsequent bloody reprisal against local indigenous Australians), neither did it deter him from coaching an indigenous cricket side (from the Western districts of Victoria) that played an MCC team at the MCG annually from 1866–69 and which toured England in 1868. Ever the larrikin, Wills had fallen foul of the authorities, which never seemed to understand his liking for indigenous Australians, and was not allowed to tour with his team. He began to drink heavily and ultimately died tragically, committing suicide by stabbing himself in the heart at the age of 44.

From Sheffield with Love

As in Sheffield, the Melbourne Rules were modified over the next few years, including introducing the important element of bouncing the ball while running, but many teams continued to play under different rules. In 1866, at a meeting similar to the ones at the Freemason's Tavern in London in 1863, delegates from Royal Park, Carlton, Melbourne and South Yarra clubs rubberstamped an updated version of the rules and the sport became known as Victorian Rules Football. With this general consensus the game snowballed and in 1877 the Victorian Football Association (VFA) was established with the Victorian Football League following in 1896; the homegrown sport that ultimately became Australian Rules football had made its mark.

One more man central to the development of the sport should be mentioned and that is HCA Harrison (16/10/36–02/09/29), dubbed the Father of the Game by Alfred Deakin in 1908. This epithet instantly dismissed the huge contribution made by the real father, the establishment-unfriendly, Wills, though the balance has been recently redressed by a statue outside the MCG of several footballers including Wills, whose crucial role is referred to on the accompanying plaque.

Harrison was both Wills' cousin and brother-in-law (he married Wills' sister); he was locally educated and regarded as the finest amateur runner of his day. He is reputed by some to have been present at the drawing up of the Melbourne Rules on May 17th 1859 and was a huge footballing talent, becoming captain of Richmond FC in 1860, replacing Wills as Melbourne captain the following year and, except for a season as Geelong captain, remaining so until he retired. He was both vice-president and president of Melbourne FC and the first vice-president of the VFA. He was winner of the annual Champion of the Colony Award – replaced by the Brownlow Medal in 1924 – a record five times (Wills won it thrice) and was the man who tried to introduce Aussie Rules to England in 1884. The English rugby authorities refused to entertain the idea of hosting a game but, as mentioned, CW Alcock welcomed the idea with open arms saying he had heard such good reports of the game from touring

Appendices

England cricketers that he would be delighted to make The Oval available. Unfortunately, insufficient finance was to be had and England did not see its first game played by professionals till 1972 when Carlton played an All Stars team, fittingly at The Oval. Although he may not have been there quite at the start as Wills was his overall contribution was far higher; he also lived a good deal longer than Wills did, dying in 1929 a month before his 93rd birthday.

Of course I must mention in passing the first Australian rugby team, the Sydney University Football Club, founded way back in 1863 but I apologise to Aussie readers because the last word goes to soccer. Association football did not take off in the same way it did in Britain probably because it was the British take on football; not only was it developing a long, long way away but it was another reminder of colonialist imperialism to the long-suffering local working classes.

Australians were evolving their own unique interpretation of the game at a time when they were establishing a national identity and the two became inextricably linked. While this put association football at something of a disadvantage there were enough people coming and going between the colony and the mother country for there to be a modest interest in it. Arthur Henry Savage, who had played for Crystal Palace and England but now lived in Australia, first suggested that the code be taken up, in a letter to the *Sydney Morning Herald* in 1877. Three days later a supporting letter was published; it was from John Walter Fletcher (11/05/47 – 28/02/18) now regarded as the father of soccer in Australia. Born in England in 1847, Fletcher attended Oxford, gaining a blue in athletics. He emigrated to Australia in the 1870s, moving to Sydney in 1876, where he worked as a teacher. He arranged and played in the country's first recognised soccer match in 1880 (with Savage on the opposing side) and established the Wanderers in Sydney August 19th 1880, the colony's first association football club. Testament to soccer's continuing links with England was the fact that the Wanderers became one of the 128 members of the English FA that year (121 were English, the other six Scottish).

The first recorded match in Australia was on August 14th 1880; the team that was to be the Wanderers (wearing white jerseys with a Southern Cross over the left breast) took on Ring's School Rugby Football team on Parramatta Common. Fletcher established the English Football Association in New South Wales in 1882 and the colony played Victoria in 1883, which, in turn, created the Anglo–Australian Football Association in 1884. The other states followed suit and united as the Commonwealth Football Association in 1912. Australia's oldest surviving soccer club is Balgownie Rangers from New South Wales, founded in 1883.

THE FIRST TRY

I was going to include this piece where it logically fell, at the end of the Australian appendix, but knowing what Aussies are like about Kiwis had second thoughts; you know: small, insignificant piece of information to the south of the Australian segment. I also have far too much respect for Kiwis as to do anything so underhand (or underarm!), so I have given them their own appendix albeit, unfortunately and inevitably… to the south of the Australian segment!

New Zealand has the honour of having the oldest club in the southern hemisphere to have played an association style (as oppose to rugby) football game: Auckland FC, founded by Charles Craven Dacre. Dacre was born in Sydney in 1848 and moved to Auckland aged 11. He was son of English-born Captain Ranulph Dacre one of the first Europeans to set foot on North Island in 1827 while sailing with the schooner, Endeavour (not the ship in which Cook travelled to Australia and New Zealand). Charles did his secondary schooling in England where he began playing football for his school, Clapham Grammar; he would also play for Clapham Rovers and the London Athletic Club. During a match on Clapham Common he sustained life-threatening internal injuries but survived, resolving to continue playing. Representing Surrey in the first inter-county football match against Middlesex in 1867 he played opposite his friend, CEB Nepean, of Charterhouse who was known as 'the best dribbler in England' and who would go on to represent Scotland in the last four 'Alcock' internationals. Dacre also worked briefly for the FA and was a cricketer of some renown with a good record at club level.

He returned to New Zealand and in July 1870 teamed up with Frank Whittaker to found Auckland Football Club. Initially playing the dribbling game using Westminster rules, by 1873 they had begun to play rugby; presumably there was not much call in New Zealand for a namby-pamby 'contact' sport with little or no violence. The same year they played the country's first 15-a-side match against North Shore Rugby Club in Auckland. Dacre continued to play for Auckland FC despite the change to rugby but in 1878 he broke his leg in a game against Cheltenham and, perhaps thinking that two serious injuries were enough, retired from football. His great-nephew, Charles Christian Dacre was one of the all-time greats of Kiwi cricket and also played soccer for his country. CC Dacre's brother, Life Marwell also played cricket for New Zealand as did his nephew, Donald Dacre Coleman.

By the way, the oldest football team in any code in New Zealand is the Nelson Football Club founded in 1868, which played a carrying game for its first two years before formally adopting the rugby union code in 1871. On May 14th 1870 they played Nelson College at the Botanical Reserve, Nelson in what was the first inter-club rugby union football match to be played in New Zealand.

THE OLD CLUB'S CLUB

To avoid confusion I have listed what are generally believed to be the oldest clubs in any code not affiliated to a school, university or the military. I have not included Guy's Hospital (rugby) because of a lack of documentary evidence to support its claims of being officially formed as a club in 1843; for the same reason Cray Wanderers (association football), who claim to have formed in 1860, are not listed. I have also omitted Trinity College Dublin University Club (c: 1856; rugby), Cambridge University Football Club (c: 1856; Cambridge Rules, later association football) and Melbourne University Football Club (c: 1859; Australian Rules) because of their university affiliations. Surrey FC (c: 1849) is omitted because of their direct connections to Surrey Cricket Club, though they are of historical significance because they produced their own set of football rules in 1849.

All clubs listed as having an unknown initial code probably played a variant most akin to the subsequent code they adopted. An '=' sign signifies that the year of inception is known but exact date unclear, meriting equal ranking. I have endeavoured to exercise balanced judgment given the conflicting views on the year of origin for many clubs; this list will surely be subject to swift alteration given the regular unearthing of new evidence. For example, Castlemaine FC (Australian Rules) now claims to have formed in June 1859, one month before Geelong, though they disbanded for a while before re-forming in 1871. It is still unclear whether their pre-1871 existence constituted a club.

Legend to rules used: AF = association football; AR = Australian Rules; CU = Cambridge University Rules, 1856; DD = Dingley Dell; HR = Harrow Rules; R = Rugby Football Union; RS = Rugby School; SR = Sheffield Rules; UIC = Unknown initial code.

1. Sheffield FC (SR, later AF) — Oct 1857
2. Liverpool Football Club (RS, later R) — Dec 1857
3. Edinburgh Academicals FC (UIC, later R) — 1857/8
4. Blackheath FC (London) (UIC, later R) — 1858
5. Melbourne FC (AR) — May 1859
6. Geelong FC (AR) — July 1859
7. Hallam FC (Sheffield) (SR, later AF) — 1860
8. Forest FC (London) (HR, later CU, later AF) — 1860
9. Manchester Football Club (UIC, later R) — 1860
= Crusaders (London) (UIC, later AF) — 1860
= Dingley Dell (London) (UIC, later DD, later AF) — 1860
12. Richmond FC (London) (UIC, later R) — 1861
= Norfolk (Sheffield) (SR later AF) — 1861

Appendices

Liverpool Football Club – founded by Old Rugbeians – is not to be confused with either St Helens Rugby League Football Club (c: 1873) or Liverpool Football Club (c: 1892; association football). In 1986 they merged with St Helen's Rugby Union Football Club (c: 1919) and became known as Liverpool St Helens Football Club.

While there is some uncertainty about the exact dates of the formation of Edinburgh Academicals and Blackheath clubs the order is correct. Blackheath FC, while formed by old boys from Blackheath School, was not directly associated with the school and is therefore included.

Dingley Dell formed their own set of rules in 1862 based on a ten-a-side game which are believed to have been used by some of the other London teams prior to the FA Laws of 1863. Unfortunately, they were not invited to the original FA meetings and it is unclear if any of their (lost) rules were ever incorporated in the Rules of the Game.

Other teams formed in 1861 include; Pitsmoor, Collegiate, Norton, Engineer and York (all of Sheffield and playing SR); Crystal Palace (UIC, later AF); Sale (UIC, later R); and Barnes (UIC, later R, though like Crystal Palace and Forest FC they were one of the 11 founder members of the FA.) Barnes' claims that it was founded in 1839, making it the oldest football club in the world, are unsubstantiated. Notts County, the oldest professional football club in the world, was formed in 1862 and originally played their own rules before adopting the FA's.

THE ETON WANDERER

Lord Kinnaird's FA Cup record
   1871–72 not in Alcock's winning Wanderers (1-0 Royal Engineers)
   1872–73 Wanderers 2-0 Oxford University. Scored. Won
   1873–74 not in (Oxford University 2-0 Royal Engineers)
   1874–75 Royal Engineers 1-1 and 2-0 Old Etonians. Captain. Lost
   1875–76 Wanderers 0-0 and 3-0 Old Etonians. Lost
   1876–77 Wanderers 2-1 Oxford University. Own goal. Won

*1877–78 Wanderers 3-1 Royal Engineers. Captain.
  Second half in goal. Scored. Won
1878–79 Old Etonians 1-0 Clapham Rovers. Captain. Won
1879–80 not in (Clapham Rovers 1-0 Oxford University)
1880–81 Old Carthusians 3-0 Old Etonians. Captain. Lost
1881–82 Old Etonians 1-0 Blackburn Rovers. Captain. Won
1882–83 Blackburn Olympic 2-1 Old Etonians. Captain. Lost*

Elysian Fields

The following venues (with relevant dates) have hosted an FA Cup Final. Replay locations are in brackets.

*1872 Kennington Oval
1873 Lillie Bridge, London
1874–92 Kennington Oval; (1875 and 1876: The Oval; 1886:
  Baseball Ground, Derby)
1893 Fallowfield, Manchester
1894 Goodison Park
1895–1914 Crystal Palace; (1901 Burnden Park, Bolton;
1902 Crystal Palace; 1910 Goodison Park;
1911 Old Trafford; 1912 Bramall Lane)
1915 Old Trafford
1920–22 Stamford Bridge
1923–2000 Wembley Stadium (1970: Old Trafford; 1981–3,
1990 and 1993: Wembley)
2000– 06 Millennium Stadium, Cardiff
2007– Wembley Stadium*

Bramall Lane hosted the replay of the 1911–12 Cup final between locals Barnsley and West Bromwich Albion, following a no score draw at Crystal Palace. Nil-nil well into extra-time, officials were getting nervous as they had expected a result and had no Plan B. Finally in the dying minutes of extra-time (after 239 minutes of cup final football; this being the first season extra-time had been played in an FA Cup final), Tufnell scored to send the Barnsley fans into raptures.

It was a fitting result – West Brom had won before and they

would win again – and a fairytale ending for the underdogs: two years before Tufnell's goal had been enough to secure a Cup Final replay against Newcastle United but Barnsley had gone down 2-0 in the replay. Penalty shootouts were first introduced in the FA Cup in 1995 but were not needed in a final until 2005 when Arsenal beat Manchester United 5-4 on penalties after a two-hour no score bore draw. Shootouts were an English invention; unsurprisingly, they were first introduced in the wonderfully eccentric Watney Cup.

Held annually pre-season from 1970–73, the cup pitted eight teams – the two highest scoring teams from each of the four divisions who had not been promoted, relegated or entered a European competition (!!) – in a one-leg knockout contest. They were first used in a 1970 semi-final; Manchester United (again) beat Hull City 4-3 on penalties after a 1-1 draw (5-4). The first to ever score a penalty in a shootout was the epitome of Seventies football, George Best, while the great Denis Law was the first to miss. United went on to lose 4-1 to Derby who had beaten Sheffield United in the other semi.

The following year the final itself was decided on penalties (a world-first) when Colchester United beat West Brom 4-3 on penalties after a 4-4 draw (8-7). The following year's final was a repeat (and a world second) when Bristol Rovers beat Sheffield United 4-3 on penalties after a 0-0 draw. The cup was scrapped after four seasons, seemingly because it never caught on. Someone get me a sponsor.

STATES OF GRACE

It is worth mentioning baseball here, as it is older than gridiron, older even than association football. Baseball is believed to have originated from the English game of rounders, which has been popular since Tudor times. Rounders' earliest written reference is not until 1744 when it was actually referred to in England as baseball, though Jane Austen calls it rounders in *Northanger Abbey* in 1798. Rounders in turn may be derived from stoolball, a game developed in the south of England perhaps as long ago as the 14th Century. Played with a 'batter' and 'baller' folklore has it that stoolball was traditionally played by milkmaids who used their stools for wickets; cricket is also believed to be descended from stoolball and one can see that a cricket wicket could be a two-dimensional representation of a milkmaid's stool.

Mentioned in *Don Quixote*, stoolball continues to be played to this day. Other traditional bat and ball games include nipsy (played in South Yorkshire); knur and spell – whose rules were published in the very first edition of the *Wisden Almanack* (Yorkshire); bat and trap – or trapball – (Kent); and billet (Lancashire).

To get back to baseball, I just wanted to add that the earliest reference to cricket was in a 1597 English court case that mentioned it as having been played fifty years earlier. This tenuously leads me to the earliest cricket international (NOT Test), which was, surprisingly, America v Canada in 1844. It was held in New York between a Toronto and a New York side; it wasn't till 1853 that the two national sides officially met – though this still makes the latter the oldest game between two national representative sides.

This, in turn, brings me back to baseball, which was first mentioned in the States in 1791, though it is unclear if this reference is to rounders. Certainly, it wasn't until 1845 that the first team to play under modern baseball rules was formed; even so, this was still twelve years before Sheffield FC. This was the Knickerbockers Club of New York who developed their own set of rules; they lost their first competitive game the following year to the New York Nine. By 1857, the year Sheffield FC formed, baseball was already forming itself into a national organisation and, within a decade, it had 400 members from coast to coast. Professionalism was introduced in 1869 and the Cincinnati Red Stockings were the early star performers winning eighty-nine games in a row. They had the famous (non-aviation) Wright brothers, Harry, who assembled and player-managed the team, and George, who later decamped to Boston to form the Boston Red Stockings, later to become the Boston Red Sox.

Appendices

Their father, John Wright, was a cricketer who migrated from Sheffield (Harry was born and raised there till he was three) to New York in 1838; he later died 25 days after Sheffield FC was founded. As with rugby and association football the introduction of professionalism caused a split in the sport in 1870, with the amateur sport withering away. The professional sport was itself hamstrung by internal wrangling and eventually two leagues emerged, the National League (est. 1875) and the American League (est. 1899); the World Series (est. 1903) is an end of season play-off between the winners of the two leagues.

A more pernicious schism was along racial lines with African Americans being excluded from professional baseball from 1868. This led to the formation of the Negro National League in 1920 by the African-American Andrew Rube Foster, and it was not until 1947 that the offensive colour bar rule was dropped. Jackie Robinson, the first player to break the colour barrier won Rookie of the Year in his first season and starred in six National League victories (and six World Series appearances including one win) in his ten years with the Brooklyn Dodgers.

Gridiron developed later; a contemporary of football and rugby. Prep school pupils led by Gerrit Smith Miller (whose grandfather was the ardent abolitionist and presidential candidate, Gerrit Smith; mother was the suffragist Elizabeth Smith Miller; sister was the suffragist Anne Fitzhugh Miller; and son was the zoologist bearing the same name) formed Oneida Football Club in Boston, America in 1861.

The club developed its own hybrid blend of rugby and association football known as the Boston Game with the emphasis on kicking the ball. When some of the players graduated to Harvard University it was taken up there – in 1871. All of the other American colleges favoured playing a form of football much more akin to soccer, though both sports used round balls. As far back as 1820 students at Princeton University were playing a game called 'ballown' which resembled soccer and in 1869 they played Rutgers University in the country's first intercollegiate football game using modified FA Laws. They all refused to play Harvard. Indeed, in 1873, representatives from

From Sheffield with Love

Princeton, Rutgers, Columbia and Yale met at the Fifth Avenue Hotel in New York City to develop the first intercollegiate code based on FA Rules with both throwing and carrying of the ball banned. Harvard who had refused to attend finally got a game against carrying opposition in 1874 against the McGill University of Montreal, Canada, who played rugby.

Two games were played, one under each set of rules, and such was Harvard's appreciation of rugby that they incorporated more carrying elements of the game into their own rules. The following year Yale agreed to play Harvard under the new rules and was obviously impressed because by 1876 representatives from Harvard, Yale, Princeton and Columbia met in Massachusetts to further develop the rules, removing most remaining elements of soccer and developing the game of American Football. In the 1880s Yale coach Walter Camp introduced a number of significant changes to make the game more like the Gridiron Football we see today.

Bibliography

I have used multiple sources to gather information from; anything derived from potentially unreliable internet or book sources has been cross-referenced. There were multiple instances of conflicting information (never truer than with Appendix 3) that I resolved by either seeking further corroborative evidence or exercising editorial judgement.

Books and articles

A Game of Our Own: The Origins of Australian Football. Geoffrey Blainey (2003)

A History of Hawthorn. Victoria Peel, Deborah Zion and Jane Yule (1993). Melbourne University Press.

An Epoch in the Annals of National Sport: Football in Sheffield and the Creation of Modern Soccer and Rugby. The International Journal of the History of Sport: 18(4) 53-87. Adrian Harvey (2001)

Association Football. Ernest Needham (1901), Reprint: Soccer Books Limited (2003)

Circus Life and Circus Celebrities. Thomas Frost. London: Chatto and Windus (1881)

Colossus: the True Story of William Foulke. Graham Phythian (2005)

Encyclopaedia of German Football Leagues 8. 1: 1890–1963. Lorenz Knieriem and Hardy Grüne (2006)

Football in Sheffield. Percy M Young (1964)

Football on Merseyside. Percy M. Young (1963)

Football's Strangest Matches. Andrew Ward (1999)

Football: The First Hundred Years – The Untold Story. Adrian Harvey (2005)

Hawthorn Peppercorns. Gwen McWilliams (1978)

History of Yorkshire County Cricket 1833–1903. Revd. R.S. Holmes (1904)

Official History of Sheffield United. Richard Sparling (1948)

Playing for money: James J Lang and emergent soccer professionalism in Sheffield. Soccer and Society: 5 (3) 336-55. Graham Curry (2004)

Sheffield Football: A History, Volume 1, 1857–1961. Keith Farnsworth (1995). Hallamshire Press.

Sheffield Football Club (Oldest in the World): Centenary History 1857–1957. Fred Walters (1957). Henry Garnett and Company, Ltd.

Sport Histories: Figurational Studies in the Development of Modern Sport. Edited by Eric Dunning (2004)

Sport in Europe: politics, class, gender. Edited by John A Mangan (1999)

Steve Bloomer: The Story of Football's First Superstar. Peter Seddon (1999)

The Boys Book of Soccer for 1947. (1947)

The Countrymen: the Story of Hallam FC. John A Steele (1989)

The Father of Modern Sport: The Life and Times of Charles W Alcock. Keith Booth (2002) Parrswood Press

The First 100 Years: the Official Centenary History of Sheffield United. Dennis Clarebrough and Andrew Kirkham (2000)

The Golden Boys: A Study of Watford's Cult Heroes. Oliver Phillips (2002)

The Official Encyclopaedia of Sheffield United. T Matthews, Dennis Clarebrough and Andrew Kirkham (2003)

The Shaping of Victorian Rules Football. Victorian Historical Journal: 60 (1). BW O'Dwyer (1989)

The Wednesday Boys: a Definitive Guide to Sheffield Wednesday Football Club. Jason Dickinson and John Brodie (2005)

Websites and Pages

Cricinfo.com
Bbc.co.uk (Shrovetide football)
The Owl Football Historian: A Drake: btinternet.com/~a.drake
black-history-month.co.uk/articles/andrew_watson.html
britannica.com/eb/article-222218
circushistory.org/Frost/Frost3.htm
classic-literature.co.uk/british-authors/16th-century/richard-carew/the-survey-of-cornwall/ebook-page-63.asp
elfinspell.com/ShearmanFootball.html
oxforddnb.com/view/article/39536
chrishobbs.com
freewebs.com/hallamfc/history
furd.org/default.asp?intPageID=25
housebarra.com/PastTimes/articles/camping.html
hallamfc.com
hubpages.com/hub/Bramall_Lane_Oldest_Major_Ground
members.tripod.com/~midgley/waltheof
wenlock-olympian-society.org.uk/
robinhoodloxley.net/mycustompage0004.htm
rsssf.com/tablese/engsupcuphist
rsssf.com/tablesa/angloscot-club
victorianlondon.org/dickens/dickens-f
soccermistral.co.uk/histref
Bocaraton rugby.com
Wikipedia.com
en.wikipedia.org/wiki/Medieval_football#_note-6
mcg.org.au
roundersonline.net
stoolball.co.uk
tradgames.org.uk
fownc.org
maxpages.com/sheffieldfc

About the author

Brendan Murphy was born and raised in Sheffield. Now an Associate Professor in psychiatry at Monash University and Director of the Southern Health Early Psychosis Service, he lives in Melbourne, Australia.